New Frontiers in HRD

Factors such as globalization, restructuring, casualization of employment and the erosion of pension rights have led to massive tensions in contemporary organizations. By exploring the boundaries of the field of human resource development, this book asks where HRD is in the middle of all of this, and presents an innovative and challenging approach to HRD theory and practice.

With contributions from a number of leading international scholars, the chapters draw upon a range of epistemologies and adopt a critically reflective perspective on the field. A key theme throughout the collection is that HRD occurs under a wide range of circumstances and situations, and can be better understood through a broader range of conceptualizations than that afforded by the dominant Anglo-American model.

The book is divided into four parts, moving from a critical perspective on the definition and boundaries of the field of HRD, through a rethinking of the human-centred nature of HRD, and the organizational context within which HRD takes place, to perspectives on the future role of HRD in the changing knowledge economy. The book's main conclusion is that HRD remains a contested concept within the more broadly contested field of organization and management theory. Yet this is neither a drawback nor weakness on the one hand, nor an advantage or strength on the other. Both threats and opportunities present themselves for the future growth of HRD as an academic field, and as an arena of professional practice.

Jean Woodall is Associate Dean and Professor of HRD at Kingston Business School. She is also the current editor-in-chief of *Human Resource Development International*. **Monica Lee** is Visiting Professor at Northumbria University, and is based at Lancaster University. She is the editor of the monograph series *Routledge Studies in Human Resource Development*, and is executive secretary for the University Forum for HRD. **Jim Stewart** is Professor of HRD at Nottingham Business School, chair of the University Forum for HRD and co-editor of three other books in this series.

Routledge Studies in Human Resource Development
Edited by Monica Lee
Lancaster University, UK

HRD theory is changing rapidly. Recent advances in theory and practice, how we conceive of organizations and of the world of knowledge, have led to the need to reinterpret the field. This series aims to reflect and foster the development of HRD as an emergent discipline.

Encompassing a range of different international, organizational, methodological and theoretical perspectives, the series promotes theoretical controversy and reflective practice.

1 **Policy Matters**
Flexible learning and organizational change
Edited by Viktor Jakupec and Robin Usher

2 **Science Fiction and Organization**
Edited by Warren Smith, Matthew Higgins, Martin Parker and Geoff Lightfoot

3 **HRD and Learning Organisations in Europe**
Challenges for professionals
Edited by Saskia Tjepkema, Jim Stewart, Sally Sambrook, Martin Mulder, Hilde ter Horst and Jaap Scheerens

4 **Interpreting the Maternal Organisation**
Edited by Heather Höpfl and Monika Kostera

5 **Work Process Knowledge**
Edited by Nick Boreham, Renan Samurçay and Martin Fischer

6 **HRD in a Complex World**
Edited by Monica Lee

7 **HRD in Small Organisations**
Research and practice
Edited by Jim Stewart and Graham Beaver

8 **New Frontiers in HRD**
Edited by Jean Woodall, Monica Lee and Jim Stewart

9 **Human Resources, Care-Giving, Career Progression and Gender**
A gender neutral glass ceiling
Beulah S. Coyne, Edward J. Coyne, Sr. and Monica Lee

10 **The Industrial Relations of Training and Development**
Jason Heyes and Mark Stuart

11 **Rethinking Strategic Learning**
Russ Vince

Also published in the series in paperback:

Action Research in Organisations
Jean McNiff, accompanied by Jack Whitehead

Understanding Human Resource Development
A research-based approach
Edited by Jim Stewart, Jim McGoldrick and Sandra Watson

New Frontiers in HRD

Edited by Jean Woodall, Monica Lee and Jim Stewart

LONDON AND NEW YORK

First published 2004
by Routledge
2 Park Square, Milton Park, Abingdon, Oxon, OX14 4RN

Simultaneously published in the USA and Canada
by Routledge

711 Third Avenue, New York, NY 10017

Routledge is an imprint of the Taylor & Francis Group

First issued in paperback 2012

Typeset in Sabon by
BOOK NOW Ltd

British Library Cataloguing in Publication Data
A catalogue record for this book is available from the British Library

Library of Congress Cataloging in Publication Data
New frontiers in HRD/edited by Jean Woodall, Monica Lee, and Jim Stewart.
p. cm.
Includes bibliographical references and index.
1. Manpower policy. 2. Manpower planning. I. Title: New frontiers in human resource development. II. Woodall, Jean, 1950– III. Lee, Monica, 1952– IV. Stewart, Jim, 1950–
HD5713 .N475 2004
658.3–dc22 2003024560

ISBN 978-0-415-31237-0 (hardback)

ISBN 978-0-415-65044-1(paperback)

Contents

Illustrations

Figures

Tables

Notes on contributors

Rona S. Beattie is Head of the Division of Human Resource Management and Development at Glasgow Caledonian University. She is a chartered fellow of the Chartered Institute of Personnel and Development (CIPD). Her research interests include line managers as developers, mentoring, human resource management (HRM) in the public sector, and voluntary sector management. She has published in edited collections, reports and in HRM, HRD and public management journals including *Employee Relations*, *Public Management Review*, *Regional Studies*, *International Journal of Training and Development* and *Management Learning*.

Stephen Gourlay is Director of Doctoral Training at Kingston Business School. He has also taught on the EUDOKMA doctoral training programme at Copenhagen Business School. He has researched on social history, technical change and unions, workplace health and safety. His present focus is on knowledge management and organizational learning. Recent publications include a critique of the SECI model of knowledge management, and a contribution towards reconceputalization of 'tacit knowledge'.

Heather Höpfl is Professor of Management at the University of Essex. She holds visiting appointments at the Humanistic University in Utrecht, the Academy of Entrepreneurship in Warsaw and the University of South Australia. She is editor of *Culture and Organization*. She publishes mainly in the area of organizational theory and has recent articles in *Journal of Management Studies*, *Journal of Organisational Change Management* and *Human Resource Development International*. She co-authored, with Monika Kostera, *Interpreting the Maternal Organisation* (Routledge 2002), and with Barbara Czarniawska, *Casting the Other* (Routledge 2002).

Joseph Kessels is Professor of HRD at the University of Twente, the Netherlands and partner in Kessels & Smit, a consultancy firm specializing in HRD topics. He co-authored, with Rosemary Harrison, *Human Resource Development in a Knowledge Economy* (Palgrave Macmillan 2003). He has a specific research interest in the characteristics of learning environments that support knowledge productivity and that facilitate innovation.

Monica Lee is Visiting Professor at Northumbria University, and is based at Lancaster University, UK. She is a chartered psychologist, a chartered fellow of CIPD and associate fellow of the British Psychological Society. She is editor of the monograph series *Routledge Studies in Human Resource Development*. She has worked extensively in Central Europe, CIS and the USA coordinating and collaborating in research and teaching initiatives. She is now concentrating on mentoring senior managers. She is intrigued by the dynamics around individuals and organizations, and most of her work is about trying to make sense of these. This can be seen in recent articles in *Human Relations*, *Human Resource Development International*, *Management Learning* and *Personnel Review*.

Jim McGoldrick is a Professor of HRD, and is Chairman of Tayside University Hospitals NHS Trust. Formerly the Vice-Principal of the University of Abertay, Dundee, where he is currently Visiting Professor of Healthcare Leadership, he is also President of the University Forum for HRD. He has published widely in HRD including *Human Resource Development: Perspectives, Strategies and Practice* (co-edited with Jim Stewart) and most recently he co-authored *Understanding Human Resource Development: A Research-Based Approach* (Routledge 2002), with Jim Stewart and Sandra Watson. In April 1998 he was awarded companionship of the CIPD.

Rob F. Poell is Associate Professor of HRD at Tilburg University in the Netherlands. He is a general editor of *Human Resource Development International* and publishes regularly in *Management Learning*, *Human Resource Development Quarterly*, *Adult Education Quarterly*, *Human Resource Development Review*, among other scholarly journals. He is a member of the Board of Directors of the Academy of HRD. His main expertise is in work-related learning and the strategies used by employees, managers and HR practitioners to organize it.

Darlene Russ-Eft is Assistant Professor of Adult Education and Higher Education Leadership at Oregon State University. She is the current editor of *Human Resource Development Quarterly*. As the former Director of Research at AchieveGlobal, Inc. and the former Director of Research Services at Zenger-Miller, she has authored books and journal articles on ethics, human resource development, leadership, research and evaluation. She is a past chair of the Research Committee of the American Society for Training and Development (ASTD) and a past member of the Board of the American Evaluation Association (AEA). She received the 1996 Times Mirror Editor of the Year Award for her research work and the Year 2000 Outstanding Scholar Award from the Academy of Human Resource Development (AHRD). Her articles can be found in *Advances in*

Developing Human Resources, *American Journal of Evaluation*, *Human Resource Development International* and *Human Resource Development Review*. Her most recent book is *Evaluation in Organizations: A Systematic Approach to Enhancing Learning Performance, and Change* (Perseus Press 2001).

Jim Stewart is Professor of HRD at Nottingham Business School. He has taught in universities since 1986 following careers in retail and in local government before working at Nottingham Business School. An active researcher and writer, Jim is the author, editor or co-editor of nine books, including two others in the *Routledge Studies in Human Resource Development* series, including *Understanding Human Resource Development: A Research-Based Approach* (Routledge 2002), with Jim McGoldrick and Sandra Watson, as well as numerous reports, articles and conference papers. Jim is also chair of the University Forum for HRD, UK editor of *Human Resource Development International* and reviews editor of the *International Journal of Training and Development*.

Russ Vince is Professor of Organisational Learning at the Business School, the University of Glamorgan and Director of the Leadership and Learning Research Unit. He serves on the International Advisory Boards of the journals *Management Learning*, *Human Resource Development International* and *Organizational and Social Dynamics*, and the Editorial Board of *Action Learning: Research and Practice*. His most recent book, which is forthcoming in the *Routledge Studies in Human Resource Development* series, is called *Rethinking Strategic Learning*.

Sandra Watson is Head of Human Resource Management at Napier University Business School, Edinburgh. Her research interests are managerial issues in human resource development. Recent publications include an analysis of managerial skill requirements in Scottish tourism and an evaluation of training initiatives in a period of downsizing in the hospital sector. She co-edited, with Jim McGoldrick and Jim Stewart, *Understanding Human Resource Development: A Research-Based Approach* (Routledge 2002).

Diana Winstanley is Senior Lecturer in Personal and Management Development at Imperial Business School, Imperial College London. She is also Deputy Director of the full-time MBA programme, a personal effectiveness trainer and a qualified counsellor. She is currently researching learning in management education and has three projects in this area on learning to practice, learning orientations and learning shock. Her latest book was with Jean Woodall on *Ethical Issues in Contemporary Human Resource Development* (Macmillan 2000), with whom she also wrote *Management Development: Strategy and Practice* (Blackwell 1998), plus books on management development and senior management competencies. She is currently writing a book on personal effectiveness. She has recent articles in *Human Resource Management Journal*, *Journal of Management Studies*, *Human Relations*, *Business Ethics: A European Review*, *Business and Professional Ethics Journal* and the *Electronic Journal of Radical Organisational Theory* on ethics and HRM, stakeholding, child labour, management competencies, sexuality in organizations and motherhood.

Jean Woodall is Associate Dean and Professor of HRD at Kingston Business School. She is also the current editor-in-chief of *Human Resource Development International*. She co-edited *Ethical Issues in Contemporary Human Resource Development* (Macmillan 2000) with Diana Winstanley, with whom she also co-authored *Management Development: Strategy and Practice* (Blackwell 1998). She has published articles on a wide range of topics including career management for women, work-related management development, ethics and HRD, HRD outsourcing and professional learning.

Part I

New frontiers in HRD

Why now? Setting the scene

1 Introduction

Jean Woodall, Monica Lee and Jim Stewart

Aims and purpose

There is evidence of prolific scholarship in the emergent field of human resource development, with a number of student texts and scholarly monographs which have been published since the mid-1990s (Stewart and McGoldrick 1996; Stewart 1999; Walton 1999; Wilson 1999; Gibb 2002). The *Routledge Studies in Human Resource Development* – a series of research monographs and edited collections under the overall editorial direction of Monica Lee – has been a particularly fruitful source of new ideas in HRD with titles including *Understanding Human Resource Development* (Stewart *et al.* 2001), *Action Research in Organisations* (McNiff 2000), *HRD and Learning Organisations in Europe* (Tjepkema *et al.* 2002), *Human Resources, Care-Giving, Career Progression and Gender* (Coyne *et al.* 2003), *Work Process Knowledge* (Boreham *et al.* 2002), *Interpreting the Maternal Organisation* (Höpfl and Kostera 2002) and *Science Fiction and Organization* (Smith *et al.* 2001).

This volume is part of that series. It shares a common origin with two other edited collections in the series, namely *HRD in Small Organisations* (Stewart and Beaver 2004) and *HRD in a Complex World* (Lee 2003). All three are the products of a UK research seminar series sponsored by the Economic and Social Research Council on *Human Resource Development: The Emerging Theoretical Agenda and Empirical Research*, jointly convened by Jean Woodall, Monica Lee and Jim Stewart, and coordinated by Jean at Kingston University. The aim of the seminar series was to provide a forum in which HRD scholars and scholar-practitioners could debate leading-edge research in HRD in a more relaxed environment than can be provided by the typical academic conference schedule. Ample opportunity was afforded for discussion and reflection on a number of themes, including defining HRD, HRD in small and medium enterprises (SMEs); HRD in Europe, HRD and complexity, human-centred approaches to HRD and revisiting adult learning theory. Two of the seminars provided a specialized core of papers for the books on small organizations and on complexity. This book draws upon papers from the whole seminar series, especially those that stood out as exploring the boundaries of the field, and particularly from the seminars on human-centred approaches to HRD and revisiting adult learning theory.

Putting together such a collection creates its own problems of thematic focus and identifying an appropriate title. The rush of preparing a proposal for the publisher resulted in what was initially a somewhat impulsive choice of *New Frontiers in HRD*. The far more reflective and constructively critical feedback of our reviewers pointed out that what sounded like a pioneering trek westwards across the 'great plains' of HRD was in danger of missing an important opportunity to take a strongly critical stance on the current context of HRD research and practice. We were in danger of making the problematic unproblematic. There are massive tensions in contemporary organizations with globalization, restructuring, casualization of employment, erosion of pension rights and a revival of Taylorist management practice. This has a considerable impact upon employees and work teams and requires us to question whether it is enough just to see HRD as a neutral bundle of techniques to improve organizational performance. Add to this an increasingly volatile geopolitical situation in which blocs and balances of power have shifted so dramatically since the late 1980s that we are now in a world where some would argue that there is but one superpower with an unflinching confidence about its manifest destiny. Where is HRD in the middle of all of this? The stream on 'a critical turn in HRD' at the third *Critical Management Studies* conference in 2003 addressed this question from a number of different perspectives, and this book is intended to add to the debate.

Certainly, from Boyacigiller and Adler (1991) onwards, a strong case has been presented that management theory, attitudes and behaviours are derived largely from that which arose in the United States from the early 1950s onwards. In other words, much of the mainstream conceptualization of management and HRD is based upon a particular culture and way of working. 'Managerialism' or the 'Americanization of management' ripples through the texts we recommend and refer to, and extends across the world – way beyond its early roots. Because it is so deeply rooted in the way in which we understand 'management' we are largely blind to its effects. It is only when we attempt to theorize or practise management or HRD in contexts that are not compatible with the 'accepted theory' that we are brought face to face with the realization that different cultures have very different views on the nature and role of management and HRD, even to the extent, for example, of how they conceptualize and deal with conflict (Lee 1999). Part of our argument in this book, therefore, is that HRD occurs under a wide range of circumstances and situations, and part of pushing back the boundaries of HRD is to better understand its nature under different or wider conceptualizations than afforded by the common model. Indeed, many would argue that a common model is not even possible let alone desirable. Attempts to identify a European model of HRD *practice*, as opposed to the normative and prescriptive models common to many academic texts, and to contrast such a model with alternatives from the United States for example, have proved unsuccessful (Sambrook *et al.* 2003). This is not to deny the usefulness or appropriateness of a core of understanding, but it is to recognize the situated nature of our theory and practice, and to acknowledge the cultural imperialism that can occur without the accommodation of such differences.

Thus we pondered whether to call this book *The Crisis in HRD*. However, we did not. We did not want to be lured into the easy temptations of critique and the dangerous seduction of a passive helplessness or a need to align ourselves and our contributors with a single 'critical' position, be it critical theory, critical realism, radical humanism or postmodernism. We wanted to be able to identify potential for change by looking back as well as by looking forward. We wanted to be able to see possibilities emerging from practice as well as from rational intellectual endeavour.

So we stayed with our original title. *New Frontiers in HRD* encapsulates the spirit of this book because it is concerned with boundaries – why they form, why and how they move, and what lies beyond. All three editors share dissatisfaction with current debate seeking to clarify and delineate the field of HRD, and this is particularly apparent in the following two chapters. For us the key pursuit is theorizing HRD, rather than presenting a particular position on HRD theory. While the latter may well have preoccupied scholarships at the end of the twentieth century (Swanson 2001; Weinberger 1998; McLean 1998), others such as Mankin (2001) and Höpfl (2000) have also examined either what might underlie HRD or the way that HRD is defined in practice (see also, for example, Sambrook 2000; Hill and Stewart 1999). Yet other writers have attempted to establish the nature of HRD through comparison with other subjects (Grieves and Redman 1999; Gourlay 2001; Sambrook and Stewart 1998). Perhaps the establishment of social closure is a typical feature of the process of professionalization, and the theoretical foundations and ultimate purpose of HRD scholarship and practice? If this is so, then this concern with definition and creating boundaries must be a necessary stage of growth. Yet it must be a stage and not a permanent block to further debate.

Overview of content

Chapters 2 and 3 engage with this issue directly. In Chapter 2, McGoldrick and his colleagues set out the difficulties in drawing together coherent streams in HRD research and writing. Examining the literature through a framework which begins with philosophy and moves through theory, academic disciplines and language to the empirical base informing current theorizing, their conclusion is that the strength of the subject, certainly as an area of academic inquiry, lies in its variety, diversity and, to an extent, its ambiguity. Rather than limiting the development of research and associated credibility, the authors of this chapter argue that both of those are enhanced by the unsettled boundaries and space of HRD. This argument draws in part on the recent academic history of HRM, and the 'troubled relationship' that might be said to exist between HRD and HRM. The authors end with a proposal that the 'holographic' metaphor originally applied to HRM by Tom Keenoy (1999) offers a positive and useful way of accommodating the rich variety of work in the field of HRD. This is appropriate to this book in the sense that holograms can be seen as operating at the *frontiers* of physical, social and virtual worlds.

Lee continues the theme of questioning the desire to 'settle questions' in any final form, especially when it comes to *defining* HRD, in Chapter 3. She argues strongly against the desire to define HRD, suggesting that not only is such definition not needed, but also it is inappropriate and counter-productive. She draws upon Heraclitus' views of 'becoming' to suggest that HRD is indefinable, and that 'to attempt to define it is only to serve political or social needs of the minute, to give the appearance of being in control'. She makes a distinction between defining HRD and drawing boundaries around it that are dynamic and situation specific. This conception of situated limits links to the idea of *frontiers* and the exploration of boundaries evident in many of the chapters in this book.

The second and third parts of the book maintain the exploration of boundaries by implication. In Part II, Chapters 4 to 7 focus upon developments in the human-centred approach to HRD. This approach is developing rapidly, largely as a reaction to the professionalization of HRD, which has been accompanied by a focus upon technique and function. A number of chapters in this book are concerned to push beyond this boundary. So a second theme concerns the *human* aspect of HRD. Despite a century-long tradition of adult learning theory, the humanistic principles which underlie this have been displaced by two forces: on the one hand by a hard-nosed focus upon the so-called business case, and on the other by rejection of the concept of the 'self' and the 'human subject'. On both counts this leaves HRD precariously balanced. An excessive preoccupation with 'adding value' can lead to a constricting focus upon short-term metrics (Lee 1995). For a field such as HRD, in which the whole rationale leads to a focus upon the mid-term and even long term, this is ultimately defeating. In addition, the dismissal of the *human-centredness* and the intra-psychic dimension of HRD leave it eviscerated as a field of both scholarship and practice. Three chapters in this book bring us back to the human dimension through an exploration of ethics and values.

It is only recently that the ethical dimension of specific human resource management practices have been examined in any depth (Winstanley and Woodall 2000; Woodall and Winstanley 2000) and only most recently has human resource development come under close ethical scrutiny (Woodall and Douglas 1999; Hatcher 2002; Stewart 2003). Hitherto most research on business ethics was focused upon issues of governance and social responsibility in relations to consumers and the community. The employee stakeholder was overlooked. A major breakthrough took place among the membership of the US Academy of Human Resource Development (AHRD), an association of scholars and scholar-practitioners, between the years 1997 and 2000. This development is traced by Darlene Russ-Eft in Chapter 4, which focuses upon how the process of professionalization led to 'articulated and shared values' and in turn to 'some standards of ethics and practice'. She shows how this emerged out of a grassroots movements among members of AHRD, into a taskforce charged with the development of a code on ethics and integrity (Academy of Human Resource Development 1999), followed by the development and publication of a set of case studies for use in teaching and training students (Aragon and Hatcher 2001). While her comparison with similar codes developed by other professional bodies is favourable, Russ-Eft does ponder on the extent to which HRD scholars and practitioners are aware of the ethical dilemmas in their work, and the extent to which this might vary cross-culturally. She concludes by calling for more research into these issues, and for more ethical debate within the pages of scholarly journals in HRD.

In Chapter 5, Rona S. Beattie reminds us that line managers exert more influence over the learning of their staff than HRD professionals. However, the behaviours they model can be inhibitory as well as facilitative. She makes a link between the underlying principles of adult learning and an ethical approach to staff supervision. This is illustrated through research into professional supervision of social workers in two not-for-profit organizations in Scotland. She argues that an ethical approach can contribute to a powerful effect upon the learning within organizations and to getting people management processes embedded within supervisor and line manager roles. The implication of this is that crude performance management systems resting simply upon targets and metrics will not necessarily be effective in ensuring that line managers play a key role in the learning and performance-improvement of their staff – especially if these staff are knowledge workers and professionals.

In Chapter 6, Diana Winstanley explores how UK HR consultants working for organizations in the charity and voluntary sector 'live' their values. This study highlights the central role that ethics and values have played in underpinning the missions of organizations in this expanding sector of employment. Not only does the nature of work in such not-for-profit organizations means that strong human-centred values are brought to bear, but also it attracts HRD consultants who claim that value congruence with their clients is essential to their way of working. Thus it is not surprising that codes of conduct and practice, although useful for surfacing some value and ethics issues, are not particularly helpful in developing value change, and can also mask contradictions between competing values. These HRD consultants were 'mavericks', working with strong sets of values in unusual and innovative ways that do not easily fit into conventional consultancy models and prescriptions of HRD practice. Again this chapter is asking us to question simplistic models of ethical compliance and also the role for HRD professionals to adopt in strongly value-driven organizations. To date most research on HRD in such organizations focuses upon the corporate commercial sector. This study indicates the different context and approaches involved in working with values and value changes in the not-for-profit sector.

The encouragement of individual professionals to engage in continuing professional development (CPD) has become a major HRD concern in recent years. However, the implicit assumptions about professional learning, and the learning contexts and processes in which professionals might participate, lie somewhat uneasily beside the conditions of professional practice. This is illustrated in Chapter 7, where Jean Woodall and Stephen Gourlay provide a critical review of the literature on professional learning as it relates to the experiences of practising UK business professionals. They conclude by arguing for the incorporation of a sociocultural perspective into research into professional learning, and outline a number of implications for future research into CPD.

In Part III, Chapters 8 to 10 continue the exploration of implicit boundaries through the examination of organizational aspects of HRD. Chapter 8 by Rob F. Poell examines the use of actor network theory in understanding learning processes experienced during work-based learning. To be more precise, the specific focus is learning through project work. Such work is though, as Poell argues, an increasingly common experience for employees and so of growing significance for work-based learning. It is also, as Poell points out, a way of organizing and designing work that potentially supports the 'holy grail' of learning through work and working through learning. The key strength of the theoretical model of actor network theory is that it focuses attention on all those involved in and who are members of the network. Thus, employees themselves, their colleagues and managers as well as HRD professionals are all involved in practising HRD. Not only this, but all are involved in determining the agenda and purpose of HRD, which means that it is not seen as exclusively a management tool to be used to achieve specified objectives. Poell goes on to identify a variety of forms that learning projects might and do take, and to examine the implications of the method, and of the application of network theory, for established ideas in adult learning and education. Poell highlights the important role of power relationships in work organizations and the related role of organization and work design, and the way work is managed, for the learning of individual employees. He also argues for constructivist positions to be adopted to inform the design of HRD research.

In Chapter 9, Russ Vince sets out the case for seeing the field of HRD as much more than individual learning. He argues that that there is a fundamental difference between individual and organizational learning, but that most traditional approaches to HRD are based upon the parameters and limitations of the first: 'The effect of such an approach has been to limit the ability of individuals and collectives to understand the many social, emotional and political issues that impact on learning and organizing.' By implication, he argues for an approach to HRD that includes and addresses such things as politics, power and emotion and legitimizes the study of these as areas of HRD alongside that of organizational structures, strategies and processes.

In Chapter 10, Heather Höpfl addresses similar issues, while looking at the impact that the plethora of change initiatives that have swept higher education in recent years has had upon the staff involved and upon the provision. She points to a number of factors, including the managerialist matrix structure and standard change practice that are routinely adopted, and argues that 'these mechanisms are counter-productive and jeopardize the very outcomes which they seek to realize'. In so doing she stands alongside Russ Vince in adopting an understanding of the business of HRD that is much broader than training and development, and also presents both the area of her concern, and HRD, as moving outside or beyond the traditional managerialist paradigm

Part IV contains the last two chapters of the book. These chapters take a wider view and look at HRD within the context of the future and the past. In Chapter 11, Joseph Kessels provides us with a new perspective on the future role of the HRD practitioner as a facilitator of learning. He takes us across the boundary between the industrial economy into the knowledge economy – a transition that will offer both new opportunities and new challenges for HRD. The continuation of traditional HRD practices for managing learning and performance – knowledge productivity – is open to question in the new knowledge economy: 'imposed performance goals, power-based managerial positions and the concept of ownership of knowledge-intensive companies in the hands of anonymous shareholders [will] inhibit knowledge productivity'. An emancipated and autonomous workforce becomes a necessity, at the same time as knowledge is increasingly socially embedded within organizations. This calls for a new approach to supporting learning – the corporate curriculum which is a 'collective learning space' that 'might become the binding force of knowledge networks and smart communities that depend heavily upon shared motivation and personal identification with the content of work'. This brings a completely new agenda for HRD recognizing that knowledge workers and autonomous professionals take charge of their own development, and that learning processes take place within the course of work. Thus the role of the HRD professional is increasingly directed towards creating an appropriate environment for this to take place, rather than specific training interventions. The new 'corporate curriculum' requires the HRD function to produce and promote, *inter alia*, processes and initiatives to support the acquisition of subject matter expertise, learning to identify and deal with new problems, the cultivation of reflective skills, and the acquisition of communication and social skills. In addition, recognizing individual autonomy in respect of motivation, feelings and identification, promoting tolerance and stimulating creative turmoil will become part of the role. In this sense, Kessels' vision looks both backwards and forwards. It looks back to the roots of adult learning theory with its focus upon individual learning experiences, emancipatory learning, and critical reflection. At the same time it looks forward to a complex world with complex, non-standard and fast-changing learning requirements.

In Chapter 12, Monica Lee reiterates some of these arguments, and provides a counterpoint to her chapter in Part I. She provides a broad and sweeping overview of organization and management theory, and how it can be linked with evolutionary and psychological understandings of human experience. From this, she postulates four perspectives that can and have been adopted to explain development, whatever that term may be attached to, e.g. management or human resource development. These perspectives are labelled maturation, voyage, emergent and shaping. Each is informed by differing positions on the nature of the world and of individual identity. Her main argument is that these perspectives are not necessarily mutually exclusive and that they can in combination provide what she terms a 'holistic' description and understanding of HRD. This may suggest a boundary, but it is one which is fluid and flexible depending on the push and pulls of the four perspectives and on the autopoietic nature of the relationships implicit in the model. So, while HRD is still not defined, Lee's model does provide a way of viewing HRD, and the notion of development in particular, which can accommodate the rich variety of current theorizing. In this respect, this final chapter reinforces the message contained in Chapter 2. It also neatly sets out the frontiers to be addressed in future research in HRD.

Summary and conclusion

It will be clear from this overview that HRD remains a contested concept in the more broadly contested field of organization and management theory. To be a contested concept though is not necessarily a drawback or a weakness. We might argue too that it is not necessarily an advantage or a strength. It is simply the case at this particular point in time. Working from that starting point, it appears logical to say that both threats and opportunities present themselves for the future growth of HRD as an academic subject and field of professional practice. Growth implies the pressing at (if not the extension) of frontiers, both processes which also presage the creation of new frontiers. This book intends to support the creation of new frontiers of HRD and so is suitably titled. The content summarized above provides the raw material. We hope that other academics, researchers, policy-makers and scholar practitioners, all of whom constitute the intended readership of the book, find the raw material useful in pressing the boundaries of HRD theory and practice.

References

Academy of Human Resource Development (AHRD) (1999) *Standards in Ethics and Integrity*, 1st edn, Baton Rouge, LA: AHRD.

Aragon, S. and Hatcher, T. (eds) (2001) *Ethics and Integrity in HRD: Case Studies in Research and Practice*, *Advances in Developing Human Resources*, 3, 1, San Francisco, CA: Berrett-Koehler.

Boreham, N., Samurçay, R. and Fischer, M. (2002) *Work Process Knowledge*, London: Routledge.

Boyacigiller, N. A. and Adler, N. J. (1991) 'The parochial dinosaur: organisational science in a global context', *Academy of Management Review*, 16, 2: 262–290.

Coyne, B., Coyne, E. and Lee, M. (2003) *Human Resources, Care-Giving, Career Progression and Gender*, London: Routledge.

Gibb, S. (2002) *Learning and Development*, Basingstoke: Palgrave.

Gourlay, S. (2001) 'Knowledge management and HRD', *Human Resource Development International*, 4, 1: 27–46.

Grieves, J. and Redman, T. (1999) 'Living in the shadow of OD: HRD and the search for identity', *Human Resource Development International*, 2, 2: 81–102.

Hatcher, T. (2002) *Ethics and HRD: A New Approach to Leading Responsible HRD*, Cambridge, MA: Perseus.

Hill, R. and Stewart, R. (1999) 'Human resource development in small organisations', *Human Resource Development International*, 2, 2: 103–124.

Höpfl, H. (2000) 'Getting to the heart of HRD', *Human Resource Development International*, 3, 2: 195–207.

Höpfl, H. and Kostera, M. (2002) *Interpreting the Maternal Organisation*, London: Routledge.

Keenoy, T. (1999) 'HRM as hologram: a polemic', *Journal of Management Studies*, 36, 1: 1–23.

Lee, M. (1995) 'Learning for work: short-term gain or long-term benefit?' *Personnel Review*, 24: 29–43.

Lee, M. (1999) 'Understandings of conflict: a cross-cultural investigation', *Personnel Review Select*, 2, 3: 138–146.

Lee, M. (ed.) (2003) *HRD in a Complex World*, London: Routledge.

McLean, G. N. (1998) 'HRD: a three-legged stool, and octopus, or a centipede?', *Human Resource Development International*, 1, 4: 375–377.

McNiff, J. (2000) *Action Research in Organisations*, London: Routledge.

Mankin, D. (2001) 'A model for human resource development', *Human Resource Development International*, 4, 1: 65–86.

Sambrook, S. (2000) 'Talking of HRD', *Human Resource Development International*, 3, 2: 159–178.

Sambrook, S. and Stewart, J. (1998) 'No, I don't want to be part of HR', *Human Resource Development International*, 1, 2: 171–188.

Sambrook, S., Stewart, J. and Tjepkema, S. (2003) 'The changing role of HRD practitioners in learning orientated organisations', in B. Nyhan *et al.* (eds) *Facing Up to the Learning Organisation Challenge: Key Issues from a European Perspective*, Luxembourg: Office for Official Publications of the European Commission.

Smith, W., Higgins, M., Parker, M. and Lightfoot, G. (2001) *Science Fiction and Organization*, London: Routledge.

Stewart, J. (1999) *Employee Development Practice*, London: FT Prentice Hall.

Stewart, J. (2003) 'The ethics of HRD', in M. Lee (ed.) *HRD in a Complex World*, London: Routledge.

Stewart, J. and Beaver, G. (eds) (2004) *HRD in Small Organisations: Research and Practice*, London: Routledge.

Stewart, J. D. and McGoldrick, J. (eds) (1996) *Human Resource Development: Perspectives, Strategies and Practice*, London: Pitman.

Stewart, J. D., McGoldrick, J. and Watson, S. (2001) *Understanding Human Resource Development*, London: Routledge.

Swanson, R. (2001) 'Human resource development and its underlying theory', *Human Resource Development International*, 4, 3: 299–312.

Tjepkema, S., Stewart, J., Sambrook, S., Mulder, M., ter Horst, H. and Scheerens, J. (2002) *HRD and Learning Organisations in Europe*, London: Routledge.

Walton, J. (1999) *Strategic Human Resource Development*, London: FT Prentice Hall.

Weinberger, L. (1998) 'Commonly held values of human resource development', *Human Resource Development International*, 1, 1: 75–93.

Wilson, J. (1999) *Human Resource Development: Learning and Training for Individuals and Organisations*, London: Kogan Page.

Winstanley, D. and Woodall, J. (eds) (2000) *Ethical Issues in Contemporary Human Resource Management*, London: Macmillan.

Woodall, J. and Douglas, D. (1999) 'Ethical issues in contemporary human resource development', *Business Ethics: A European Review*, 8, 4: 249–261.

Woodall, J. and Winstanley, D. (2000) 'The ethical dimension of human resource management', *Human Resource Management Journal*, 10, 2: 5–20.

2 Philosophy and theory in HRD

Jim McGoldrick, Jim Stewart and Sandra Watson

Introduction

This chapter draws upon the emerging body of research in HRD, primarily UK based, which provides the underpinning for the conceptual, theoretical and practical advance of HRD. We aim to provide an overview of many of the conceptual and theoretical concerns surrounding the meaning and understanding of HRD. These issues and concerns relate to both the ontological and epistemological perspectives on HRD, which in turn influence our vision of researching and understanding HRD. The chapter offers a contribution to the ongoing debate surrounding the theoretical foundations of HRD (Walton 1999; Lynham 2000) and the purpose and value of HRD professional practice (Holton 2000). It presents an analysis of the key tenets of the various positions in these debates. In doing so, it provides something of a comparison of American and European conceptions of HRD. This informs the overview of the diversity of research philosophies, processes and practices currently being applied in the United Kingdom. We also draw on the work of Keenoy (1999), a sharp critic of the literature of HRM, and try to apply his critique into a better conceptual understanding of HRD by developing a metaphor of HRD as a 'hologram'.

Theoretical context

The process of defining HRD by academics, researchers and practitioners is proving to be frustrating, elusive and confusing (see, for example, Sambrook 2001, 2003; see also Lee, Chapter 3 in this volume). This suggests that HRD has not established a distinctive conceptual or theoretical identity (Garavan *et al.* 2000; Hatcher 2000). The process of defining HRD is *frustrated* by the apparent lack of boundaries and parameters; *elusiveness* is created through the lack of depth of empirical evidence of some conceptual aspects of HRD. *Confusion* arises over the philosophy, purpose, location and language of HRD. This is further complicated by the epistemological and ontological perspectives of individual stakeholders and commentators in the HRD arena (Swanson *et al.* 2000). All research, to varying degrees, is tied to a particular theoretical framework and to a general body of knowledge. This, in turn, is the product of a complex interplay of philosophical arguments. Thus the 'complication' noted by Swanson *et al.* (2000) is perfectly natural but renders the task of analysing the 'meaning' of HRD more difficult. Inevitably this draws us into the realm of philosophy.

Philosophical and conceptual dimensions

As Swanson *et al.* (2000: 1126) argue, 'philosophy is a systematic examination of the assumptions that underlie action.' Therefore, in order to understand action, in this case HRD research, it is necessary to engage with philosophies of HRD to make explicit the rationales underpinning competing perspectives. They put forward three interactive elements of the philosophical framework of HRD. These are, first, *ontology* (how we see our world), second, *epistemology* (how we think about our world) and, third, *axiology* (the values that determine how we should and actually act in research and practice). The dynamic relationship of these three elements will influence an individual's understanding and expression of HRD. Therefore it is useful and appropriate to address philosophical issues in attempting to understand HRD. Recently this has been strongly reinforced by the publication of a thoughtful collection of reflections on the philosophical foundations of *HRD practice* by leading US academics in the field of HRD (Ruona and Roth 2000).

The philosopher Thomas Kuhn first introduced the idea of scientific paradigms in his path-breaking book *The Structure of Scientific Revolutions* in 1962. This book has proven to be seminal in the development of theory and research in the social sciences and is likely to have an equally profound and enduring influence on the conceptual and theoretical development in HRD. The concept of paradigms, introduced by Kuhn (1962), is often used to describe philosophical frameworks informing and guiding scientific research. McAndrew (2000) usefully applies this notion in analysing significant influences on HRD theory and practice.

One of the best known paradigmatic frameworks is that developed by Burrell and Morgan (1979). They suggest four broad paradigms, which affect the development of social theory. The *functionalist paradigm* assumes an objective, social reality, which can be empirically analysed and understood through application of scientific methods. Social systems are seen as inherently concerned with stability and continuity to serve regulatory purposes. The *interpretive paradigm* assumes that individuals and their interactions create social reality, subjectively. Multiple social realities are created, maintained and changed, and there is no single objective entity to be analysed and understood. However, in common with the functional perspective, the interpretive paradigm assumes an underlying pattern and order in the social world, that is a regulatory focus, rather than a change orientation.

The *radical humanist paradigm* assumes that reality is socially and subjectively created and therefore not capable of objective analysis, seeing social institutions as negative in the sense of constraining and controlling human thought, action and potential. These negative aspects tend to alienate rather than focuses on positive outcomes. The concern is with radical change rather than regulation. The *radical structuralist paradigm* assumes that social systems have independent, concrete and objective existence and are capable of scientific analysis. This perspective also encompasses social systems as oppressive and alienating and assumes an inherent drive for radical change in society. A related perspective based on the philosophical work of Roy Bhaskar has been applied to the theory and practice of HRD by Hamblett *et al.* (2002) to persuasive effect.

Variants of these arguments are evident in the emergence of new perspectives on HRD framed as *post-positivist* (Trochim 1999) and *critical realist* (Sayer 2000; Hamblett *et al.* 2002) positions. The former of these develops elements of the Burrell and Morgan (1979) functionalist and interpretive paradigms while the critical realist perspective takes forward a concern with meaning and interpretation that echoes the radical humanist and radical structuralist paradigms. However, these have not crystallized into a simple bipolarization. Rather the whole area is characterized by *paradigm incommensurability*, which in turn reflects an impact on methodological development (for a more detailed discussion of these issues see Aldrich 1992). There are also important theoretical developments in the field of organization studies where there is a growing literature around the issue of realism and critical realism in management research which would be of great interest to those of us engaged in the process of 'theorizing' HRD (Ackroyd and Fleetwood 2000). The work of Hamblett and his colleagues already referred to is an example of this. Their use of the critical realist philosophy of Bhaskar in analysing HRD raises doubts about the taken-for-granted performance benefits associated with functionalism, and about the taken-for-granted emancipatory benefits associated with the interpretive paradigm.

To date, there appears to be little sustained and detailed attention given to philosophical influences on HRD, but as Kuchinke (2000: 32) argues, 'paradigm debates can deepen theory and provide the foundation for new research'. This view is supported by Swanson *et al.* (2000) among others, who identify implications of philosophy for research, theory building, practice and the evolution of HRD. The role of the varying paradigms discussed here, representing as they do different philosophical frameworks, in shaping HRD theory and practice is well illustrated by the work of Lynham (2000). It is evident that a significant outcome of adopting different paradigms will be varying emphasis on the possible alternative purposes of HRD.

This variety of perspectives demonstrates vividly that there is no dominant paradigm of HRD research (see also McGoldrick *et al.* 2002). It also illustrates what may be meant by 'paradigm incommensurability' in organizational research. However, such a position is healthy. There is no *single lens* for viewing HRD research and there are *many voices* expressing opinions. It may be that, as HRD academics become more sophisticated in theorizing, then greater clarity and paradigm commensurability will occur. It may also be the case that the increasingly influential discourse of postmodernism, which is strongly established in the field of organization studies (Alvesson and Deetz 1999; Burrell 1999) and is now evident in the literature of strategic change, will come to have an impact on HRD researchers (Ford and Ford 1995). Some early examples of this include Rigg and Trehan (2003) and Holmes (2003).

Much of the foregoing discussion resonates with the debates on the development of organization theory in the early 1990s. In particular Ackroyd's (1992) argument for the academic space for organization theory offers a sharp critique of paradigmatic analysis which he characterized as 'a positive brake on the development of a new discipline' (p. 102) by seeking 'exclusive control of authoritative knowledge of the field' (p. 103). These remarks have interesting implications for those engaged in defining the academic space for HRD. Progress in the growing maturity of HRD research and theorizing may though be signalled by collections such as those edited by Lee (2003) and by Elliott and Turnbull (2004).

Purpose of HRD

Lying behind the main philosophical debates concerning the nature of HRD, there is a concurrent set of debates concerning the purpose of HRD. According to Holton (2000) the debates on purpose centre on the *learning* versus *performance* perspectives. Should HRD practice focus on the well-being of the individual or should interests of the shareholders predominate? This section presents a rudimentary map of what the various claims of the purpose of HRD might be. Hatcher (2000) proposes that HRD research should focus on the economic benefits, systems theory, social benefits and ethics of HRD, and thus indirectly attempts a reconciliation of these two perspectives. Kuchinke (2000) presents a classification of schools of thought according to the central focus of the developmental activity: *person-centred, production-centred* and *principled problem-solving*, each deriving from different philosophical traditions. Gourlay (2000: 99) in attempting to clarify the nature of HRD states that 'it focuses on theory and practice relating to training, development and learning within organisations, both for individuals and in the context of business strategy and organisational competence formation'.

Garavan *et al.* (2000) articulate three perspectives of HRD as being concerned with *capabilities, psychological contracts and learning organization/ organizational learning*. Each of these is associated with different root disciplines. They also imply different purposes in their prescriptions for HRD practice. There is also variability in relation to the purpose of HRD arising from the root disciplines seen to be underpinning HRD. These include adult education, instructional design and performance technology, psychology, business and economics, sociology, cultural anthropology, organization theory and communications, philosophy, axiology and human relations theories (Willis 1997, cited by Walton 1999). There is also a running subterranean debate within the field of HRD on the 'discipline' status of some these root disciplines. As well as variability of purpose, conceptual propositions derived from and built on these root disciplines also influence individual perspectives of HRD. For example, in the typology devised by Garavan *et al.* (2000) the capabilities perspective is primarily associated with human capital theory and the application of economics in a resource based view of the firm. In a similar vein, Weinberger (1998) identifies systems theory as being distinct from learning theory in relation to their influence on HRD, leading to different formulations on the nature and purpose of HRD practice.

What is apparent from the above commentary is that there is no consensus over the conceptual-theoretical identity of HRD and related purpose. In addition, some of the main strands that can be argued to be apparent in these different views have themselves been subject to criticism in their own terms, rather than from the platform of a competing perspective. For example, the economic concept of human capital which informs and to an extent rationalizes the performance perspective is challenged by the newer concept of social capital (Stewart and Tansley 2002). Our understanding of learning – indeed the very notion of learning itself, which obviously underpins the learning perspective – has also been challenged as a valid or useful concept (Holmes 2003). What is clear though, and of interest here, is that the assumed or declared purpose of HRD is contingent upon both philosophical and theoretical perspectives.

Boundaries and parameters of HRD

This discussion demonstrates that the multidisciplinary nature of HRD makes precise definition difficult. There is some evidence in the literature of ideological or descriptive-normative models for aspects of HRD. For example Walton (1999) has identified 'Strategic HRD' as a distinctive, almost freestanding, dimension of HRD. Similarly, the much-discussed idea of the Learning Organization (Senge 1997) is a good example of the ways in which the normative prescriptive models are used as the basis for examining current practice (Dibella and Nevis 1998). HRD is often presented as different to training and development with the focus being on learning and development for the organization as well as the individual (see for example Harrison 2002; Gibb 2002). There is often a futuristic focus, with prescribed contingent outcomes. Although there are often attempts to address both the practice and the conceptual aspects of HRD, the drive to express HRD in relation to models, frameworks and typologies, could result in a distancing between rhetoric and reality, similar to that found in HRM debates. As Hatcher argues, 'Without a focus on the theoretical foundations of research and practice, HRD is destined to remain *atheoretical* in nature and poor practice will continue to undermine its credibility' (Hatcher 2000: 45, emphasis added).

Historically, the development of HRD can be traced from training and instructional design, to training and development, to employee development, to human resource development (Jacobs 2000). Traditionally, the field of HRD was defined by practice, not from a theoretical frame or set of research (Lynham 2000). More recently, the emergence of HRD-related journals has presented an opportunity to define the field on basis of theory and practice (Jacobs 2000). There is also a blurring of the boundaries in relation to the affiliation of researchers. Many early US researchers emanated from either an instructional design or an adult educational base. Jacobs (2000) has reported that there are an increased number of manuscripts coming from business schools. This trend is a reversal of the European and UK situation. In the United Kingdom, HRD is very much the child of the explosion of HRM literature in the 1980s and 1990s (McGoldrick and Stewart 1996).

In addition, the scope of HRD research can be seen to be expanding, with recent focus on areas that were not traditionally considered to be within the domain of HRD. These include organizational leadership, organizational values, workforce development issues at the societal level and labour economics (Donovan and Marsick 2000).

Multidisciplinary foundations and an expanding scope both have the effect of expanding the discursive resources and therefore language available to and used by HRD academics and practitioners (Sambrook 2001). This last point is worth a little more elaboration, particularly with respect to Hatcher's (2000) remark (noted earlier) concerning the poverty of HRD practice being a function of the poverty of HRD theory. Rather than seeking to stake a claim to particular territory, HRD should be looking to enhance its capability to theorize on the basis of a solid research base. As already noted, there is no single lens through which HRD is viewed, nor should there be. The debates which are now emerging from the AHRD in the United States and the University Forum for HRD in Europe indicate a growing vitality for the development of good HRD theory. In taking these discussions and debates forward, it is essential to pay close attention to issues of language and meaning.

Language of HRD: 'jargon-ridden' and 'meaning-hidden'?

There is a clear and continuing paradox concerning the language used in the discourse of HRD. Walton (1999: 54) neatly sums it up as follows: 'this constant concern with meaning and learning and their subtleties/shades/tones/cadences by those responsible for HRD can paradoxically be (yet another) reason why the HRD language appears so jargon-ridden and meaning-hidden.' He continues:

> Words are being asked to express the ambiguities faced by those trying to translate the subtleties of meaning into learning frameworks and language that hopefully capture all the nuances of actual experience and associated reflection, conceptualisation and experimentation.
>
> (Walton 1999: 54)

Social processes through which this has been attempted involve the construction of linguistic categories and an alteration in the received meaning of existing expressions. New terms in HRD include lifelong learning and psychological contracts, while terms with scope for new meaning include competence and competencies, integration, teamwork, communication and commitment. Although all of these are useful to describe practices, conceptually there is a danger that these denote rhetorical, often managerial, aspirations and desired states of being. A lack of effective linguistic categories to clarify what is happening within HRD could result in a combination of illusion and allusion, as there are no definitive words to signify its identity.

Many of Walton's concerns resonate with Legge's (1995) sharp critique of rhetoric and reality of HRM. However, this point is challenged by Sambrook (2000, 2001), who provides an analysis which draws no distinction between rhetoric and reality or words and action. In her view rhetoric is reality and words constitute action. From this approach, she is able to formulate a typology of 'ideal types' which is capable of accommodating discourse from both academic disciplines and professional practice. Such typologies, as well as those suggested by Garavan *et al.* (2000) and Lynham (2000) may well be useful in capturing and making sense of current variety of discourses within the HRD domain. However, a proliferation of linguistic terms with variable meanings has obvious consequences for investigating empirical experience.

Empirical elusiveness

Empirical elusiveness (Keenoy 1999) derives from an *inability to show* that HRD has a substantive presence in organizations. In some respects the issues surrounding the empirical absence or presence of HRD are analogous with those discussed earlier with respect to the conceptual parameters and boundaries. The American Society for Training and Development Research Committee identified two major empirical gaps in relation to evidence as being between practitioners and researchers, and between practitioners and senior executives (Dilworth and Redding 1999). Several European commentators, including Harrison (2002), have found little empirical evidence of 'Strategic HRD' in organizations. Others including Sambrook (1998) identify divergence in the stories told by HRD practitioners and non-HRD managers and employees. These studies suggest a need for closer collaboration between researchers and practitioners in order to build more accurate empirical evidence. Such a need has been expressed by both

European (Hamlin *et al.* 1998; Hamlin 2002) and American (Lynham 2000) academics.

Locations of HRD

Locations of HRD can be understood in two senses: first, as a description of a physical or sectoral location, and second and more importantly, as a feature of the process of organizational design. Reconfiguration of contemporary organizations, the emergence of the small business sector and continued growth in non-standard forms of employment are extending the perimeters of HRD activity. Internal creation of independent business units and growth of outsourcing, subcontracting and down sizing are all impacting on the structures and boundaries of organizations. Similarly the notion of 'employee' appears increasingly transient (Stewart and Tansley 2000); employment security is less salient, with apparent continuing growth in temporary, part-time, subcontract and agency work. As a consequence HRD can no longer be seen to operate within the traditional boundaries of an organization, but spread its influence to the development of those outside, on whom it depends (Walton 1996, 1999). In addition the SME sector is likely to provide a growing location for HRD practice, which may imply an expansion of the meaning of HRD (Hill and Stewart 2000; Stewart and Beaver 2004).

Summary

What is apparent from the discussion so far is that there is no consensus over the conceptual-theoretical identity of HRD. The concept is indeed complex and complicated (Vince 2003). It can be seen to constitute multiple, shifting, competing and contingent identities, dependent on philosophical perspectives and influenced by the range of methodological dimensions derived from the literature and from the continuing analysis of ongoing research work.

Critical analysis

It is part of our argument that conceptually HRD is still in the intellectual shadows of HRM particularly with respect to HRD research in the United Kingdom (McGoldrick and Stewart 1996; Harrison 2002). It is instructive, however, to see all the lessons that HRD academics can learn from the theoretical development of HRM. Since its emergence in the late 1980s there have been two distinct strands to the literature advancing HRM. The first of these has been the solid development of texts and journal publications. The second has been a highly critical, even polemical, literature questioning the academic and root discipline claims of HRM (Watson 2003). The strongly critical literature is exemplified by Keenoy and Anthony's (1992) portrayal of HRM as 'metaphor' and Legge's (1995) critique of the rhetoric of HRM.

One of the sharpest critics is Tom Keenoy (1999), who has written a deeply polemical review of the rise of HRM – which he dubs 'HRMism'. The article is both challenging and stimulating, and poses questions as relevant to the emerging debates about HRD as to the discussion of HRM. His argument is that HRM concepts, practices and theory are 'a continuing source of controversy, confusion and misapprehension.' Indeed, he goes further and argues: 'At the centre of this unfolding obfuscation lies an infuriating but curious paradox: despite mounting evidence of conceptual fragmentation, empirical incoherence and theoretical vacuity, HRMism has gone from strength to strength' (Keenoy 1999: 1). These charges of conceptual fragmentation, empirical incoherence and theoretical vacuity may equally be applied to HRD. However, emerging from his polemical discourse there is a potentially useful metaphor for HRD.

A holographic metaphor?

The key argument that we wish to advance here, in contradistinction to the way that Keenoy's argument is developed, is that utilizing the metaphor of a hologram enables the reconciliation of intrinsic confusions and contradictions of conceptual, theoretical and empirical identities of HRD to be understood. 'Holograms are projected images which, as we shift our visual field in relation to them, appear to have contours, depth and, in some cases, movement' (Keenoy 1999: 9). The hologram is comprised of two distinct, discrete technological and social processes, which are entwined. Both must occur simultaneously for the hologram to exist. Human social action and perception are an integral part of the process required to construct the image. Holograms can be described as 'techno-social' artefacts with a complex ontology (Keenoy 1999: 10). Each is real, but each exists in a different domain. We see only what we are looking for. In order to see the other side, the shaded, deeper side of its identity, we need to change our perspective. The hologram provides a metaphor, which depicts 'social reality' as multidimensional, multicausal, mutually dependent and constantly changing. The holographic reality is accessible only through a reflexive epistemology, which explicitly acknowledges the role of human beings in creating 'social reality'.

The following quotation from Keenoy is modified and substitutes HRD for HRM:

> The more [HRD] is undermined by conventional academic analysis, the stronger it seems to have become. Viewed from a holographic perspective this paradox is a consequence of employing a limiting two-dimensional epistemology. . . . Trying to fragment the phenomena and then mapping each fragment against a predetermined definition could be responsible for failure to 'see' [HRD] for what it is.
>
> (Keenoy 1999: 10–11)

For Keenoy all of those implicated (in HRD) may hold different 'conceptual-projections' of HRD, which are likely to contradict their actual experience of HRD. From this HRD can be seen as a series of mutually expressive phenomena, which are transient (Keenoy 1999: 17). Therefore it is impossible to conclude that HRD does not exist and impossible to conclude that it does exist (see also Sambrook 2001). HRD exists in so far as it is the process of coming into being. Although we may not be used to conceptualizing HRD as social phenomena in this way, such a conception is already present in the learning organization discourse, which is depicted as a continuous and never-ending process (Sun 2003).

The holographic metaphor of HRD has some attraction for some of the reasons that Keenoy is sceptical. While most of this chapter has argued that HRD has no singular identity, if it is understood as a hologram it could be defined as singular. HRD's singularity would be defined through the properties of the hologram which could be described as 'the fluid, multi-faceted, integrated social artefacts', which are the 'continuing-outcome' of contextualized learning. HRD then serves as the *collective noun* for the various concepts, theories and methods devised to manage and control learning. This definition embodies our earlier argument concerning the complex interplay of competing ontological, epistemological and methodological assumptions, which assist in understanding the reality of HRD. The benefits of the holographic metaphor are the following:

- It acknowledges anomaly, uncertainty, ambiguity, multiple identities, multiple interpretations and transience. It is sensitive to the problem of linguistic expression.
- It permits the encompassment and softening of contradictions and paradoxes of different perspectives of HRD.
- It emphasizes the analytical significance of the mutually involved processes of social and discursive construction, that is the role of social actors in reconstructing reality, while being components of reality.
- It provides interesting methodological questions concerning empirical research. This does not necessarily mean the abandonment of conventional modernist methodology, but emphasizes the need for greater interpretative sensitivity. It requires analytical space to accommodate paradox, ambiguity and instability as normal predictable outcomes within the praxis relationship.

The holographic metaphor seems to offer an alternative to the dualistic limitations of the modernist perspective and avoids the 'limitless relativism' found in some varieties of social constructionism.

The use of metaphors in HRD is not a new phenomenon by any means. Short (2000) provides an excellent review of the use of metaphors. However, the attractions of the holographic metaphor are that it allows for a whole new perspective radically different to those currently associated with the debates on HRD. It provides a perspective, which is grounded in the belief that social reality has to be understood as a 'fluid, unfolding *process* of social accomplishment' and, in addition, 'draws our attention to the experiential nature of observation and the *observational nature of experience.* "Reality" is a fuzzy *shimmer* between these two movements' (Keenoy 1999: 18, original emphases).

The implications for theorizing and methodological development afforded by consideration of the holographic perspective may not yet amount to a new paradigm. However, it does offer a counter to the initial charges that may be laid at the door of HRD theory of conceptual fragmentation and theoretical vacuity. The methodological implications for research design are immense and challenging. But that is a matter for another chapter and another time.

Conclusion

We have offered a detailed analysis of the theoretical context of HRD research by focusing initially on the philosophical and conceptual dimensions. We argued that HRD has no dominant paradigm, at least in the United Kingdom. There is no single lens for viewing HRD and indeed there are many voices articulating particular perspectives. In relation to our questions on the purpose of HRD we found that there is no consensus over the conceptual-theoretical identity of HRD and related purpose. The purpose is contingent upon both philosophical and theoretical perspectives. Arguments on the theoretical foundations of HRD also constitute the core of debates on its scope and boundaries.

We also discussed at length the issues of the boundaries and parameters of HRD where we argued that rather than seeking to stake a claim to particular territory, HRD should be looking to enhance its capability to theorize on the basis of a solid research base. We also addressed the language of HRD as central to advancing theory and research. Such is the significance of the language of HRD that we concluded that the distinction between rhetoric and reality in HRD is a false one. Finally, in the theoretical overview we examined the empirical elusiveness and locations of HRD and argued that both of these were intimately bound up with the changing forms and designs of organizations and the need therefore for research in HRD to address these changes.

The concluding section focused on the holographic metaphor as a novel perspective on HRD. Our thinking in this regard is at an early stage but we felt it provided the basis of a paradigm through which HRD can be expressed as a transient phenomenon more difficult to explain than understand. It is also seen as useful in developing new explanatory models of what HRD 'is', 'might be' or 'can be'. Although there is no agreement on what HRD means, it is nonetheless researched, practised and taught.

Acknowledgement

This chapter is an updated version of J. McGoldrick, J. Stewart and S. Watson (2001) 'Theorizing human resource development', *Human Resource Development International*, 4, 3: 343–356 http://www.tandf.co.uk/journals/routledge/13678868.html

References

Ackroyd, S. (1992) 'Paradigms lost: paradise regained?', in M. Reed and M. Hughes (eds) *Rethinking Organisation: New Directions in Organisation Theory and Analysis*, London: Sage.

Ackroyd, S. and Fleetwood, S. (2000) 'Realism in contemporary organisation and management studies', in S. Ackroyd and S. Fleetwood (eds) *Realist Perspectives on Management and Organisations*, London: Routledge.

Aldrich, H. E. (1992) 'Incommensurable paradigms? Vital signs from three perspectives', in M. Reed and M. Hughes (eds) *Rethinking Organisation: New Directions in Organisation Theory and Analysis*, London: Sage.

Alvesson, M. and Deetz, S. (1999) 'Critical theory and postmodernism: approaches to organisational studies', in S. Clegg (ed.) *Studying Organisation Theory and Method*, London: Sage.

Burrell, G. (1999) 'Normal science, paradigms, metaphors, discourses and genealogies of analysis', in S. Clegg (ed.) *Studying Organisation Theory and Method*, London: Sage.

Burrell, G. and Morgan, G. (1979) *Sociological Paradigms and Organisational Analysis*, London: Heinemann.

Dibella, A. J. and Nevis, E. C. (1998) *How Organizations Learn: An Integrated Strategy for Building Learning Capability*, San Francisco, CA: Jossey-Bass.

Dilworth, J. and Redding, R. L. (1999) 'Bridging gaps: an update from the ASTD research committee', *Human Resource Development Quarterly*, 10, 3: 199–202.

Donovan, L. L. and Marsick, V. J. (2000) 'Trends in the literature: a comparative analysis of 1998 HRD research', *Proceedings of the Academy of Human Resource Development*, North Carolina.

Elliott, C. and Turnbull, S. (eds) (2004) *Critical Thinking in HRD*, London: Routledge.

Ford, J. D. and Ford, L. W. (1995) 'The role of conversations in producing intentional organisational change', *Academy of Management Review* 20, 3: 541–570.

Garavan, T. N., Gunnigle, P. and Morley, M. (2000) 'Contemporary HRD research: a triarchy of theoretical perspectives and their prescriptions for HRD', *Journal of European Industrial Training*, 24, 1, 2, 3 and 4: 65–93.

Gibb, S. (2002) *Learning and Development: Processes, Practices and Perspectives at Work*, Basingstoke: Palgrave Macmillan.

Gourlay, S. (2000) 'Knowledge management and HRD', *HRD Research and Practice across Europe Conference Proceedings*, Kingston University, Kingston upon Thames.

Hamblett, J., Holden, R. and Thursfield, D. (2002) 'The tools of freedom and the sources of indignity', in J. McGoldrick *et al.* (eds) *Understanding HRD: A Research Based Approach*, London: Routledge.

Hamlin, B. (2002) 'Towards evidence based HRD practice', in J. McGoldrick *et al.* (eds) *Understanding HRD: A Research Based Approach*, London: Routledge.

Hamlin, B., Reidy, M. and Stewart, J. (1998) 'Bridging the research–practice gap through professional partnerships: a case study', *Human Resource Development International*, 1, 3: 273–290.

Harrison, R. (2002) *Learning and Development*, London: CIPD,

Hatcher, T. (2000) 'A study of the influence of the theoretical foundations of human resource development on research and practice', *Proceedings of the Academy of Human Resource Development*, North Carolina.

Hill, R. and Stewart, J. (2000) 'Human resource development in small organisations', *Journal of European Industrial Training*, 24, 1, 2, 3 and 4: 105–117.

Holmes, L. (2003) 'The learning turn in education and training: liberatory paradigm or oppressive ideology?' *Proceedings of Third International Conference on Critical Management Studies*, Lancaster University, 7–9 July.

Holton, III, E. F. (2000) 'Clarifying and defining the performance paradigm of HRD', *Proceedings of the Academy of Human Resource Development*, North Carolina.

Jacobs, R. L. (2000) 'Developing the boundaries of HRDQ and HRD', *Human Resource Development Quarterly*, 11, 1: 1–3.

Keenoy, T. (1999) 'HRM as hologram: a polemic', *Journal of Management Studies*, 36, 1: 1–23.

Keenoy, T. and Anthony, P. (1992) 'HRM: metaphor, meaning and morality', in P. Blyton and P. Turnbull (eds) *Reassessing Human Resource Management*, London: Sage.

Kuchinke, P. K. (2000) 'Development towards what end? An analysis of the notion of development for the field of human resource development', *Proceedings of the Academy of Human Resource Development*, North Carolina.

Kuhn, T. S. (1962) *The Structure of Scientific Revolutions*, Chicago, IL: University of Chicago Press.

Lee, M. (ed.) (2003) *HRD in a Complex World*, London: Routledge.

Legge, K. (1995) *Human Resource Management: Rhetoric and Reality*, London: Macmillan.

Lynham, S. A. (2000) 'Theory building in the human resource development profession', *Human Resource Development Quarterly*, 11, 2: 159–178.

McAndrew, A. E. (2000) 'Scientific paradigms and their implications for a vision of HRD', *Proceedings of the Academy of Human Resource Development*, North Carolina.

McGoldrick, J. and Stewart, J. D. (1996) 'The HRM/HRD nexus', in J. Stewart and J. McGoldrick (eds) *Human Resource Development: Perspectives, Strategies and Practice*, London: Pitman.

McGoldrick, J., Stewart, J. and Watson, S. (eds) (2002) *Understanding HRD: A Research Based Approach*, London: Routledge.

Reed, M. (1992) 'Introduction', in M. Reed and M. Hughes (eds) *Rethinking Organisation: New Directions in Organisation Theory and Analysis*, London: Sage.

Reed, M. and Hughes, M. (eds) (1992) *Rethinking Organisation: New Directions in Organisation Theory and Analysis*, London: Sage.

Rigg, C. and Trehan, K. (2003) 'Reflections on working with critical action learning', *Proceedings of Third International Conference on Critical Management Studies*, Lancaster University, 7–9 July.

Ruona, W. E. A. and Roth, G. (eds) (2000) *Philosophical Foundations of Human Resource Development Practice, Advances in Developing Human Resources*, 7, San Francisco, CA: Berrett-Koehler.

Sambrook, S. A. (1998) 'Models and concepts of human resource development; academic and practitioner perspectives', unpublished PhD thesis, Nottingham Trent University.

Sambrook, S. A. (2000) 'Talking of HRD', *Human Resource Development International*, 3, 2: 159–178.

Sambrook, S. A. (2001) 'HRD as an emergent and negotiated evolution: an ethnographic case study in the British national health service', *Human Resource Development Quarterly*, 12, 2: 169–191.

Sambrook, S. A. (2003) 'A "critical" time for HRD', *Proceedings of the Third International Conference on Critical Management Studies*, Lancaster University, 7–9 July.

Sayer, A. (2000) *Realism and Social Science*, London: Sage.

Senge, P. (1997) *The Fifth Discipline*, London: Century Business.

Short, D. (2000) 'Analysing HRD through metaphor: why, how, and some likely findings', *Proceedings of the Academy of Human Resource Development*, North Carolina.

Stewart, J. and Beaver, G. (eds) (2004) *HRD in Small Organisations: Research and Practice*, London, Routledge.

Stewart, J. and McGoldrick, J. (eds) (1996) *Human Resource Development: Perspectives, Strategies and Practice*, London: Pitman.

Stewart, J. and Tansley, C. (2002) *Training in the Knowledge Economy*, London: CIPD.

Sun, H. C. (2003) 'Conceptual clarifications for "organisational learning", "learning organisation" and a "learning organisation"', *Human Resource Development International*, 6, 2: 153–166.

Swanson, R. A., Lynham, S. A., Ruona, W. E. and Torraco, R. J. (2000) 'Theory building researching HRD – pushing the envelope!', *Proceedings of the Academy of Human Resource Development*, North Carolina.

Trochim, W. K. (1999) 'Positivism and post-positivism: research methods', *Knowledge Base*, 2nd edn, http://trochim.human.cornell.edu/Kb/positivism.htm

Vince, R. (2003) 'Towards a critical practice of HRD', *Proceedings of the Third International Conference on Critical Management Studies*, Lancaster University, 7–9 July.

Walton, J. (1996) 'The provision of learning support for non-employees', in J. Stewart and J. McGoldrick (eds) *Human Resource Development: Perspectives, Strategies and Practice*, London: Pitman.

Walton, J. (1999) *Strategic Human Resource Development*, London: FT Prentice Hall.

Watson, T. (2003) 'Towards a grown-up and critical academic HRM – and the need to grow out of infantile "Hard and Soft HRM"', *Proceedings of the Third International Conference on Critical Management Studies*, Lancaster University, 7–9 July.

Weinberger, L. A. (1998) 'Commonly held theories of human resource development', *Human Resource Development International*, 1, 1: 75–93.

Willis, V. J. (1997) 'HRD as evolutionary system: from pyramid building to space walking and beyond', *Proceedings of the Academy of Human Resource Development*, Atlanta, GA.

3 A refusal to define HRD

Monica Lee

Introduction

In the early 1990s I started a master's course at Lancaster University in the United Kingdom (an MSC in HRD (by research) designed to lead to both professional and academic qualifications for international cohorts of senior HRD professionals). In the first workshop of each cohort, people were getting their bearings and feeling what the course might be like. Two months later, after people had been back at work and started to reflect upon links between the academic and professional sides of their lives, they attended the second workshop, and the feel of the group would change from a rather polite coming together to a ravenous demanding caucus.

The defining of HRD became paramount in most people's minds. It was as if they believed that once they knew the definition of HRD then they would understand what HRD 'is'. They would then be able to manage their jobs, and the course; their future study and work roles will be laid out in front of them, such that so long as they knew where the path was, they could achieve excellence through sheer hard work. These views shifted quite rapidly, but for that workshop, if I failed to define HRD for them, then, as course designer and leader I would be preventing them from achieving; furthermore, how could I design a course without knowing what I was doing?

In addition, during and since the establishment of *Human Resource Development International* (an international journal devoted to developing theory and practice in HRD), I have been regularly asked for my definition of HRD, for publicity, for guidance to contributors, and so on. I refused.

Despite (at times, intense) pressure I have succeeded in refusing to define HRD since the early 1980s, and this chapter represents a rehearsal of the justifications that I used then, and since, for my obdurate behaviour. In this chapter I argue that there are philosophical, theoretical, professional and practical reasons for my refusal and, indeed, that HRD, as tacitly 'defined' by our experiences, would be harmed by anything more than such an emergent tacit approach.

I shall tie this account around that of the master's programme that I mentioned earlier. This programme was terminated after running for only four cohorts, yet, unlike many master's programmes, it generated income and proved to be extremely successful with the students, many of whom say that it has fundamentally changed their lives. The problem was not quality either, as the majority of students achieved exceptionally good academic results, even though several came with very little prior academic experience. The problem was that it adopted a philosophy and practice fundamentally different from that of 'normal' academe.

The philosophical case for refusing to define HRD

I used the design of this programme to explore some of my ideas of adult education, and, having only recently joined university life after twenty years' working for others and myself in the field, I did not fully realize quite how unusual my ideas would seem to the 'system'.

I designed my master's programme in accordance with how I understood my role as an HRD professional, and as an educator of others. It seemed to me as an HRD professional that while I carried a central core of understanding from each experience that came my way, 'I' and 'my understanding' shifted and changed according to that experience, and each experience influenced, and was influenced by, future experiences. I could never say 'this is the organization', 'this is my role' and 'this is what I am doing' as I could never manage to complete or finalize any of these states. Similarly, as an educator, I could not identify with any firm body of knowledge and say 'this is what is needed'. I could see that people needed knowledge, but that most of what they needed would be situation specific; the knowledge needed by an Angolan participant would be very different from that needed by someone working in Hong Kong; working multinationally needed different knowledge and skills than working with SMEs; working in the voluntary sector appeared fundamentally different from working with the corporate fat-cats, and so on. I could see that people needed different knowledge and skills, and that they would need to shift and change, to emerge into new roles and 'selves'. However, I could not build a course that specified that; instead I built one that refused to specify, or at least, the only specification was for the areas of focus on the different workshops, the form (not the content) of the assessed research projects and international placement, and the form of process that occurred over the different days of each workshop.

An overview of the programme taken from the brochure (see Figure 3.1) shows that it roughly consisted of eight four-day workshops over one and a half years, and was assessed through three guided work-based research projects, an international placement, a learning log and a dissertation. Following a Kolbian pattern, I designed the process of each workshop to force a focus on the academic (theory), followed by one on the professional (self within group) (reflection), and then the individual (planning), before the return to work (experience).

During the first two days of each workshop I invited specialists who I

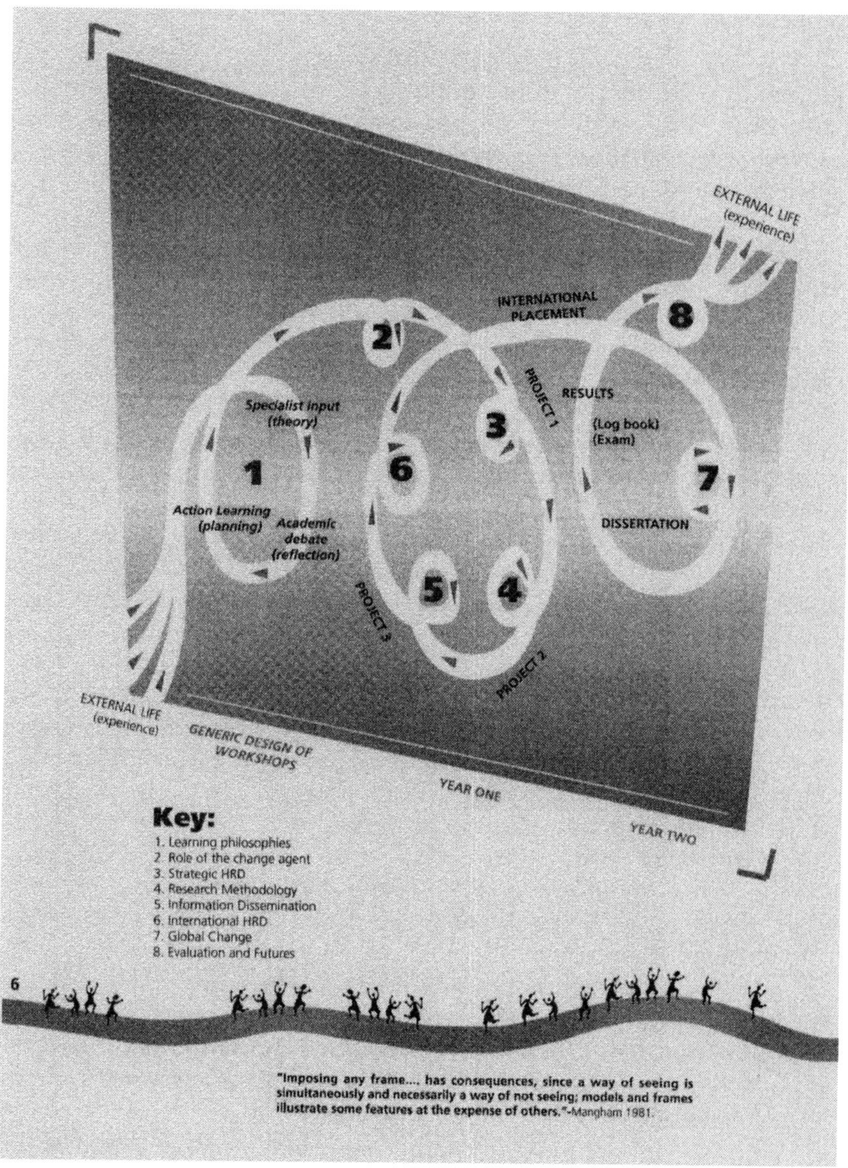

Figure 3.1 Outline of the MSc HRD (by research).

knew would present different views to come and talk to the group about the topic (half a day each), with specific instructions to be controversial and to follow their pet theories. For each half-day the group lived in the world of that specialist and, given the diversity of each group, there was lots of discussion and hard questioning. I would refuse to clarify, and insist that each person had to come to their own decisions on the differing views presented.

I was very determined in ensuring that the third day shifted to one of *no* content. It was called 'academic debate' as it was set aside for the group to work with the ideas from the previous two days and with their own processes, contextualizing theory with practice. This was, initially, hard for the participants, and proved to be very hard for co-tutors (more of that later). The majority of participants came from commerce-based pressured lives where they had to be doing something. Quite often the group got stuck, and occasionally I would jump in with some exercise or idea to shift them, but despite the real pain sometimes associated with the processes of self within group, each group eventually came to value the creation of a reflective space in this way.

While the whole programme was based on principles of action learning (Lee 1996), the fourth day made this more explicit. The group split into subgroups of about six people each, and these were run as a facilitative action learning set. Each person would have about an hour (even if they said they didn't want it!) in which to address whatever issues they wished. These normally started as work issues, but quickly shifted to individual or group issues, and then, over the next year, moved increasingly towards issues associated with completing the dissertation.

I designed the course like this because it felt the best way to foster what I wanted to achieve, namely the fostering of reflective practitioners able to develop and marry best practice with academic credibility and personal strength. I was not fully aware, at the time, of my underlying philosophical assumptions in doing so, or the extent to which they would be alien to the majority of my immediate academic community.

As Chia states

> Contemporary Western modes of thought are circumscribed by two great and competing pre-Socratic cosmologies or 'world-views', which provided and continue to provide the most general conceptual categories for organising thought and directing human effort. Heraclitus, a native of Ephesus in ancient Greece, emphasised the primacy of a changeable and emergent world while Parmenides, his successor, insisted upon the permanent and unchangeable nature of reality.
>
> (Chia 1997: 74)

Parmenides' view of reality is reflected in the continued dominance of the 'belief that science constitutes, by far, the most valuable part of human learning and accomplishment'. He argues that this leads to an atomistic conception of reality in which 'clear-cut, definite things are deemed to occupy clear-cut definite places in space and time', thus causality becomes the conceptual tool used for linking these isolates, and the state of rest is considered normal while movement is considered as a straightforward transition from one stable state to another.

> This *being* ontology is what provides the metaphysical basis for the organisation of modern thought and the perpetration of a system of classificatory taxonomies, hierarchies and categories which, in turn, serve as the institutionalised vocabulary for representing our experiences of reality. A *representationalist* epistemology thus ensues in which formal knowledge is deemed to be that which is produced by the rigorous application of the system of classifications on our phenomenal experiences in order to arrive at an accurate description of reality.
>
> (Chia 1997: 74, original emphases)

A *being* ontology is conceptualized with one 'true' reality, the units of which are tied together in a causal system. The truth is out there, we just have to find it!

The Heraclitean viewpoint offers a *becoming* ontology in which

> how an entity *becomes* constitutes *what* the actual entity *is*; so that the two descriptions of an actual entity are not independent. Its 'being' is constituted by its 'becoming'. This is the principle of process. . . . The flux of things is one ultimate generalisation around which we must weave our philosophical system.
>
> (Whitehead 1929: 28 and 240, original emphases)

Cooper (1976) suggests that within such a *process* epistemology the individuals involved feel themselves to be significant nodes in a dynamic network and are neither merely passive receivers nor dominant agents imposing their preconceived scheme of things on to that which they apprehend. All are the parts of the whole, and the parts, and the whole, change and develop together. From this point of view, there are both one and many realities, in which I 'myself' comes into being through interacting with these and am constituted within them, and the knowing of these is never final or finished.

John Keats (1817) is described by Chia as the originator of the term 'negative capability',[1] as a personal quality necessary for 'living' within a process epistemology, and Chia continues:

> Negative Capability involves the resisting of conceptual closures . . . when dealing with affairs of the world. It is an injunction for us to 'stay with the experience' and to wallow in the open-endedness and indeterminacy of that experience, soaking it up until we are saturated with it. Conceptual resistance thereby creates the necessary 'space' for the formulation of personal insights, and from it the development of the form of managerial foresight that Whitehead (1933) spoke of.
>
> (Chia 1997: 83)

These notions gave me a peg on which to pin my understanding of why my programme did not suit some of my colleagues; it (and I) was coming from a fundamentally different philosophy to that which they adopted. In essence, my world was one of becoming, while theirs was one of being. A programme that generated its own content was fine by me, but an anathema to them, as was a programme in which the process was structured but the (majority of the) knowledge wasn't; in which the 'students' had full responsibility for their own work, and in which the 'teacher's role was to enforce negative capability rather than closure.

I was lucky to start the programme with staff who accepted this way of working. Unfortunately they were not core to the department (or 'traditional' academics) and were replaced by colleagues who found it very hard to understand why I placed any importance on what they saw as 'anti-academic-activities', such as refusing to structure the third day or to define my terms. This replacement was partly political (and I won't go into that here) but also occurred because of the sheer dominance of the Parmenidesean viewpoint within academe. Its insistence upon there being only one reality or one 'right way' meant that there was no room for alternative paradigms. Indeed, for some, there was no ability to see that alternative paradigms existed, let alone understand that they might be associated with different (but equally valid) forms of operationalization.

Philosophically, then, I do not wish to define HRD because to do so would be alien to my worldview.

The theoretical case for refusing to define HRD

My theoretical case for refusing to define HRD is that I do not believe that it can be done in a meaningful way. Most would agree that, to be meaningful, the definition of something needs to encapsulate the properties or qualities of that which is being defined, such that it can be recognized uniquely from the definition and thereby distinguished from those that are not being defined.

This sort of description of what a definition might be, however, is, in itself, one of *being* rather than *becoming*. We could, however, say that a definition of something need not be fixed or permanent, but instead, it could take the form of a working definition; if enough people use a word in a particular way, and know what each other means by it, more or less, then there is tacit agreement about the meaning of that word and its qualities, such that it could be deemed to be *becoming* defined.

We might, therefore, get a rough feeling for a word by looking at the way in which it is used. In Lee (1997a) I report an attempt I made to develop a working definition of the word 'development'. I examined promotional literature aimed at HRD professionals and found four different ways in which the word 'development' was used. In the first approach that I identified, 'development as maturation' was used as if to refer to a predetermined 'stage-like' and inevitable progression of people and organizations. 'Development' is seen as an inevitable unfolding, and thus the 'developmental' force is the process itself, which, in turn, defines the end-point. The 'system', be it an individual, a group or an organization, is seen as being a coherent entity with clearly defined boundaries existing within a predictable external environment; the organization is discussed as if it were a single living element, whose structures, existence and change are capable of being completely understood through sufficient expert analysis. Concepts such as empowerment and change-agency are irrelevant in an approach that is essentially social determinism, with no place for unpredictable events or freedom of individual choice.

In the second meaning, 'development as shaping', people are seen as tools who can be shaped to fit the organization. Here, development is still seen to have known end-points, but these are defined by some one or something external to the process of development. The organization is stratified and 'senior' management define the end point for 'junior' management; the wishes of the corporate hierarchy create the developmental force. This approach assumes that there is something lacking, some weakness or gap, that can be added to or filled by the use of the appropriate tools or blueprint, and that such intervention is necessary. Individuals (their aspirations and their values, as well as their skills) are malleable units that can be moulded to suit the wider system. 'Empowerment' and 'individual agency' can be part of the developmental agenda, but not in their own right; they are acceptable developmental end-points only if ratified by senior management, and 'empowerment' becomes a tool to enhance performance and decision-making (within limits).

'Development as voyage' is as a lifelong journey upon uncharted internal routes in which individuals construe their own frames of reference and place their view of self within this, such that each of us construct our own version of 'reality' in which our 'identity' is part of that construct. This is described as an active process in which individuals are continually reanalysing their role in the emergence of the processes they are part of, and in doing so also confronting their own ideas, unsurfaced assumptions, biases and fears while maintaining a core of ethicality and strong self concept (Adler 1974). 'Development' involves a transformative shift in approach that enables critical observation and evaluation of the experience, such that the learner is able to distance themselves from it rather than 'replay' it; experiencing becomes a way of restoring meaning to life (Vasilyuk 1984). The external world (including organization and management) might mirror or catalyse 'development', but it is the individual who is the sole owner and clear driving force behind the process. 'Empowerment' would be within the individual's own terms, and might have little regard for organizational objectives.

'Development as emergent' is the fourth approach that I identified. Here 'development' is seen to arise out of the messy ways by which societal aspiration becomes transformed into societal 'reality'. 'The individual's unique perceptions of themselves within a social reality which is continuously socially (re)constructed' (Checkland 1994); in which 'individuals dynamically alter their actions with respect to the ongoing and anticipated actions of their partners' (Fogel 1993: 34) and in which they negotiate a form of communication and meaning specific and new to the group, and relatively unaccessible or undescribable to those who were not part of the process (Lee 1994). 'Self-hood' is a dynamic function of the wider social system (be it a family grouping, a small or medium sized enterprise, a large bureaucracy, or a nation, or parts of each) and as that system transforms so do 'I'. Emergent development of the group-as-organization is seen to be no different from development of any social system, and is not consistently driven by any single subsection (be it senior management or the shop-floor). Discussion about planned top-down or bottom-up change is irrelevant, as the words themselves imply some sort of structure to the change. This approach is, of course, in direct conflict with traditional ideas that organizational change is driven by senior management, however, Romanelli and Tushman (1994) offer empirical support for rapid, discontinuous transformation in organizations being driven by major environmental changes.

It is very simple to place these in a 2 × 2 matrix, as shown in Figure 3.2. The 2 × 2 matrix is pervasive and well understood in management, but it is a tool of being, rather than becoming. The lines are solid and impermeable, the categories fixed. Instead, we can examine these areas as areas of concentration, in which it is as if the most concentrated 'essence' of that which we are examining is in the centre of the area, and, as it diffuses outward, it mingles with the essences of the other areas (Figure 3.3).

Despite finding alternative ways of representing these findings, which might meet problems of how to represent the sorts of working definitions associated with becoming, we cannot avoid the fact that there appear to be four fundamentally different working definitions of 'development'. Each of these carries with it a particular view of organization, and of the nature and

		IDENTITY	
END-POINT		UNITARY	CO-REGULATED
	KNOWN	MATURATION Development through inevitable stages	SHAPING Development through planned steps
	UNKNOWN	VOYAGE Development through internal discovery	EMERGENT Development through interaction with others

Figure 3.2 A 2 × 2 matrix of 'development'.

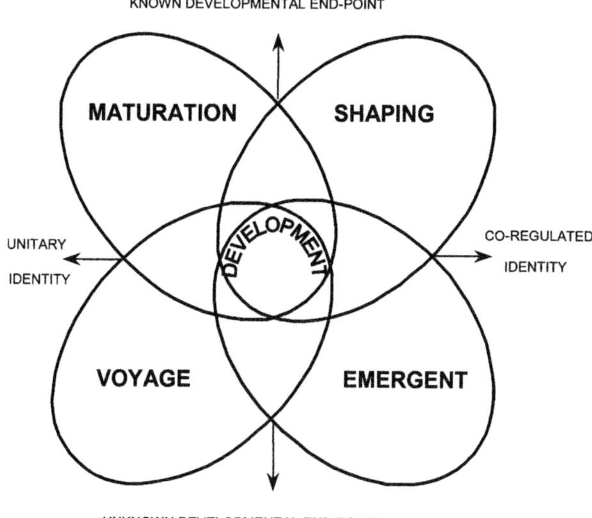

Figure 3.3 Four forms of 'development' (after Lee 1997a).

role of HRD, and is used under different circumstances. When talking of our own development we normally address it as if it is a voyage. When senior managers talk of organizational development they normally talk of it as if it were shaping. When social theorists talk of development they normally adopt a maturational or emergent perspective (depending upon their theoretical bent). 'Development' is clearly not a unitary concept.

The professional case for refusing to define HRD

The many ways in which the word 'development' can be used indicates the many different roles that the professional 'developer' might adopt. For example the role of the developer in the maturational system has the sureness of the (relatively) uninvolved expert consultant who charts the inevitable unfolding of the stages. The developer within a shaped system is the process expert who can not only clearly help senior management identify an enhanced future, but also apply the tools necessary to ensure that such a future is achieved. Such developers sell a 'better' (and otherwise unobtainable) view of the future (to individuals, groups and organizations) and the blueprint to get there. Those that are being 'developed' are encouraged/moulded to meet the end criteria, regardless of whether such criteria are enhanced skills, positive attitudes or the achievement of corporate objectives. The role of the developer within the system as voyage is one of helping others to help themselves (see, for example, Rogers 1951, 1959). The developer brings 'expert' skills that help individuals to recognize their self-imposed bounds and widen their horizons, but does so without calling upon the 'power' of expertise that describes a particular path and end-point as 'best' for the individual concerned. In emergent systems there is little role for a 'developer' as the developer holds no 'unique' or special status. Developers are as similar and as different as each other member is, and although they (perhaps) have fewer vested interests in political machinations (and thus might be able to view circumstances more objectively), they are as directly involved in the life of the organization as any of the individuals they are supporting in co-development.

Let us step back for a bit, and take a Parmenidesean view of the world, and examine what is meant by the definition of HRD. In this worldview we have the 2 × 2 matrix rules, and four different definitions of the word 'development', only one of which can be what we really 'mean' (the other three need to be renamed – but that is not important to us here). When we talk about *human resource* development, however, the situation becomes clearer. A 'human resource' is a commodity – something to be shaped and used at the will and needs of the more powerful. The role of the HRD professional is clear, and, by implication, so is the nature of organization and management. Senior management set the objectives within a clearly defined organizational structure, in which HRD is a subset of the larger HRM function. If we accept the common meaning of the words, then there is no alternative to HRD as an activity and profession in which development is about shaping individuals to fit the needs of the organization (as defined by senior management). Integrity, ethics and individual needs are not important within this conceptualization (and need be considered only if the circumstances call for hypocritical lip-service to them).

A Parmenidesean definition of HRD, therefore, might be along the lines of 'the shaping of the employees to fit the needs of the employer'. This definition of HRD effectively limits HRD to 'training'. It is questionable, however, whether that definition was ever fully adopted by the HRD professions. It is, perhaps, the professional and qualifying bodies, more than any others, which feel the need to define HRD. They need to do so, as, in order to patrol their boundaries and maintain their standards, they need to establish what those standards are. Some might still see HRD in this way, but for many, the profession has (slowly) moved on to incorporate notions of integrity and ethics, and also to reflect, at least in part, the notion that people are central to the organization, and thus the strategic role that their development can play.

The professional bodies have, in general, adopted a practice-based view of HRD, in which they attempt to promote what they see as 'best practice' (within their own contexts) through the establishment of their professional standards. In establishing professional standards, however, they run the risk of strangling growth in the profession by stipulating so closely what the practice of HRD is, that it is unable to become anything else.

The master's in HRD programme that I mentioned earlier did offer professional recognition, however I tried to avoid the limiting nature of 'professionalization' by working with other members of EURESFORM to establish professional recognition through the attainment of learning outcomes, rather than standards.[2] This meant that the individuals took responsibility of evidencing that they had met the outcomes (either during the course or otherwise) and the learning outcomes could be rapidly adjusted as the needs of the profession changed. This system continues to operate and provide European professional recognition, but appears to be slipping more towards what is, in effect, the 'validation' of courses and back-door standardization. Negative capability is *very* hard to foster!

The practical reason for refusing to define HRD

Pressure towards standardization and thus the defining of HRD seems an inevitable part of professionalization and qualification structures. However, as illustrated in Lee *et al.* (1996), 'standardization' across disparate systems of HRD is likely to have been achieved through cultural imposition, with the accepted 'standards' or definition in practice, belonging to those cultures with the loudest voices. Even if the rhetoric is of the dominant culture, the practice often remains that of the hidden or underlying culture (Lee 1998). The idea, therefore, of a generally acceptable definition of HRD achieved via the processes of standardization becomes particularly unrealistic when we look at the degree of variation in practice across the globe. It is simply not practical.

If we abandon the notion of establishing a single working definition of HRD, we still have open the possibility of defining HRD according to what actually happens in different situations. Thereby attempting to establish situated working definitions. Some people need and use such definitions for their jobs, but as soon as these definitions are encased in course brochures, syllabi, professional standards, organizational literature, or other such statements of fact, they stop becoming and ARE. As discussed earlier, however, HRD theorists and professionals are increasingly talking and acting as if the process that we call HRD is dynamic and emergent.

Perhaps the only way to address the need to encapsulate what is meant by 'HRD' is to refrain from 'defining' as the encapsulated meaning includes elements that are much wider than 'real' HRD as seen in a Parmenidesean worldview. Instead we should seek to draw permeable outlines around this complex of activities that we all know and, for want of any other term, choose to call HRD.

Conclusion: emergent HRD

One way of addressing this issue might be to focus again on the 'emergent' system of development. I describe this as reflecting the messy ways by which societal aspiration becomes transformed into societal 'reality'. Society 'develops' with no clear end-point and with its emergent activities as the drive behind change, rather than the edicts of the hierarchy (Lee 1997b). From this perspective, HRD could be seen as that which is in the processual bindings of the system, which links the needs and aspirations of the (shifting) elements of the system, between and across different levels of aggregation, as they are in the process of becoming.

Throughout the master's in HRD I felt unable to explain this concept in a way that it made sense in abstract terms; my method of 'explaining' it was to maintain negative capability, and let it emerge, each person putting it into their own words and situations. 'HRD' was different for each person and emerged out of their experiences: 'It is not enough to insist upon the necessity of experience, nor even of activity in experience. Everything depends upon the quality of experience which is had . . . every experience lives in further experiences' (Dewey 1938).

I was lucky to be able to run my master's course as I did for four cohorts since most institutions would not have even accepted its notion of self-generating content. Having ensured that its systems of verification and quality management were sufficient, Lancaster University was happy for it to continue indefinitely. It was particular individuals who caused it to close, largely through fear of the different and a desire to control the uncontrollable. The Heraclitean *becoming* lost to the Parmenidesean *being* in a fight in which the becoming was gagged and the being held the power!

By virtue of this chapter, while acknowledging how very hard it is at times to live in a Heraclitean world, I wish to redress the balance and propose that, certainly as far as HRD is concerned, there is no alternative. I will not define HRD because it is indefinable, and to attempt to define it is only to serve political or social needs of the minute, to give the appearance of being in control.

Acknowledgement

This chapter is largely based upon work presented in M. Lee (2001) 'A refusal to define HRD', *Human Resource Development International*, 4, 3: 327–342 http://www.tandf.co.uk/journals/routledge/13678868.html

Notes

1 'And at once it struck me, what quality went to form a man of Achievement . . . meaning Negative Capability, that is when a man is capable of being in uncertainties, mysteries, doubts, without any irritable reaching after facts and reason' (Keats, letters of 21 December 1817).

2 This work was funded through the auspices of a European Community Research Grant.

References

Adler, P. S. (1974) 'Beyond cultural identity: reflections on cultural and multicultural man', *Topics in Culture Learning*, vol. 2, Honolulu: East–West Culture Learning Institute.

Checkland, P. (1994) 'Conventional wisdom and conventional ignorance', *Organisation*, 1, 1: 29–34.

Chia, R. (1997) 'Process philosophy and management learning: cultivating "foresight" in management', in J. Burgoyne and M. Reynolds (eds) *Management Learning: Integrating Perspectives in Theory and Practice*, London: Sage.

Cooper, R. (1976) 'The open field', *Human Relations*, 29, 11: 999–1017.

Dewey, J. (1938) *Experience and Education*, New York: Collier.

Fogel, A. (1993) *Developing through Relationships: Origins of Communication, Self and Culture*, Hemel Hempstead: Harvester Wheatsheaf.

Keats, J. (1817) 'Letter to George and Tom Keats', 21, 27 December, in R. Gittings (ed.) *Letters of John Keats*, Oxford: Oxford University Press.

Lee, M. M. (1994) 'The isolated manager: walking the boundaries of the microculture', *Proceedings of the British Academy of Management Conference*, Lancaster, UK.

Lee, M. M. (1996) 'Action learning as a cross-cultural tool' in J. Stewart and J. McGoldrick (eds) *Human Resource Development: Perspectives, Strategies and Practice*, London: Pitman.

Lee, M. M. (1997a) 'The developmental approach: a critical reconsideration', in J. Burgoyne and M. Reynolds (eds) *Management Learning: Integrating Perspectives in Theory and Practice*, London: Sage.

Lee, M. M. (1997b) 'Strategic human resource development: a conceptual exploration', in R. Torraco (ed.) *Academy of Human Resource Development Conference Proceedings*, Baton Rouge, LA: AHRD.

Lee, M. M. (1998) 'Understandings of conflict: a cross-cultural investigation', *Personnel Review*, 27, 3: 227–242.

Lee, M. M. (2001) 'A refusal to define HRD', *Human Resource Development International*, 4, 3: 327–343.

Lee, M. M., Letiche, H., Crawshaw, R. and Thomas, M. (eds) (1996) *Management Education in the New Europe*, London: Routledge.

Rogers, C. R. (1951) *Client Centred Therapy*, Boston, MA: Houghton Mifflin.

Rogers, C. R. (1959) 'A theory of therapy, personality, and interpersonal relationships as developed in the client-centred framework', in S. Koch (ed.) *Psychology: A Study of a Science*, vol. 3, New York: McGraw-Hill.

Romanelli, E. and Tushman, M. L. (1994) 'Organisational transformation as punctuated equilibrium: an empirical test', *Academy of Management Journal*, 37: 1141–1166.

Vasilyuk, F. (1984) *The Psychology of Experiencing: The Resolution of Life's Critical Situations*, English translation 1991, Hemel Hempstead: Harvester Wheatsheaf.

Whitehead, A. N. (1929) *Process and Reality*, New York: Free Press.

Whitehead, A. N. (1933) *Adventures of Ideas*, Harmondsworth: Penguin.

Part II

Developments in the human-centred approach to HRD

4 In search of ethics and integrity in HRD

Darlene Russ-Eft

Introduction

The title of this book is *New Frontiers in HRD*. For some researchers and practitioners, a discussion of ethics and integrity as a 'new' frontier may seem questionable. After all, a researcher might ask, 'So, what new research needs to be undertaken, and how will this work contribute to theory-building?' Practitioners might ask more down-to-earth questions, such as 'What ethical issues might I encounter? And, if such dilemmas do occur, how will any of this theoretical and research work enhance my own practices? Bottom-line, what contribution will this make to learning and performance in my organization?'

This chapter will attempt to address these questions. It will begin by defining human resource development. It will then present various ethical frameworks and identify the position taken by this author. It will discuss the ways in which ethics defines a profession, will provide some examples from various professions and professional organizations, including the Academy of Human Resource Development, and will compare the work of AHRD with that of other associations. Finally, it will attempt to address the 'so what' questions raised by researchers and by practitioners.

Defining HRD

The term human resource development implies that the work is focused on human beings, as opposed to rats (in a psychology lab) or fruit flies (in a biology experiment). We should note, however, that such a statement could be considered as a purely anthropocentric, and some may argue that human beings do impact both rats and fruit flies. Indeed, Hatcher (2002: 43) states that anthropocentrism 'enables the continuation of irreparable harm to the environment, which also inevitably threatens human well-being'. Nevertheless, as a practical or utilitarian matter, we must recognize that HRD theory, research and practice focuses on human beings and the processes, systems and organizations created by human beings.

As for HRD itself, a variety of definitions have appeared in the literature (Carnevale *et al.* 1990; Chalofsky 1992; Nadler 1970, 1983; Nadler and

Nadler 1990; Russ-Eft 1996; Swanson 1989; Walton 1999; Wimbiscus 1995) and the definition still appears to be of major concern (Russ-Eft 2000b). So, using the research method of looking up the various words in the dictionary, Russ-Eft (2000b) provided the following definition, using the *American Heritage Dictionary* (Berube 1982).

> First, 'human' or 'human being' is defined as 'a member of the genus *Homo* and especially of the species, *Homo sapiens*' (p. 627). Then the term 'resource' includes the definition 'means that can be used to advantage; available capital assets' (p. 1052). Finally, 'development' is defined as 'the act of developing' which involves 'realizing the potentialities' (p. 389).
>
> (Russ-Eft 200b: 50)

This dictionary approach to defining HRD actually points out some of the controversies within the field – whether focusing on humans or the processes and systems created by humans, or focusing on human or other resources as an economic consideration, or focusing on the development of humans, teams, processes, systems or organizations.

Whatever the definition of HRD, however, we need to probe further to examine ethics within HRD or an ethical agenda. So, let us turn to some consideration of ethics.

Defining ethics and ethical frameworks

Let us begin by defining what is meant by 'ethics' by applying the dictionary method. According to the *American Heritage Dictionary* (Berube 1982: 467) ethics is 'a principle of right or good conduct; a system of moral principles or values'. The definition continues, however, to include 'the rules or standards governing the conduct of the members of a profession' (p. 467). This last point will be elaborated in a later section of this chapter.

Given that HRD operates in the 'corporate' or 'organizational' world, we may want to consider what is discussed in terms of 'corporate ethics'. Clarence C. Walton (1977), president of the Catholic University of America, wrote the following as part of the Fifty-second American Assembly at Arden House:

1 Ethics involves critical analysis of human acts to determine their rightness or wrongness in terms of two major criteria: truth and justice.
2 Business ethics extends the range of criteria whereby human actions are judged to include such things as societal expectations, fair competition, the aesthetics of advertising and the use of public relations, the meaning of social responsibilities, reconciling corporate

> behaviour at home with behaviour abroad, the extent of consumer sovereignty, the relevance of corporate size, the handling of communications, and the like.
>
> (Walton 1977: 10)

Thus, we can assume that ethics involves some moral judgement as to whether an act is 'good or bad' or 'right or wrong'. Some of the components or aspects of this judgement involve such intangibles as truth, justice, and social responsibilities. Indeed, such ideas link to those described in the literature on corporate social responsibility (Carroll 1979, 1999).

Even though agreement may be reached as to the definition of ethics, agreement as to the 'ethical agenda' may be difficult to achieve, particularly if there is not clarity as to the various theoretical viewpoints and approaches. One approach is that of 'situation ethics' or 'relativism' (Fletcher 1966; Des Jardins 1993) in which there can be no single ethical stance. Rather, an ethical position is viewed as applicable to a specific situation or context. In stark contrast is that of absolutism in which some set of universal ethics holds. Although such absolutism can lead to intolerance (Hatcher 2002) and the potentially inappropriate application of certain cultural norms (Hofstede 2001), it also allows for the development of ethical codes.

Beyond relativism and absolutism, there are other issues and frameworks to consider. As discussed by Hatcher and Aragon (2000a) and Hatcher (2002), one might use a teleological approach to ethical decision-making. This comes from the Greek 'teleos', which means 'end' or 'goal.' In this case, the consequence of an act is of greatest concern. In contrast is that of the deontological approach. The word comes from the Greek 'deon' which signifies 'duty' or 'that which is binding'. In this case, the moral rightness of an act is considered more important than the consequence of that act. Alternatively, we may want to adopt a theological ethics. Then, the particular theological or religious perspective would become paramount. Finally, we may want to use an environmental perspective. According to Hatcher (2002: 38), 'environmental ethics focus on environmental and ecological controversies that threaten our planet and humanity and raise questions about what we value'.

My position is that in order to develop any sort of ethical code or agenda one must reject a completely relativistic approach in favour of some, albeit limited, stance. I tend to favour an approach that focuses on the consequences of the actions, although ethical codes and agendas tend to describe certain desired moral actions rather than the consequences of those actions. Nevertheless, presumably those actions are ones that will tend to lead to the desired consequences.

Given these various frameworks, let us now consider the application of ethics within the context of HRD.

Ethics and the professionalization of HRD

Human resource development can be considered as a field that has existed in some form for thousands of years or as a relatively new field. Certainly, ever since specific 'jobs' have existed, some form of on-the-job training has been provided to those new to the job. More recently, however, the field of HRD has become formalized and professionalized.

Part of the expansion, formalization and professionalization of HRD involves the development of associations to support the professionals in the field. The Academy of Human Resource Development is one such association that was established in 1993 by a group concerned that the American Society for Training and Development (ASTD) failed to distinguish between atheoretical and theoretical practice.

Another aspect of the professionalization of HRD involves the development of an ethical code. According to *Webster's Dictionary* (1969: 680) 'profession' is defined as 'a calling requiring specialized knowledge and often long and intensive academic preparation.' Furthermore, a 'professional' is defined as one who is 'characterized by or conforming to the technical or ethical standards of a profession' (p. 680). Indeed, Gellerman *et al.* (1990: 8) claim that 'ethical standards are central to understanding what constitutes proper conduct as well as expectations of the virtues professionals should possess.' Similarly, Shadish *et al.* (1995: 1) state: 'Professions are marked by a number of features rarely shared by academic specialties. One of these is a code of ethics or standards that professionals aspire to follow.'

Beyond such statements supporting the development of an ethical code, however, recent HRD scholars described some of the traits or characteristics that distinguish a profession. Table 4.1, adapted from Burns *et al.* (2001) and Ruona and Rusaw (2001), indicates some of these characteristics. It should be noted that this table includes only characteristics shared by two or more authors and does not include some of the unique traits identified by some of these authors.

As can be seen from Table 4.1, 'organized and specialized body of knowledge' as well as 'articulated and shared values' appear as traits of a professional across all five sets of authors. Furthermore, 'standards of ethics and practice' and some form of 'educating and training professionals' appear in four of the five authors.

It may be that the organized and specialized knowledge in a field leads to some articulated and shared values. Both of these may lead, in turn, to some standards of ethics and practice, which are then used in educating and training professionals in the field. This finding tends to confirm the statement by Gellerman *et al.* (1990) that some set of standards forms a central core for any profession, including that of HRD.

In addition, Table 4.2 (adapted from Ruona and Rusaw 2001) takes each of the characteristics appearing in Table 4.1 and outlines the ways in which HRD has progressed towards professionalization.

Table 4.1 Synthesis of characteristics of a profession

Characteristic	*Cutlip* et al. *(1985)*	*Gellerman* et al. *(1990)*	*Pace* et al. *(1991)*	*Swanson (1982)*	*Wilensky (1964)*
Provides a unique and essential service recognized by the community	X		X		
Develops organized and specialized body of knowledge	X	X	X	X	X
Defined area of competence			X	X	X
Articulated and shared values	X	X	X	X	X
Standards of ethics and practice (interpreted and enforced)	X	X		X	X
Monitors the practice and its practitioners		X		X	
Educates and trains professionals	X	X	X		X

Source: adapted from Ruona and Rusaw 2001; Burns *et al.* 2001.

As can be seen from Table 4.2, HRD has progressed along the various traits characterizing a profession. Of greatest importance, following the argument of Gellerman *et al.* (1990), is that of developing a formal code of ethics. The following section provides some of the history of that effort.

History of work on the AHRD standards on ethics and integrity

In a town forum at the 1996 Academy of Human Resource Development, Victoria Marsick (1996) and Ron Jacobs (1996) discussed whether the academy should have a code of integrity. Marsick (1997) later published some of her remarks in the *Human Resource Development Quarterly*. At the next annual meeting of the academy in 1997, a lunchtime Food-for-Thought session discussed some of the ethical dilemmas facing both researchers and practitioners. A group from that gathering developed a session at the 1998 AHRD meeting to identify some of the issues in the areas of research, practice and teaching. During this same time period, the academy sponsored pre-sessions focused on ethics and integrity. From these various sessions and discussions, the AHRD board along with more and more members became convinced that the academy should develop a code on ethics and integrity, particularly given the mission of 'leading the Human Resource Development Profession through research'.

Table 4.2 An overview of HRD's progress towards professionalization

Characteristic	*HRD's progress*
Provides a unique and essential service that is recognized by the community	• A 2002 *State of the Industry* report (Van Buren and Erskine 2002) indicates a modest increase from 2000 to 2001 in the amount being spent on training and on the use of learning technologies. The '2002 Industry Report' (Galvin 2002) suggested that about $54 billion would be spent in 2002 on learning and development efforts in US-based organizations. Such information yields some evidence that organizations are looking to HRD for unique and essential services.
Develops organized and specialized body of knowledge	• The Academy of Human Resource Development was established in 1993 with a vision to lead the profession through research. Regional conferences currently take place annually in the United States, Europe and Asia. • Four research-based journals have been established since 1996: (1) *Human Resource Development Quarterly*, (2) *Human Resource Development International*, (3) *Advances in Developing Human Resources*, (4) *Human Resource Development Review*.
Defined area of competence	• Many competency models have been produced, most notably including McLagan (1998) and Rothwell (1996).
Articulated and shared values	• Ruona (2000) reported results of a qualitative study exploring core beliefs underlying HRD.
Standards of ethics and practice (interpreted and enforced)	• The Academy of Human Resource Development published *Standards on Ethics and Integrity* (AHRD 1999). • ODI, considered to be part of HRD, published its twenty-second revision of its International Code of Ethics (Organization Development Institute 1999).
Monitors the practice and its practitioners	• The current AHRD Committee on Ethics and Integrity is discussing issues of enforcement. • HRD's literature includes more about certification (Ellinger 1998) and alternative ways to monitor for quality and ethical practice (Hatcher 2002).
Educates and trains professionals	• There are numerous academic programmes in HRD and closely related topic areas in the United States (White 1999; Kuchinke 2002) and internationally. • ASTD has begun offering certificate programmes all over the United States in an effort to educate on specific competencies.

Source: adapted from Ruona and Rusaw 2001.

Beginning in the spring of 1998, a taskforce was formed to develop such a code. The taskforce included Janet Z. Burns (Georgia State University), Peter J. Dean (University of Tennessee and Wharton School of the University of Pennsylvania), Tim Hatcher (University of Louisville), Fred Otte (retired,

Georgia State University) and Hallie Preskill (University of New Mexico), with Darlene Russ-Eft (then from AchieveGlobal, Inc.) as committee chair. This group began its work by reviewing the ethical statements and/or standards from several organizations. These organizations included the American Educational Research Association (AERA), American Evaluation Association (AEA), American Management Association (AMA), American Psychological Association (APA), Society of Human Resource Management (SHRM), and the Organization and Human Systems Development (OD-HSD) group. After reviewing documents from these organizations, the group prepared a draft document titled 'Academy of Human Resource Development Standards on Ethics and Integrity'. This same group then sponsored a keynote session at the 1999 academy conference (Burns *et al.* 1999) focused on a discussion and reaction to these standards. Based on the comments from the AHRD board and the keynote session, a final document was prepared and approved by the board in November 1999 and published by AHRD (1999). At the same time, the board decided to designate the members of the group as the AHRD Committee on Ethics and Integrity.

Table 4.3 presents a listing of the major sections and the various topics included in the AHRD Standards. It should be noted that, in addition to standards related to HRD research, practice and teaching, there are general principles that underpin and support the specific standards.

Beyond creating the AHRD Standards, the Committee on Ethics and Integrity recognized a need for continuing discussion and presentation of ethical issues. These efforts have focused on both presentations and publications. At each annual meeting, the committee has presented one or more sessions in order to engage academy members in discussion and action on ethical concerns. Committee members have published descriptions of the standards in a variety of publications (e.g., Dean 1999; Hatcher and Aragon 2000a, 2000b; Hatcher 2002).

Abstract ethical statements, such as the AHRD Standards, cannot in and of themselves provide guidance to researchers and practitioners. Therefore, recognizing the need for further clarity, the committee embarked on the development of a set of case studies. At the 2000 academy conference, the AHRD Committee on Ethics and Integrity sponsored an innovative session to describe the development of case studies and to solicit contributions from the membership (Burns *et al.* 2000).

Following that session, Russ-Eft (2000a) argued for the need for case studies in ethics and integrity for use in teaching and training students, scholars, and practitioners. Aragon and Hatcher (2001) proceeded to assemble and edit case studies illustrating most of the standards. Each of the case studies describes a specific ethical dilemma, such as differences in pay for US trainers as compared with Tanzanian trainers working at the same centre (Bates 2001) or issues of confidentiality in experiential training (Woodall 2001). Then the case presents some focus questions, undertakes an analysis of the dilemma, and identifies applicable standards. Thus, the

Table 4.3 Academy of Human Resource Development Standards on Ethics and Integrity

General principles	Competence; Integrity; Professional responsibility; Respect for people's rights and dignity; Concern for others' welfare; Social responsibility
General standards	Boundaries of competence; Maintenance of expertise; Basis for research and professional judgements; Description of HRD professionals' work; Respecting others; Non-discrimination; Exploitative relationships; Misuse of HRD professionals' work; Multiple relationships; Consultations and referrals; Third party request for services; Delegation to and supervision of subordinates; Documentation of professional and research activity; Records and data; Fees and financial arrangements; Accuracy in reports to payers and funding; Sources; Referrals and fees; Research and evaluation in professional context
Research and evaluation	Data collection; Responsibility; Compliance with law and standards; Institutional approval; Informed consent; Incentives to participants; Deception in research; Interpretation and explanation of research and evaluation results
Advertising and other public statements	Definition of public statements; Statements by others; Avoidance of false or deceptive statements; Media presentations
Publication of work	Reporting of research and evaluation results; Plagiarism; Publication credit; Duplicate publication of data; Release of data; Professional reviewers; Ownership of intellectual property
Privacy and confidentiality	Discussions of the limits of confidentiality; Protection of confidentiality; Maintenance and ownership of records; Disclosures; Consultations; Confidential information in databases; Use of confidential information for didactic or other purposes
Teaching and facilitating	Design, development, implementation, and evaluation of programmes; Descriptions of programmes; Accuracy, objectivity, and professionalism in programmes; Limitation on training and instruction; Assessment of performance
Resolution of ethical issues and violations	Familiarity with ethics; Informal resolution of ethical violations; Conflicting pressure with organizational demands; Improper complaints; Resolution of ethical issues; Cooperation with ethics committees

document provides a teaching tool, as well as further guidance to scholars and practitioners.

Comparison of the AHRD Standards with other ethical codes

The AHRD Standards do not exist in a vacuum; rather they reflect the standards and principles set forth by other related organizations. Indeed, the taskforce that developed the AHRD Standards examined and adapted the work of some of these other associations in creating the standards. Some organizations, such as the American Psychological Association, have existed for many decades and have created and revised their ethical codes several times. Other organizations, such as the American Evaluation Association, have a shorter history, with their ethical code as the original statement. Still others, such as the *International Organizational Development Code of Ethics* (IOD: ODI 1999), though in existence since 1981, have been revised numerous times (twenty-two times for IOD). The length and detail of the various ethical codes also provides some interesting comparisons or as stated by Rossi (1995: 55) these vary from being 'very detailed and encyclopaedic in coverage to being relatively general'. The most detailed of the ethical codes comes from APA with over 9000 words, while those of ASTD, the IOD and SHRM appear to be the most succinct at about 200, 900 and 1000 words respectively. The remaining codes vary in length and detail from over 2000 to 6000 words. Rossi (1995: 55), furthermore, claimed that 'detailed codes exist in professional fields in which consensus has been reached over substance and methods and that weak codes flourish in associations in which members are divided on such matters'. Thus, it should be noted that, of the codes described, only APA includes a quasi-judicial body set up to enforce the code.

Of most interest, however, is a comparison of the content of these various codes. Table 4.4 presents a comparison of the major principles set forth in the ethical codes adopted by the various associations. As can be seen, principles of respect for people's rights and dignity, competence and professional development, integrity, and professional responsibility appear in almost all of the codes. Principles of concern for others' welfare, social responsibility, confidentiality, and objectivity, fairness and justice appear in some of the codes. Finally, there are principles that appear in only one of the sets of codes, such as systematic inquiry, beneficence and nonmaleficence, and ethical leadership. These latter principles appear to be of concern to one particular group of researchers or practitioners.

Conclusion: HRD and the ethical agenda

The work on the AHRD Standards and more recently on the ethical case studies (Aragon and Hatcher 2001) builds a good foundation for an agenda, but it does not provide a complete agenda. Indeed, some might argue that not enough has really happened and that the work has just begun. Therefore, the following paragraphs describe some specific research, teaching, and training, and other activities that are needed.

Of immediate concern is determining the extent to which HRD scholars and practitioners are aware of and familiar with the AHRD *Standards on Ethics and Integrity*. This could be undertaken as a survey of the AHRD membership. In addition, it would be useful to know whether other related organizations and their members are aware of these standards. Some of these

Table 4.4 Comparison of various codes of ethics including those of the Academy of Human Resource Development, Academy of Management, American Evaluation Association, American Educational Research Association, American Psychological Association, American Society for Training and Development, Organization and Human Systems Development and the International Organization Development Code of Ethics and Society for Human Resource Management

Principles	*AHRD*	*AOM*	*AEA*	*AERA*	*APA*	*ASTD*	*IOD*	*SHRM*
Competence and professional development	X	X	X	X		X	X	X
Integrity	X	X	X	X	X	X	X	
Professional responsibility	X	X			X	X	X	X
Respect for people's rights and dignity	X	X	X	X	X	X	X	X
Concern for others' welfare	X		X					
Social responsibility	X	X	X				X	
Confidentiality	X				X	X		
Systematic inquiry			X					
Objectivity, fairness and justice		X			X			X
Beneficence and nonmaleficence					X			
Ethical leadership								X

other organizations would include the Academy of Management (AOM), the American Society for Training and Development, International Society for Performance Improvement and the Society for Industrial and Organizational Psychology, as well as the organizations discussed in an earlier section of this chapter. Furthermore, with such studies, one could determine the extent to which various groups within HRD are aware of and familiar with the standards. Of particular interest would be an examination of the awareness level of HRD practitioners.

A series of empirical studies are needed to examine the extent to which HRD scholars and practitioners are aware of the ethical dilemmas in their work. A model for such a study appears in the work of Newman and Brown (1992) and Morris and Cohn (1993). Both studies examined violations of ethical standards among evaluators. The Newman and Brown study compared novice evaluators, those who had moderate knowledge of evaluation, and those who were experienced in evaluation. In contrast, Morris and Cohn (1993) surveyed members of the American Evaluation Association. These studies helped to identify the most frequent and most serious kinds of ethical dilemmas for evaluators. Such empirical studies are needed in the field of HRD. In addition, they would determine the extent to which the types of dilemmas identified are the same or different across various scholar and practitioner groups. This information will help to identify areas where further research or training may be needed. In addition, the research itself will bring some awareness to scholars and practitioners of the types of dilemmas faced by others in the field.

The AHRD *Standards on Ethics and Integrity* provide a good first step toward the development of an ethical code for HRD. We must, however, recognize that the standards were developed with an American and western European bias. Therefore, some research should be undertaken to determine which aspects of the AHRD Standards may be appropriate or inappropriate in which cultures. This research could begin with a survey such as those undertaken by Newman and Brown (1992) and Morris and Cohen (1993). Another type of survey could simply ask scholars and practitioners from non-western cultures to react and comment on the standards. Such a reaction piece might be similar to the work of Hendricks and Conner (1995) in obtaining and presenting comments on the AEA Guiding Principles from evaluators in different countries. A third method might include some ethical dilemmas from the case study book, asking scholars and practitioners from a variety of cultures to complete the analysis portion. Such an approach might help to identify cultural or situational differences. A final alternative would be to conduct a critical incident study asking for specific examples of ethical dilemmas (see Flanagan (1954, 1974) or Russ-Eft (1995) for more details on the method). This last alternative may also contribute to a compilation of ethical dilemmas faced by scholars and practitioners along with some suggestions for resolution of those dilemmas.

Beyond a series of research studies, much as those may be needed, the agenda must include more publicity, along with some training and education. A half-day or day-long seminar, for example, would provide an opportunity for further training and education. But, this publicizing, training and educating must go beyond the walls of AHRD and the university and move into the corporate world. Thus, the members of the AHRD Committee on Ethics and Integrity might consider presenting sessions at meetings of related practitioner associations, such as ASTD and ISPI, discussing the standards and the case studies and their utility in organizational practice.

Another means of publicizing the issues surrounding ethical decision-making in HRD would involve the creation of a column devoted to ethical issues to be included in one of the journals in the field. An example of such a column in the field of evaluation appears in each issue of the *American Journal of Evaluation*. The editor of the column (currently Michael Morris) prepares a brief case of an ethical dilemma. He then asks two different evaluators to comment on the case. These commentaries provide the evaluation scholar and practitioner with two different approaches to the ethical dilemma (see Russ-Eft 1999 for an example). A column of this sort in one of the AHRD HRD journals would help to increase awareness of the ethical challenges existing in the field. In addition, it would bring attention to the AHRD Standards, as well as other ethical codes that may be used by HRD scholars and practitioners.

A final agenda item facing the AHRD Committee on Ethics and Integrity is to undertake a thorough review and revision of the standards. The revision effort might include a thorough review of other ethical codes similar to the presentation in this chapter; the purpose of the review would be to identify possible additional areas to include in the revised statement, such as that of 'ethical leadership'. In addition, such a review and revision process would need to incorporate the ideas and recommendations coming from western and non-western scholars and practitioners. By undertaking some of the other parts of the agenda described above – specifically surveying non-western HRD scholars and practitioners as well as using non-westerners commentaries in a journal column devoted to ethical issues – the AHRD Standards may become more global in their viewpoints.

References

Academy of Human Resource Development (1999) *Standards on Ethics and Integrity*, 1st edn, Baton Rouge, LA: AHRD.

Aragon, S. R. and Hatcher, T. (eds) (2001) *Ethics and Integrity in HRD: Case Studies in Research and Practice*, *Advances in Developing Human Resources*, 3, 1, San Francisco, CA: Berrett-Koehler.

Bates, R. A. (2001) 'Equity, respect, and responsibility: an international perspective', in S. R. Aragon and T. Hatcher (eds) *Ethics and Integrity in HRD: Case Studies in Research and Practice*, *Advances in Developing Human Resources*, 3, 1, San Francisco, CA: Berrett-Koehler.

Berube, M. S. (ed.) (1982) *The American Heritage Dictionary*, 2nd edn, Boston, MA: Houghton Mifflin.

Burns, J. Z., Dean, P. J., Hatcher, T., Otte, F. L., Preskill, H. and Russ-Eft, D. (1999) 'Standards on ethics and integrity', in R. Torraco (ed.) *Academy of Human Resource Development 1999 Conference Proceedings*, Baton Rouge, LA: AHRD.

Burns, J. Z., Hatcher, T. and Russ-Eft, D. (2000) 'Confronting professional values and ethical issues: an innovative session on development of a casebook on ethics and integrity', in K. P. Kuchinke (ed.) *Academy of Human Resource Development 2000 Conference Proceedings*, Baton Rouge, LA: AHRD.

Burns, J. Z., Russ-Eft, D. and Wright, H. F. (2001) 'Codes of ethics and enforcement of ethical conduct: a review of other organizations and implications for AHRD', in O. Aliaga (ed.) *Academy of Human Resource Development 2001 Conference Proceedings*, Baton Rouge, LA: AHRD.

Carnevale, A. P., Gainer, L. J. and Villet, J. (1990) *Training in America: The Organization and Strategic Role of Training*, San Francisco, CA: Jossey-Bass.

Carroll, A. B. (1979) 'A three-dimensional conceptual model of corporate social performance', *Academy of Management Review*, 4: 497–505.

Carroll, A. B. (1999) 'Corporate social responsibility', *Business and Society*, 38: 268–295.

Chalofsky, N. (1992) 'A unifying definition for the human resource development profession', *Human Resource Development Quarterly*, 3, 2: 175–182.

Cutlip, S. M., Center, A. H. and Broom, G. M. (1985) *Effective Public Relations*, 6th edn, Englewood Cliffs, NJ: Prentice Hall.

Dean, P. J. (1999) 'Editorial: standards on ethics and integrity for professors and professionals in the field of learning and performance improvement and for the practice of HRD/HPT', *Performance Improvement Quarterly*, 12, 3: 3–4.

Des Jardins, J. R. (1993) *Environmental Ethics: An Introduction to Environmental Philosophy*, Belmont, CA: Wadsworth.

Ellinger, A. D. (1998) 'Credentialing in the workplace: human resource development practitioners should strive for certification', in R. J. Torraco (ed.) *Academy of Human Resource Development 1998 Conference Proceedings*, Baton Rouge, LA: AHRD.

Flanagan, J. C. (1954) 'The critical incident technique', *Psychological Bulletin*, 51, 4: 327–358.

Flanagan, J. C. (1974) *Measuring Human Performance*, Palo Alto, CA: American Institutes for Research.

Fletcher, J. (1966) *Situation Ethics: The New Morality*, Philadelphia, PA: Westminster.

Galvin, T. (2002) '2002 Industry Report', *Training*, October: 24–33.

Gellerman, W., Frankel, M. S. and Ladenson, R. F. (1990) *Values and Ethics in Organization and Human Systems Development: Responding to Dilemmas in Professional Life*, San Francisco, CA: Jossey-Bass.

Hatcher, T. (2002) *Ethics and HRD: A New Approach to Leading Responsible Organizations*, Cambridge, MA: Perseus.

Hatcher, T. and Aragon, S. R. (2000a) 'A code of ethics and integrity for HRD research and practice', *Human Resource Development Quarterly*, 11, 2: 179–185.

Hatcher, T. and Aragon, S. R. (2000b) 'Rationale for and development of a standard on ethics and integrity for international HRD research and practice', *Human Resource Development International*, 3, 2: 207–219.

Hendricks, M. and Conner, R. (1995) 'International perspectives on the Guiding Principles', in W. R. Shadish, D. L. Newman, M. A. Scheirer and C. Wye (eds) *Guiding Principles for Evaluators, New Directions for Program Evaluation*, vol. 66, San Francisco, CA: Jossey-Bass.

Hofstede, G. (2001) *Culture's Consequences: Comparing Values, Behaviors, Institutions, and Organizations across Nations*, 2nd edn, Thousand Oaks, CA: Sage.

Jacobs, R. (1996) 'Human resource development with integrity', in E. F. Holton III (ed.) *Academy of Human Resource Development 1996 Conference Proceedings*, Minneapolis, MN.

Kuchinke, K. P. (2002) 'Institutional and curricular characteristics of leading graduate HRD programs in the United States', *Human Resource Development Quarterly*, 13, 2: 127–144.

McLagan, P. (1989) 'Models for HRD practice', *Training and Development*, 43, 9: 49–59.

Marsick, V. (1996) 'Performance with integrity: thoughts on a code of conduct for HRD that reflects adult development theory', in E. F. Holton III (ed.) *Academy of Human Resource Development 1996 Conference Proceedings*, Minneapolis, MN.

Marsick, V. (1997) 'Reflections on developing a code of integrity for HRD', *Human Resource Development Quarterly*, 8, 2: 91–94.

Morris, M. and Cohn, R. (1993) 'Program evaluators and ethical challenges: a national survey', *Evaluation Review*, 17, 6: 621–642.

Nadler, L. (1970) *Developing Human Resources*, Houston, TX: Gulf.

Nadler, L. (1983) *Clearinghouse on Adult, Career, and Vocational Education*, Columbus, OH: ERIC Clearinghouse on Adult, Career, and Vocational Education.

Nadler, L. and Nadler, K. (1990) *Developing Human Resources: Concepts and a Mode*, 3rd edn, San Francisco, CA: Jossey-Bass.

Newman, D. L. and Brown, R. D. (1992) 'Violations of evaluation standards: frequency and seriousness of occurrence', *Evaluation Review*, 16, 3: 219–234.

Organization Development Institute (1999) *International Organization Development Code of Ethics*, dated 1991. Available online http//:members.aol.com/ODInst/ethics/html

Pace, W. R., Smith, P. C. and Mills, G. E. (1991) *Human Resource Development: The Field*, Englewood Cliffs, NJ: Prentice Hall.

Rossi, P. H. (1995) 'Doing good and getting it right', in W. R. Shadish, D. L Newman, M. A. Scheirer and C. Wye (eds) *Guiding Principles for Evaluators, New Directions for Program Evaluation*, vol. 66, San Francisco, CA: Jossey-Bass.

Rothwell, W. J. (1996) *ASTD Models for Human Performance Improvement: Roles, Competencies, and Outputs*, Alexandria, VA: ASDT.

Ruona, W. E. A. (2000) 'Philosophy and core beliefs in human resource development: a journey for the profession and its professionals', in W. E. A. Ruona and G. Roth (eds) *Philosophical Foundations of Human Resource Development*, San Francisco, CA: Berrett-Koehler.

Ruona, W. E. A. and Rusaw, A. C. (2001) 'The role of codes of ethics in the human resource development', *Academy of Human Resource Development 2001 Conference Proceedings*, Baton Rouge, LA: AHRD.

Russ-Eft, D. (1995) 'Defining competencies: a critique', *Human Resource Development Quarterly*, 6, 4: 329–335.

Russ-Eft, D. F. (1996) 'Looking through a new lens: different views of human resource development', in H. Preskill and R. L. Dilworth (eds) *Human Resource Development in Transition: Defining the Cutting Edge*, Baton Rouge, LA: AHRD and ISPI.

Russ-Eft, D. (1999) 'Can this evaluation be saved?', *American Journal of Evaluation* 20: 590–597.

Russ-Eft, D. F. (2000a) 'A case for case studies on HRD ethics and integrity', *Human Resource Development Quarterly*, 11, 2: 101–103.

Russ-Eft, D. (2000b) 'That old fungible feeling: defining HRD', in W. E. A. Ruona and G. Roth (eds) *Philosophical Foundations of Human Resource Development*, San Francisco, CA: Berrett-Koehler.

Shadish, W. R., Newman, D. L., Scheirer, M. A. and Wye, C. (eds) *Guiding Principles for Evaluators, New Directions for Program Evaluation*, vol. 66, San Francisco, CA: Jossey-Bass.

Swanson, R. A. (1982) 'Professionalism: the high road or the low?', *Vocational Education Journal*, 57, 2: 22–24.

Swanson, R. A. (1989) 'Pick a system, any system', *Human Resource Quarterly*, 3, 3: 213–214.

Van Buren, M. E. and Erskine, W. (2002) *State of the Industry: ASTD's Annual Review of Trends in Employer-Provided Training in the United States*, Alexandria, VA: ASTD.

Walton, C. (1977) *The Ethics of Corporate Conduct*, Englewood Cliffs, NJ: Prentice Hall.

Walton, J. (1999) *Strategic Human Resource Development*, London: Pearson Education.

Webster's Seventh New Collegiate Dictionary (1969) Springfield, MA: G. and C. Merriam.

White, K. (1999) *The 1998 ASTD Directory of Academic Programs*, Alexandria, VA: ASTD.

Wilensky, H. L. (1964) 'The professionalization of everyone?' *American Journal of Sociology*, 70: 137–158.

Wimbiscus, J. J., Jr (1995) 'The classification and description of human resource development scholars', *Human Resource Development Quarterly*, 6: 5–34.

Woodall, J. (2001) 'Adventure training and client confidentiality', in S. R. Aragon and T. Hatcher (eds) *Ethics and Integrity in HRD: Case Studies in Research and Practice, Advances in Developing Human Resources*, 3, 1, San Francisco, CA: Berrett-Koehler.

5 Line managers, HRD, ethics and values

Evidence from the voluntary sector

Rona S. Beattie

Introduction

Previous explorations of HRD and ethics have focused on HRD professionals (Walton 1999; Hatcher and Aragon 2000; Woodall and Douglas 2000; Beattie and McDougall 2002). This research builds on that work but focuses on the line manager's role in supporting workplace learning.

The context of this study is the voluntary sector utilizing two large social care voluntary organizations, Richmond Fellowship Scotland (RFS) and Quarriers. These organizations were selected because of the sector's distinctive values, which Steane (1997: 6) describes as 'affiliative and humane'. In this study the organizational values and learning climate were explored to investigate whether or not human-centred approaches to social care were transferred to HRD practice.

The chapter first discusses the interaction between HRD, values and ethics. It then explores the rationale for line managers having a central role in workplace learning, before considering the role of HRD in voluntary organizations, particularly the contribution of supervision to learning. This is followed by a description of the research methodology utilized before presenting findings, and discussing the implications for a range of stakeholders.

HRD, values and ethics

HRD practitioners have traditionally been described as having responsibility for facilitating relatively permanent changes in individual and group behaviour (Walton 1999). Garrick (1998) notes that the 'humanistic' position held by many HRD practitioners believes that people will be more productive when they feel work is personally meaningful and not simply an instrumental means to another end. However, some concern has been expressed about 'attitude modification activities that go beyond encouraging task-orientated specific behaviours . . . and which entail trying to convince individuals of the appropriateness of taking on a set of broad-based, culturally specific organisational values' (Walton 1999: 561–562). Walton's questions concerning the validity of HRD practitioners being propagators of organizational values and HRD's role in changing behaviours or attitudes could be applied equally to line managers undertaking developmental responsibilities and roles.

Fisher and Rice (1999) argue that organizations will only act ethically when members are skilled at thinking about, and coping with, ethical issues and are underpinned by an organizational culture that encourages ethical awareness and debate. They continue that ethical leadership should focus on developing an organizational moral ethos where people are more likely to act ethically. It could therefore be argued that managers are pivotal to such ethical development and that line managers, at all levels, should act as role models to ensure that appropriate values and ethics are consistently expressed and acted upon.

Knowles (1984: 97) argues that organizations 'teach by everything they do, and often they teach opposite lessons in their organisational operation from what they teach in their educational program'. Clearly line managers play a critical role in operational activities. Knowles then argues that:

> A democratic philosophy [that we might expect in a voluntary organisation] is characterised by a concern for the development of persons, a deep conviction as to the worth of every individual, and faith that people will make the right decisions for themselves if given the necessary information and support.
>
> (Knowles 1984: 98)

He continues that climate setting is probably the most crucial element in the whole process of HRD.

Knowles (1984) and Brookfield (1986, cited in Garrick 1998) have identified a range of principles and characteristics, reflecting a concern for ethics and values, that facilitate adult learning and create a conducive learning climate. These include voluntary participation in and ownership of learning; mutual respect; collaborative facilitation; freedom of expression and sharing of information; the encouragement of critical reflection; and learners and facilitators of learning being involved in a continual process of activity, reflection and collaborative analysis.

Woodall and Douglas (2000) argue that learning style theory also has an ethical dimension though more from a utilitarian perspective, compared to Knowles' (1984) deontological perspective where the absolute rights of the learner are central. With the former, HRD professionals (or line managers) are more likely to select learning interventions which are seen as being useful rather than what the learner necessarily wishes. In addition, Schein (1993) has argued that for individuals to change they need to feel psychologically safe to engage in learning and they 'must have a motive, a sense of direction and the opportunity to try out new things without fear of punishment' (Schein 1993: 91). Woodall and Douglas (2000) however note that not all

HRD activities provide such psychological safety, particularly those involving value change.[1] Finally, Tough's (1979) model of the 'ideal helper' in learning emphasizes the need for the helper to respect the needs and rights of the individual learner:

> the ideal helper views his interaction with the learner as a dialogue, a true encounter in which he listens as well as talks. His help will be tailored to the needs, goals and requests of this unique learner. The helper listens, accepts, responds, helps. These perceptions of the interaction are in sharp contrast to those of 'helpers' who want to control, command, manipulate, persuade, influence and change the learner.
>
> (Tough 1979: 195, cited in Knowles *et al.* 1998: 91)

Line managers as facilitators of learning

Since the early 1990s there has been growing recognition of the devolution of HRD responsibilities to line managers, as part of the wider devolution of HRM (e.g. Mumford 1993; Bevan and Heyday 1994; Heraty and Morley 1995). Indeed Salaman (1995: 5) has argued that key managerial competences are those which 'support the management of performance or the management of learning'. Heraty and Morley (1995) argue that such devolution can be highly effective as line managers are well placed to assess training needs and deliver training in the workplace. Higgins and Thomas (2001) have found that receiving high levels of developmental assistance can increase employee commitment to the organization.

However, the effectiveness of managers in supporting workplace learning depends significantly on whether they have the requisite knowledge, skills and attitudes (Leicester 1989; Heraty and Morley 1995; Institute of Personnel and Development (IPD) 1995; Thomson *et al.* 2001). Concerns have also emerged about the willingness of line managers to undertake development roles, the insufficient training provided for these roles and increased managerial workloads (IPD 1995; Cunningham and Hyman 1999). Until the mid-1990s, however, there has been limited research into what managers actually *do* to facilitate learning (Mumford 1993; Heraty and Morley 1995; IPD 1995; Horowitz 1999). As a consequence of this paucity of research, we have limited understanding of what behaviours managers demonstrate in developmental interactions (Ellinger and Bostrom 1999). However, due to a resurgence in recognition of the workplace as a site of 'natural learning' (Burgoyne and Hodgson 1983) there has been increasing awareness of the need to consider the developmental responsibilities and behaviours of line managers both from academic (e.g. Marsick and Watkins 1997; Ellinger and Bostrom 1999) and policy perspectives (e.g. Scottish Council for Voluntary Organizations (SCVO) 1999; National Skills Task Force (NSTF) 2000; IPD 2000).

Although there is an extensive literature on developmental roles that managers may play, such as mentor and coach, much of this literature is prescriptive, and there are relatively few examples of substantive research and empirical studies, as Horowitz (1999: 187) highlights: 'The HRD literature is somewhat normative and rhetorical in exhorting line managers to take responsibility for training and development'. An honourable exception to this substantive and empirical deficit is the work of Ellinger and Bostrom (1999) who explored the coaching behaviours, which they clustered into empowering and facilitating categories, of corporate sector managers in the United States. However, they interviewed only managers, whereas this study has also listened to the 'employee voice'.

Based on another empirical study (McGovern *et al.* 1997), this time into the devolution of HRM, it was found that effective devolution had been inconsistent across a range of private and public sector organizations. Indeed McGovern *et al.* concluded that their findings were contrary to the 'developmental humanism' that underpins many models of HRM and they consequently argue that 'developmental humanism under-estimates the extent to which short-term pragmatism is embedded in capitalist enterprises' (McGovern *et al.* 1997: 27). There is therefore a need for empirical research, such as this, into the developmental behaviours of managers. Furthermore this study has been conducted in not-for-profit voluntary organizations whose values are not based on capital accumulation and whose cultures may therefore be more receptive to developmental humanism. Lessons may also be learned for other sectors from managers who are well used to having developmental responsibilities as part of the supervisory function associated with social care.

HRD in the voluntary sector

Osborne (1996) has identified a range of challenges facing HRD in the UK voluntary sector. These include:

- the changing environment and context of voluntary organizations;
- the changing pattern of social and community needs;
- the diversity and distinctiveness of the voluntary sector;
- the rise of the contract culture and managerialism;
- the importance of equal opportunities and anti-discriminatory practice;
- the changing national framework for vocational training.

A survey of the Scottish voluntary sector workforce found that such challenges, including the increasing demand on the sector for accountability, were leading to greater adoption of quality standards and HRD practices (SCVO 1999): 35 per cent of all respondents held or were committed to achieving a quality standard, Investors in People (IiP) being the most popular. The Voluntary Sector National Training Organization (VSNTO) has also encouraged voluntary organizations to become involved in national standards, such as Scottish and National Vocational Qualifications (SVQs/NVQs), as part of their campaign for lifelong learning which acknowledges that 'the workplace can be the ideal setting for learning' (VSNTO 2001: 1).

The SCVO survey found that 52 per cent of voluntary organizations had a formal training policy, and 60 per cent had a training budget. Organizations with over £1 million income per annum spent 2.4 per cent of their income on training; 67 per cent of all and 90 per cent of large organizations had formal induction programmes for new staff. Some 46 per cent of staff work in organizations with formal appraisal systems, and this rises to 79 per cent in large organizations; 25 per cent of organizations also provided accredited training, such as SVQs. Such accreditation of workplace learning is becoming increasingly important given the Scottish Social Services Council's requirement to have substantial numbers of care staff qualified by 2006 – a form of learning where managers can play a pivotal role in terms of facilitation and assessment. Over 95 per cent of paid staff reported that they had training opportunities within their organization, of which 85 per cent had utilized these opportunities.

Beattie *et al.* (1994) found that voluntary sector managers generally had a positive attitude towards HRD. However, respondents identified that their limited exposure to management development hindered their ability to meet and identify the development needs of their staff. SCVO (1999) identified that the activities most commonly undertaken by managers are support and supervision, and that people management skills were the most frequently mentioned development need for managers. The important role of supervision in people management will be discussed further.

Supervision in social care

Within the field of social care supervision provides a framework for managers to support workplace learning. Supervision has been defined as:

> a means of developing and controlling the quality of service, taking account of the needs and rights of users and the quality of staff performance. The needs and rights of staff must also be attended to, in order to get the best from them.
>
> (Hughes and Pengelly 1997: 6)

Supervision has been described as a process where one individual helps another to improve their work performance (Wiener 1995), through regular meetings (Brown and Bourne 1996). It allows managers to ensure that employees are coping, doing what they should be doing and as well as they can. From the employee's perspective supervision provides an opportunity to review their work to ensure that it meets expectations, to get support, and to reflect upon individual development needs and career progression

(Wiener 1995). Sawdon and Sawdon (1995) argue that the three functions of supervision – managing, teaching and supporting – need to be regarded holistically, with no one function given predominance. However, as do Brown and Bourne (1996), they do acknowledge that there is the potential for inequity to arise due to the power relationship implicit in supervision relationships. They argue that this can be minimized as:

> The effective supervisor does not deny her/his power and authority but uses it to ensure with the supervisee that s/he is clear about what is required and how they are meeting or not meeting those requirements together. The effective supervisor does not lean over backwards nor abrogate power and authority. S/he shares the responsibility for dealing with the pain and complexity of vulnerable life situations in a manner which promotes the supervisee's own sense of worth.
>
> (Sawdon and Sawdon 1995: 9)

From their discussions with employees Brown and Bourne (1996) have found that it tends to be facilitative interventions that are lacking and suggest that there is a need to train social care managers in these skills. Indeed,

> understanding how people learn, facilitating and indeed accelerating these processes, is critical and underpins the educative function of supervision . . . The teacher/supervisor is seen as a facilitator, joining the learner/supervisee in a process of enquiry, and mutual challenge rather than an expert transmitter of knowledge.
>
> (Sawdon and Sawdon 1995: 7)

Hughes and Pengelly (1997) also stress the need for supervisors to be aware of differences in learning styles, and their impact on which stage of the learning cycle individuals are more likely to be comfortable. In practice they have found limited exploration of such adult learning factors within the supervisory context.

Finally, to be effective the supervisory relationship must be built on 'mutual trust and respect for individual knowledge and experience, and must seek to preserve non-judgemental attitudes to personal and cultural differences' (Stanners 1995: 178).

Such trust and respect provide the foundation for the

> Openness and security that comes from feeling valued at whatever level in an organisation is the only path to the sort of reflection and constructive criticism which entails speaking one's mind and voicing one's feelings, even when feeling foolish and vulnerable. Silence is the enemy of supervision wherever it takes place.
>
> (Sawdon and Sawdon 1995: 30)

This study has explored whether managers within voluntary organizations can be classified as 'ideal helpers' supporting ethical development which requires 'considerable respect for individual privacy, self-esteem, dignity and autonomy' (Woodall and Winstanley 2000: 284). In particular the role of the social care model of supervision is explored as a framework for 'ethical helping'.

Research methodology

This study adopted a phenomenological approach utilizing participant observation and in-depth interviews, exploring critical incidents with respondents representing four stakeholder groups. These were junior employees (n = 32), first line managers (FLM, n = 12), senior line managers (SLM, n = 10) and key informants, including HRD specialists (KI, n = 6). The managers selected were regarded as good or competent developers by their organizations. Relevant organizational documentation was also explored. Much of the presentation of primary data uses the indefinite pronoun to minimize the potential identification of individual respondents.

Findings

Case study organizations

Quarriers and Richmond Fellowship Scotland (RFS) have grown rapidly and diversified since the mid-1990s. For example, they are increasingly delivering services, such as support for people with learning disabilities, within individuals' communities rather than in large-scale residential projects. Key informants in both organizations felt that the organizations were now at a critical point in their organizational life cycles. The challenges now facing the organizations included retaining their cutting edge innovation, while controlling the level of bureaucracy that inevitably accompanies growth. At the time of this research RFS employed around 700 staff and Quarriers nearly 1000. Both organizations have well-developed HRD strategies and practices, (including supervision), are recognized as Investors in People and provide training for managers as developers. They also aspire to be learning organizations. Both organizations therefore provided appropriate environments to explore the developmental behaviours of line managers.

Both organizations stress the value of human-centred approaches implicit in the social care model of care. Their respective mission statements encapsulate this:

> To strive to ensure that the best possible high quality services continue to be delivered in respect of individuals with mental health difficulties or learning disability. This aims to meet these individuals' rights,

> aspirations and needs . . . in assuming as much power and control as possible over their own lives.
>
> (Richmond Fellowship Scotland 1997)

> To work together to overcome personal and social disadvantage, inspire optimism, create opportunity and offer choice to children, families and others in need of support.
>
> (Quarriers 1999: 1)

Person-centred planning is central to this philosophy and involves social care provision being driven by the individual, rather than being professionally led, ‘by really looking at the individual and what their needs and wants are’ (KI 6). As part of this ethos, and contained in the organizations’ strategic objectives, an explicit link is made between practice towards service users and staff. This involves the organizations promoting models of positive social care and good practice in running community support services, and in the supportive relationship the organizations have with their staff. New employees are introduced to the values of each organization through their induction programmes and other training courses. During an induction course one chief executive stressed their organization’s values as ‘standing on the same platform of humanity as people we serve; working together *with* [the respondent’s emphasis] the individual; not doing things to people’. A course on core values gave participants an opportunity to examine their own values and the influence of these in their own work.

My own observation of and discussions with staff confirmed that they generally believed that the organizations possessed positive and appropriate values that were practised by and affected many staff. Two examples are provided here from staff at different levels: ‘[The culture] values and focuses on the needs of the individuals, their dreams and aspirations. It gets staff to think about the dreams and aspirations of service users and tries to help them achieve as much as possible’ (Employee 32) and ‘the culture is very much about being an enabling organization and enabling not only the clients . . . but also the members of staff’ (SLM 10). A key informant also hoped that employees felt these values. ‘I would like to think that staff, who work directly with those values with service users, experience the same kind of values in their interrelationship with staff at whatever level in the organisation’ (KI 1). However, there was recognition that the bureaucracy associated with growth and the impact of the ‘contract culture’ (see also Cunningham 2001) presented challenges, as noted by a junior employee: ‘it has had to become contracting, outcome oriented . . . mostly to do with the culture that we bid for contracts in . . . There is more in terms of outcomes and objectives for us to meet’ (Employee 30).

As employers the organizations were described positively by staff, for example: ‘I know from my personal experience that the [manager] and team leaders are always trying . . . to do the best for every staff member so that it helps our service users' (Employee 9).

The chief executives of both organizations stressed their organizations' commitment to HRD because if 'service users have the capacity to grow and develop, staff need to be facilitators and educators'.

There were common themes emerging from RFS and Quarriers' HRD strategies. These included the desire to maintain IiP accreditation, recognition of the role of line managers in HRD, individual responsibility for learning and the expansion of accredited training, such as SVQs. There were also explicit links made between learning and quality, with both HRD strategies aiming to support the continuous improvement of staff and, ultimately, services. Another common feature was the use of language emphasizing learning rather than training, as exemplified by a junior employee.

> I think as an organization they are into staff development and learning . . . I think at one time everybody thought that meant going on a training day but now we're into recognizing different ways of learning such as reading, getting a video or just having small coaching sessions.
>
> (Employee 25)

Central to their HRD strategies are the organizations' supervision and appraisal policies, which provide a framework for line managers to review the development of their staff, and 'to enhance individual performance in order to improve the quality of services' (Quarriers 1996).

The objectives of these policies, reflecting the supervision literature above, are to ensure that all staff:

- carry out responsibilities to the organization's agreed standards and receive constructive feedback;
- are provided with appropriate support;
- have appropriate skills development and CPD opportunities;
- are consulted and involved in decision-making regarding their individual work;
- enjoy equality of opportunity.

(RFS 1998)

Two types of supervision were recognized. First, informal supervision involved *ad hoc* consultation on day-to-day issues and discussions with a supervisor during everyday work. By contrast formal supervision is a planned and recorded one-to-one session, with an agreed agenda, provided every three to four weeks. The session is expected to be a maximum of one hour, however I found several examples where supervision exceeded this. Respondents described supervision as a good source of learning and support:

> In my previous job I never got any supervision or reviews. I never had any opportunity to air my concerns or say anything at all about my job or about what I was doing or what I thought about anything that I was doing. Since I came here it's been very in-depth . . . [*How have you felt about this and are you clear about that?*] . . . I think it is really, really, good.
>
> (Employee 3)

Many of the examples of developmental interactions reported below took place within the supervisory context.

Both organizations provide training courses to help managers with their developmental responsibilities. These include courses on supervision, appraisal, training for trainers, and coaching, and are designed to maximize links with practice. Increasingly, such training incorporated input on aspects of adult learning and learning organization theory to help managers understand how they and others learn. Respondents confirmed that managers and staff were either already working with tools such as learning style questionnaires or considering how to incorporate this knowledge into their developmental interactions. Managerial responsibilities for HRD are also made explicit in their own supervision and appraisal meetings, and in job descriptions.

Line managers' behaviours

Within both organizations it was recognized that line managers play an important role in influencing the learning climate within their areas of operation. For example, one key informant recognized that 'managers are understanding that learning is a cultural activity at the heart of service delivery, it's not separate' (KI 1). A major element of this study was to identify the behaviours that managers demonstrated in the workplace that facilitated or inhibited employee learning and contributed to the development of a positive learning climate (for a full list of behaviours see Table 5.1). Relatively few inhibitory incidents were identified, and should be seen in the context of generally positive learning relationships. Illustrative examples of behaviours facilitating or inhibiting ethical and values-based HRD are provided in Table 5.1 and discussed below.

Caring behaviours

Given the organizations' social care context it is not surprising that caring behaviours, demonstrating managers valuing employees, emerged strongly from the analysis of interview data. All managers demonstrated caring behaviours such as supporting, encouraging, being committed and involved. A senior manager explained that they supported first line managers dealing with staff management problems because they got satisfaction from helping

Table 5.1 Comparison of facilitative and inhibitory behaviours

Facilitative behaviours	*Inhibitory behaviours*
Caring: supporting, encouraging, being approachable, reassuring, being committed or involved and empathizing	• Not being assertive • Not giving time • Being task orientated
Informing	Withholding information
Being professional: role modelling, standard-setting, planning and preparing	
Advising: instructing, coaching, guiding and counselling	Being dogmatic
Assessing: providing feedback and recognition; identifying development needs	Not assessing
Thinking: reflective or prospective thinking, clarifying	Not thinking
Empowering: delegating, trusting	Controlling
Developing developers	
Challenging	

their managers cope with the stress that could arise from such situations. A more harrowing example of providing support to staff identified by several managers was helping staff cope with service user bereavement. One described such support as 'a kind of emotional support . . . I was here for the person on the day and the day after I spoke to them. I then followed up a week later' (FLM 7).

Several managers demonstrated caring behaviours that were recognized as encouraging, particularly when helping staff with problems.

> I suppose the language that they use with you, their tone, how they are sitting, the questions they are asking – they're very encouraging. It's not the heavy hand of your line manager coming down. It's well 'OK you're having problems, let's look at why this is a problem for you'. They look very comfortable and very at ease, which makes me feel at ease . . . They are also careful in the words they use, there's no what I call negative words . . . it's very much about me and how I feel.
>
> (Employee 23)

Another of the caring behaviours demonstrated was being committed to and involved in staff development, that took place mainly in managers' own time.

> I really felt I had a commitment to [Employee 15] to get them through it [an HNC course] so it didn't really bother me that we were doing it in

> our own time . . . we did most of the stuff at my place, sitting in cafes, up at the library . . . we'd do things like they would come in an hour early . . . and I would stay an hour late across sleepovers.
>
> (FLM 5)

However, there was also some evidence managers occasionally did not give this time, mainly due to managerial workloads. The consequence of not having sufficient time meant some managers felt that they rushed development activities and ended up being directive, rather than giving staff time to think things through. A senior manager recognized that 'there are times I've thought I should have taken the extra half-hour, created a half-hour from somewhere and just asked questions and then just gone and left them with it' (SLM 9).

A few critical incidents demonstrated managers behaving non-assertively. One line manager acknowledged that early in their managerial career they had lost their temper when reprimanding a member of staff. 'I went on a bit of a tirade, left the [individual] feeling wrecked but probably not very clear about how [they were] going to approach and sort these issues out' (FLM 10). Following this incident the manager apologized to the employee and successfully resolved the situation, the manager having recognized that the individual would have 'learned nothing' from their first interaction. In some instances managers were identified as being too task focused to the detriment of people development. One first line manager commented that supervision with their senior manager had 'been so task orientated I don't really feel there's been space to look at what I need to do in terms of my own personal learning and development' (FLM 8).

Informing behaviours

One of Knowles' (1984) preconditions for a positive learning climate was openness in information sharing. One employee who described their manager as a 'pool of information' summed up the importance of this behaviour, while a key informant recognized that sharing information and not using knowledge as a 'power tool' was critical for the establishment and maintenance of developmental relationships (KI 4). The developmental behaviours in this category included sharing knowledge, ideas and experience, and providing access to resources and experiences that would enhance knowledge. Employees were also encouraged to learn from each other. There were also examples of two-way learning and recognition by managers that it was important to learn from staff. The willingness of some managers to engage in two-way learning is demonstrated by a junior employee:

> We discuss each time something different and come from all angles about how I could deal with that and what I would do. At times you

> don't actually think of things that [they've] thought of and at times I think of things [they've] not thought of.
>
> (Employee 22)

Managers indicated that they enjoyed sharing their knowledge, particularly in areas where they felt confident. However, there was recognition that managers needed to feel safe to share information.

There were several instances where managers were not so open about sharing information and experiences. One first line manager comparing their previous and current managers found that the former had not shared as much knowledge because they 'felt threatened by me' (FLM 10). A senior manager also recognized that as they were establishing themself in their current role they had not given their staff opportunities to work with external agencies being more 'more concerned that I knew the people and how things worked'. They now recognized that this would have been 'quite inhibiting' for individuals who could have had something to contribute to such interactions (SLM 7). This was now being addressed by giving them 'that level of exposure and letting them have a chance to get the broader picture as well'. Another manager recognized that they had not involved or informed staff fully in certain activities because of commercial sensitivities which meant staff had 'no sense of responsibility and no sense of control of the situation' (SLM 10). There was also some evidence that managers did not always transfer tacit knowledge effectively, as was demonstrated by an employee, temporarily promoted to cover for their manager, who observed: 'It was all the bits in between that [they have] in [their] head that hadn't been put down. Maybe if I had observed [them] doing a few things that would have been better' (Employee 13).

Being professional

Within the professional behaviours' cluster, role modelling was identified by staff as particularly important. The example presented below demonstrates a team member describing how they have learned from their manager about ethics in social care. In this example the manager persuaded staff that a service user who would have normally been transferred to another setting should stay. The employee felt that this demonstrated the manager's 'professional' commitment to the service user and had prompted this employee to try and behave more flexibly.

> It's a difficult thing to learn because once you've come out of the restrictions of a policy you're on your own and you really have to justify what you're saying and I don't know that I would have bothered to take that risk in the past. But now I think I would be more inclined to do that . . . It's not a standard or particular way of filling in a form or

> completing a unit, it's different from that . . . it's more looking at your overall ethics and management.
>
> (Employee 30)

Throughout this study there were examples of staff mirroring their managers' behaviours. For example one employee commented: 'If you think somebody is a good manager then you try to model yourself on how would they maybe handle this' (Employee 25). While the research has provided clear evidence of staff valuing managers as role models they did not view their managers uncritically nor did they emulate everything their managers did. 'It's about taking different bits and pieces, just watching how they do things' (SLM 3).

While no examples were identified in this sample, it could be argued that the risk of staff modelling inappropriate behaviour is possible.

Advising behaviours

While these behaviours included direct instruction the predominant behaviours – coaching, guidance and counselling – saw managers and employees collaborating in learning. A team leader who had worked with their current manager over a range of projects described how the manager had guided them, even when they were not working together. In effect the manager appears to have adopted a mentoring role.

> Basically throughout my whole time here [they've] pointed me in the right direction [they're] always giving me information and ideas about things, advising me to go on and take the training [they've] been very supportive in giving me [their] advice.
>
> (Employee 22)

There were, however, instances when managers behaved in a more directive, even dogmatic, fashion, either in terms of how a task was achieved or the speed at which the task was undertaken. First line managers demonstrated this behaviour more commonly, particularly when they were relatively new to the role. Several of these incidents were reported historically i.e. the managers recognized that they had behaved this way in the past but now they were more confident in their managerial role, they recognized that this was inappropriate behaviour. A consequence of dogmatic behaviours meant staff might find it difficult to challenge their managers, as described by one employee who found it 'really difficult to put something across that might differ from their [manager's] opinion' (Employee 6).

Another consequence might be that staff could lack confidence in their own abilities, as recognized by a first line manager who had pushed staff too quickly to perform a new task.

> [I'd] driven them to go and do something that they're not at the stage of being comfortable doing and they therefore do it badly. That then gives them the cycle of 'I'm not good at that' and therefore they do it badly.
> (FLM 6)

Giving feedback and recognition

Employees saw feedback and recognition as important because it let them know how they were doing and removed uncertainty. They appreciated receiving praise and got a boost from being told they had done well, which increased their confidence. Staff also indicated that they wanted feedback to be specific and prompt, to reduce worry as demonstrated here:

> [They're] very honest, which is great because you don't have any worries that 'oh maybe I'm not doing that as well as I should be?' [They] tell you straight away, straight down the line . . . You know exactly where you are going, what you need to do. [They] always give you feedback and [they] always let you know when you've done something well.
> (Employee 22)

Managers, employees and key informants recognized the effective provision of constructive feedback as being a key behaviour of developmental managers.

> They're even good at turning something that hasn't worked into a learning curve for you. They don't make you feel that the world has collapsed . . . it leaves the individual feeling that was OK . . . I think they're very good at getting you to explore how to fix things rather than coming in with the answers. People that are not good at developing people are just good at telling you that you can't do it but they don't show you how to do it.
> (KI 6)

Several staff identified previous managers (outwith the sample) that had not provided appropriate feedback which contrasted sharply with the highly effective feedback they got from their current managers, for example:

> [I'd] assumed that [I was] doing all right because I haven't had any negative feedback . . . Then after a few months something did come up, it wasn't a major issue, but the manager said to me maybe you shouldn't have done that . . . I felt that all of the good work up until that point had been disregarded and that it was only the negative thing that was picked on.
> (Employee 24)

This demonstrates the confusion, uncertainty, and even hurt, felt by staff caused by inadequate feedback.

Thinking behaviours

Supervision was often the context in which thinking behaviours were revealed, as it was used to 'look for opportunities in learning from one situation to the next' (SLM 6).

Within the supervision process the encouragement to reflect revealed that managers and employees were considering the impact of learning styles, particularly where the 'supervisor' and the 'supervisee' had contrasting styles. There were examples of 'reflector supervisors' recognizing that reflection could be challenging to those with more 'active' learning styles. In such instances they would encourage supervisees to think about what they had done, or about what they might do in the future, by giving them time to think and using questions to facilitate thinking. 'Active supervisees' found these sessions stretching and challenging, but ultimately most felt they were beneficial by helping them to capitalize on the complementary styles of themselves and their managers. The important factor was that differences in learning style were recognized and discussed as observed by this key informant:

> There's no point telling the activist to sit there and you need to do the theory first because you've lost them. It's been really helpful for me to think about the different learning styles and how people learn and then try to tailor things to that person.
>
> (KI 6)

Trusting

Trusting behaviours included both parties in the learning relationship being able to trust each other -'getting them to trust you, trust is the big thing' (FLM 5) – thus enabling the open and honest dialogue necessary for learning. One line manager described how this enabled them to raise sensitive issues with their senior manager that they could not discuss with anyone else in the organization.

> We've hopefully been very honest with each other . . . I'll go to them at times when I think I need the support or just to get things off my chest and I don't want to do it to my staff because the last thing they want to see is me being negative. I see that as [the manager's] role if I want to mouth off.
>
> (FLM 11)

Discussion

The key question posed in this study was whether or not the humanistic values and ethics of adult learning were present in RFS and Quarriers. From this empirical study clear evidence has emerged that a human-centred approach to HRD, particularly within supervision, was present within these organizations. It is argued here that such regular contact enabled the development of the trust critical for effective learning relationships. Overall, the managers studied here did provide significant evidence of the facilitative behaviours that Sawdon and Sawdon (1995) found lacking in their study. These behaviours were encouraged and developed by the organizations' cultures, HRD policies and the training provided to managers, identified as critical in SCVO's (1999) survey. However, it should be noted that managers did not always behave consistently as demonstrated by evidence, albeit relatively limited, of inhibitory behaviours.

The respect for individuals could be seen in the caring behaviours demonstrated by all managers. These behaviours were much more prevalent in this study than in Ellinger and Bostrom's (1999): a confirmation of the need to conduct HRD research across a range of organizational settings (for a fuller comparison of this study's findings with Ellinger and Bostrom's, see Table 5.2). Such behaviours appear to have played an important part in creating a learning climate where people were willing to approach managers for help and support. Where non-assertive behaviour was occasionally demonstrated this contributed to staff feeling that they could not always approach their manager, or that their needs were not being recognized. In addition, the recognition, by staff and managers that feedback, even where

Table 5.2 Comparison of facilitative behaviours

Ellinger and Bostrom's behaviours (1999)	*Beattie's behaviours (2003)*
Empowering cluster	
Question framing	Thinking
Being a resource	Informing
Transferring ownership	Empowering
Holding back	Thinking
Facilitating cluster	
Providing feedback	Providing feedback
Working it out together	Thinking
Creating and promoting a learning environment	Preparing and planning; identifying development needs
Setting and communicating expectations	Assessing, clarifying
Stepping into other	Empathizing
Broaden perspectives	Thinking
Using analogies, scenarios	Thinking
Encouraging others to facilitate learning	Developing developers

negative, should be given constructively, shows the value placed on respecting individual personality.

Freedom of expression and the sharing of information require an open and positive learning climate (Knowles 1984). Generally this appears to be present in RFS and Quarriers and is underpinned by the organizations' values, and caring behaviours demonstrated by managers. In addition managers generally welcomed sharing their experience and expertise through provision of information, coaching and guidance. There was however recognition that managers need to feel confident to engage fully in such activities. Therefore not only learners, but managers also need to feel psychologically safe (Schein 1993; Woodall and Douglas 2000) to facilitate learning. There was limited evidence that staff were not getting full access to information or experiences, sometimes due to commercial sensibilities, that prevented them seeing the full context of particular situations. This could contribute to lack of understanding or feelings of lack of involvement.

Advising behaviours, such as coaching and guidance, enabled staff to learn in a collaborative and active manner. However, where managers behaved dogmatically, they could become less approachable and may not have been able to provide sufficient psychological safety (Schein 1993; Woodall and Douglas 2000) for the freedom of expression necessary for effective learning. Finally, trust was also recognized by respondents as enabling managers and supervisees to engage in the open and honest discussion, which Stanners (1995) and Sawdon and Sawdon (1995) see as pivotal for effective learning.

The need for collaboration in defining individual goals, planning and implementing learning and work activities and evaluating them, was evident in the supervision process; a process that replicated person-centred planning for service users. Within supervision another key principle of adult learning was identified – critical reflection. The importance of making time available for staff to engage in reflective and prospective thinking was recognized, particularly given the demanding and hands-on nature of much of the work. There was however some recognition that this process did not come easily to all individuals, especially those with more active learning styles, and thus there was some evidence of the tension between utilitarian and deontological perspectives in learning practice.

The managers studied within RFS and Quarriers clearly demonstrate much of Tough's (1979) vision of the 'ideal helper', particularly respecting the needs and the rights of the individual learner. However, they do occasionally demonstrate the controlling behaviours which Tough perceives as unhelpful. Tough (1979) also suggests that influencing learners is not helpful. It could however be argued in this, and indeed other contexts, that such behaviour is acceptable if the ultimate goal is meaningful to the learner as noted by Garrick (1998). In this study managers were generally trying to influence employees to behave in a way that would value the rights of service users, a value-set in which (to this observer) individual employees appeared to believe.

Finally, the extent to which staff observed their managers' behaviour in the workplace and looked for appropriate role models demonstrates the importance of managers being aware of their actions. Staff clearly respected some managers as role models and aspired to follow their example. What was less clear was how many managers were aware of the potential influence their 'professional' and 'ethical' leadership could have on employees, a critical element in the creation of an organizational moral ethos identified by Fisher and Rice (1999). How this can be addressed will be discussed further.

Conclusion: implications of this study

A range of lessons for five stakeholder groups emerges from this study. First, for voluntary organizations the good practice demonstrated in RFS and Quarriers, through the organizational frameworks provided for learning and their line managers' behaviours, should be considered by other voluntary organizations, especially given the increasing regulation of social care in Scotland and the increasing demand to have more qualified staff. In particular, it is suggested that other voluntary organizations should explore how they can emulate the learning climates created in both organizations.

Second, public and private sector organizations, as well as absorbing the lessons above, should reflect on the powerful impact that supervision had on learning within RFS and Quarriers, and consider how to adapt such an approach to meet the needs of their own organizations. However, an issue for such organizations to think about is the span of control that line managers have and whether it is small enough to enable them to know their employees' needs and abilities sufficiently.

Third, a challenge often faced by HRD specialists is getting line managers to take employee development seriously. This was addressed effectively in the case study organizations by including people management responsibilities in managerial supervision sessions, appraisals and job descriptions. Central to effective and ethical facilitation of learning by line managers were the supervisory system and the extensive training in HRD knowledge and skills provided by the respective HRD functions.

Fourth, the key lesson for managers is the reminder that, after individuals themselves, they are the most important influence on an individual's learning in the workplace. To enhance their performance it is suggested that managers need to be informed of the behaviours that facilitate and inhibit learning, which have been identified in this study. Of particular importance is the need to inform managers that their behaviours are closely observed by staff, as was demonstrated by the latter's identification of role modelling as a facilitative behaviour, and therefore managers need to consider what example they are setting employees by their actions. Managers also need to be advised of the need to make their tacit knowledge more explicit, as if they do not, employees may have insufficient knowledge to do their jobs, which could result in feelings of stress.

Fifth, academics should consider utilizing the findings of this study in management learning curricula. I contend that the outcomes of this study could inform specialist HRD modules on academic diploma and master's programmes, as well as the Learning and Development and Management Development standards of the CIPD's professional education scheme for human resource specialists. The knowledge gained from this study could also be used to inform the small but growing provision of voluntary sector management education in UK universities and colleges.[2]

In conclusion by ameliorating the empirical deficit in our knowledge of how line managers develop staff it is hoped that this study has offered further insight into managerial behaviours by observing managerial practices in a sector often neglected by management and HRM scholars.

Notes

1 Woodall and Douglas (2000) explore this dilemma in relation to three approaches to value change: outdoor development, NLP and Gestalt.

2 I am programme leader for the Certificate in Management Studies (for the Voluntary Sector) at Glasgow Caledonian University.

References

Beattie, R. and McDougall, M. (2002) 'Ethical issues in HRD research', in J. McGoldrick, J. Stewart and S. Watson (eds) *Understanding Human Resource Development: A Research-Based Approach*, London: Routledge.

Beattie, R., McDougall, M. and Solomon, S. (1994) *Scottish Voluntary Sector Industry Training Organization – Feasibility Study*, unpublished report for SCVO and the Department of Employment.

Bevan, S. and Hayday, S. (1994) *Towing the Line: Helping Managers to Manage People*, Brighton: Institute of Manpower Studies.

Brookfield, S. D. (1986) *Understanding and Facilitating Adult Learning: A Comprehensive Analysis of Principles and Effective Practices*, San Francisco, CA: Jossey-Bass.

Brown, A. and Bourne, I. (1996) *The Social Work Supervisor*, Buckingham: Open University Press.

Burgoyne, J. and Hodgson, V. (1983) 'Natural learning and managerial action: a phenomenological study in the field setting', *Journal of Management Studies*, 20, 3: 387–399.

Cunningham, I. (2001) 'Employment issues in the UK voluntary sector' – guest editorial, *Employee Relations*, 23, 3: 223–225.

Cunningham, I. and Hyman, J. (1999) 'Devolving human resource responsibilities to the line: beginning of the end or a new beginning for personnel', *Personnel Review*, 28, 1–2: 9–27.

Ellinger, A. and Bostrom, R. (1999) 'Managerial coaching behaviours in learning organizations', *Journal of Management Development*, 18, 9: 752–771.

Fisher, C. and Rice, C. (1999) 'Managing messy moral matters: ethics and HRM', in J. Leopold, L. Harris and T. Watson (eds) *Strategic Human Resourcing: Principles, Perspectives and Practices*, London: FT/Pitman.

Garrick, J. (1998) *Informal Learning in the Workplace*, London: Routledge.

Hatcher, T. and Aragon, S. (2000) 'Rationale for and development of a standard on ethics and integrity for international HRD research and practice', *Human Resource Development International*, 3, 2: 207–220.

Heraty, N. and Morley, M. (1995) 'Line managers and human resource development', *Journal of European Industrial Training*, 19, 10: 31–37.

Higgins, M. and Thomas, D. (2001) 'Constellations and careers: toward understanding the effects of multiple developmental relationships', *Journal of Organizational Behavior*, 22, 3: 223–247.

Horowitz, F. (1999) 'The emergence of strategic training and development: the current state of play', *Journal of European Industrial Training*, 23, 4–5: 180–190.

Hughes, L. and Pengelly, P. (1997) *Staff Supervision in a Turbulent Environment: Managing Process and Task in Front-Line Services*, London: Jessica Kingsley.

Institute of Personnel and Development (IPD) (1995) *Personnel through the Line*, London: IPD.

IPD (2000) *Success through Learning: The Argument for Strengthening Workplace Learning*, London: IPD.

Knowles, M. (1984) *The Adult Learner: A Neglected Species*, Houston, TX: Gulf.

Knowles, M. S., Holton III, E. F. and Swanson, R. A. (1998) *The Adult Learner: The Definitive Classic in Adult Education and Human Resource Development*, Houston, TX: Gulf.

Leicester, C. (1989) 'The key role of the line manager in employee development', *Personnel Management*, March: 53–57.

McGovern, P., Hope-Hailey, V. and Stiles, P. (1997) 'Human resource management on the line?', *Human Resource Management Journal*, 7, 4: 12–29.

Marsick, V. and Watkins, K. (1997) 'Lessons from informal and incidental learning', in J. Burgoyne and M. Reynolds (eds) *Management Learning: Integrating Perspectives in Theory and Practice*, London: Sage.

Mumford, A. (1993) *How Managers Can Develop Managers*, Aldershot: Gower.

National Skills Task Force (NSTF) (2000) *Third Report of the National Skills Task Force: Tackling the Adult Skills Gap – Upskilling Adults and the Role of Workplace Learning*, London: DfEE.

Osborne, S. (1996) 'Training and the voluntary sector', in D. Billis and M. Harris (eds) *Voluntary Agencies: Challenges of Organization and Management*, London: Macmillan.

Quarriers (1996) *Supervision Policy*, Bridge of Weir: Quarriers.

Quarriers (1999) *Strategic Plan 1999–2002*, Bridge of Weir: Quarriers.

Richmond Fellowship Scotland (1997) *Corporate Plan, 1997–2000*, Glasgow: RFS.

Richmond Fellowship Scotland (1998) *Staff Supervision and Appraisal Policy, 1998*, Glasgow: RFS.

Salaman, G. (1995) *Managing*, Buckingham: Open University Press.

Sawdon, C. and Sawdon, D. (1995) 'The supervision partnership: a whole greater than the sum of its parts', in J. Pritchard (ed.) *Good Practice in Supervision: Statutory and Voluntary Organizations*, London: Jessica Kingsley.

Schein, E. (1993) 'How can organizations learn faster? The challenge of entering the green room', *Sloan Management Review*, winter: 85–92.

Scottish Council for Voluntary Organizations (SCVO) (1999) *Working in the*

Voluntary Sector: A Report of Research to Map the Voluntary Sector and its Training Needs in Scotland, Edinburgh: SCVO.

Stanners, C. (1995) 'Supervision in the voluntary sector', in J. Pritchard (ed.) *Good Practice in Supervision: Statutory and Voluntary Organizations*, London: Jessica Kingsley.

Steane, P. (1997) 'Strategy across sectors – the influence of values', paper presented at the *Second International Research Symposium on Public Services Management*, Birmingham, 11–12 September.

Thomson, A., Mabey, C., Storey, J., Gray, C. and Iles, P. (2001) *Changing Patterns of Management Development*, Oxford: Blackwell.

Tough, A. (1979) *The Adult's Learning Projects*, Toronto: Ontario Institute for Studies in Education.

Voluntary Sector National Training Organization (VSNTO) (2001) *Would You Credit it? A Guide on Scottish and National Vocational Qualifications for the Voluntary Sector*, Edinburgh: VSNTO.

Walton, J. (1999) *Strategic Human Resource Management*, Harlow: FT Prentice Hall.

Wiener, R. (1995) 'Supervision in a residential/day care setting', in J. Pritchard (ed.) *Good Practice in Supervision: Statutory and Voluntary Organizations*, London: Jessica Kingsley.

Woodall, J. and Douglas, D. (2000) 'Winning hearts and minds: ethical issues in human resource development', in D. Winstanley and J. Woodall (eds) *Ethical Issues in Contemporary Human Resource Management*, London: Macmillan.

Woodall, J. and Winstanley, D. (2000) 'Concluding comments: ethical frameworks for action', in D. Winstanley and J. Woodall (eds) *Ethical Issues in Contemporary Human Resource Management*, London: Macmillan.

6 Working with values

A study of HR consultants in the charity and voluntary sectors

Diana Winstanley

Introduction

There has been growing interest in work on ethics and values in human resource development (Beattie and McDougall 2000; McLagan 1989; Hatcher 2002). Recently more attention has been directed towards human resource development consultants, and how they work (see, for example, Aragon and Hatcher 2001; Woodall and Douglas 2000). The research reported here explores the work of human resource consultants in the under-researched UK not-for-profit (NFP) sector, focusing particularly on their values and how they are put into practice through their work. It is not just in HRD that the NFP sector is neglected, it is also notably absent from leading texts on managing values in organizations (such as McEwan 2001; Fisher and Lovell 2003).

This chapter begins with an exploration of the challenges facing the NFP sector, and the role of HRD in addressing them. It highlights the central role that ethics and values have played in underpinning the sector and therefore by implication, HRD in this area. The findings of a research project into working with these values are then reported, where it is argued that it is not only the NFP sector that brings values to bear, but also the HRD consultants themselves who work with and through their values. The HRD consultants in this area are found to be an unusual group of 'mavericks' working with strong value sets in unusual and innovative ways. The chapter concludes with a discussion of the ways in which values play a part in the work of an HRD consultant in the NFP sector, but warns against over reliance on codes of practice or on templates which go against the ethos of the practitioners in this area.

HRD in the not-for-profit area

The UK NFP sector is an important area for HRD because of its size, diversity and activity base. It has achieved an unprecedented status since the mid-1990s as it has grown considerably in size and stretched its activities to encompass new forms of organization. For example income received by UK charities amounts to more than £16 billion a year, equivalent to about 1.5 per cent of gross domestic product (Johnson 1997; Key Note 2001). Only fifteen charities receive over £100 million a year, and the top 7.9 per cent of charities between them get 92.5 per cent of the registered charitable sector's income, while 72.8 per cent of the sector, whose income is less than £10,000 a year, share 1.4 per cent of its total income. Not all organizations in the NFP sector qualify as charities, and so even these figures under-represent the sheer scale of this third force, alongside the private and public sectors. The traditional definition of the objectives of charities, as specified by the Charity Commission and outlined in the Charities Digest (2003), is with relation to 'the relief of poverty, or for the advancement of education, or for the advancement or religion or for other purposes beneficial to the community.' This has largely become an anachronism, as the developments in the NFP sector have stretched the boundaries laid down for a bygone age.

A number of writers on the NFP sector trace some of the managerial challenges that beset this area. For example Adirondack (1998) places the aims and purposes as well as the legal framework at the centre of her invaluable text on the need for management development in this sector. Likewise Connors (2001), Drucker (1990), Handy (1988), Hudson (1999) and Wilbur (2000) build up a strong case to consider this as a distinct area requiring the development of expertise and capability beyond that currently in evidence, and with its own knowledge base. The need for HRD is ironically overshadowed by the difficulties in resourcing this at all, let alone delivered by in-house HRD. Table 6.1 charts some of these challenges, and they are discussed below. Without the support of HRD they could easily defeat the large established organizations, not to mention the huge periphery

Table 6.1 Managerial challenges facing the not-for-profit sector

Type 1 challenges: to be a charity
- Identifying the purpose
- Developing the purpose
- Dealing with mixed activities
- The legal requirements on a charity

Type 2 challenges: external winds of change
- Moving from private to public to the third sector
- New regulations and government legislation
- Competition
- The infiltration of business-like concepts
- New funding streams

Type 3 challenges: the management development agenda
- Voluntary but not amateur
- Developing capability in strategy, fundraising, financial management, information systems and IT, human resources
- Maintaining morale through organizational change

of new, small and growing enterprise. It is not just the growing size of this sector, but also its nature, activities and the rate of change that make it a particular challenge for HRD.

The first category in Table 6.1 relates to the aims and purposes of the organizations themselves. Handy (1988: 12) outlines a classification of NFP organizations using five main categories of voluntary organization according to purpose – mutual support and self-help groups (such as Alcoholics Anonymous), service delivery providers (such as Save the Children) and research, advocacy and campaigning (such as the Child Poverty Action Group or Greenpeace), common interest groups such as Glenans (a sailing association) and intermediary bodies (such as the Councils for Voluntary Services). The reality is that this can be further split into a myriad of activities, with many organizations mixing these purposes (something that Handy warns against). For example the National Childbirth Trust enables new parents to support each other as well as provide information and antenatal and postnatal classes, in addition to campaigning to make the birth experience a better one. It is easy for organizations to lose sight of their original objectives, or drift into new activities, and they may need support in enabling dialogue with members, trustees and funders over changing directions.

Underlying the aims of not-for-profit organizations are sets of values, and these values are strongly embedded in the root and origin of their existence. Therefore any HRD in this sector has to take account of these values, and be sensitive to them in both the content and process of the work. However, this value-laden context is surrounded by a complex web of legal and financial obligations, specifications and limitations, as outlined thoroughly by Adirondack (1998), who recognizes the difficulties such organizations have keeping abreast of such changes. NFP organizations need continual development in human resources capability to stay within the law, remain financially stable, and benefit from advantageous tax laws and rates relief. For example section 505 of the Income and Corporation Taxes Act 1988 exempts gifts to charities from tax, and extends this to trade. Charity shops also experience 80 per cent relief from mandatory local authority rates, and 20 per cent relief from discretionary rates. So for new and growing not-for-profit organizations the need for consultancy support and development in this area can be vital.

A second set of challenges in Table 6.1 outline changes in NFP organizations brought by external 'push' factors. These can arise from new regulations or government legislation, competition, or even the transfer of organizations or their activities from one sector into another. Government has influenced these developments through a plethora of legislation, regulations, directives and incentives, primarily in the public sector, but has also affected charities by means of funding and grants tied to policy changes. The complexity of legislation impacting upon the NFP sector has developed apace as new employment law has emerged, for example in relation to contracts of employment, the minimum wage, working time regulations, changes in maternity leave, the introduction of parental leave, recognition of trade unions, and the right to be accompanied at disciplinary hearings. As well as the Employment Relations Act there is also legislation on human rights and on data protection.

Housing is an area where the expansions in the NFP sector has replaced public provision. Where public housing had once been within the direct ownership and control of local government, increasingly this has been outsourced to social organizations and the public provision has been met by a rise in the number and size of independent housing trusts. Changes such as this have brought the NFP sector into new forms of funding provision with more stringent requirements for organizations to be organized and managed in a professional and transparent way. This is illustrated in the introduction of 'best value' practices in local government which have been cascaded on down to their partner organizations in the NFP sector.

Once again consultants are at the forefront of enabling charities to develop themselves for their changing environment. In particular, funding streams are changing and charities have looked for new ways of funding activities, moving away from a reliance on grants and donations, and towards greater marketing, sales and trading activities. In 1947 Oxfam opened its first shop, followed by Sue Ryder opening a number of shops in the 1950s. The number of charity shops has grown such an extent that according to Mintel (2001) it comprises more than 100 organizations running in excess of 7,000 shops, which generate more than £400 million annual turnover. Charities such as Shelter and Oxfam have all developed their strategies for developing a high street presence alongside budget shops in the private sector.

Changes such as these have all led to a third set of challenges – a formidable management agenda for development of strategy, fundraising, financial management, information systems, IT and human resources. Many NFP organizations have found it necessary to improve their management practice, both for internal reasons, and in order to secure funding. Thus management practices widespread in other sectors have filtered into the charity and voluntary sector: performance management, training models (such as Investors in People), quality assurance models, and particularly those processes concerned with measurement and evaluation. Underlying many of these internal changes is the move away from the NFP sector being seen as run by 'voluntary amateurs' to more professional organizations with strategies for branding their image, products and services. These changes also require the sector to maintain the morale and commitment of armies of volunteer workers. For some organizations this means not just keeping pace with the private sector, but being at the forefront of innovative organizational structures and human resource practices. The value-laden basis of many NFP organizations, where profit maximization is irrelevant and financial viability and survival are related to broader social aims, leads to some unique and unusual practices. For example flat pay policies, such as are found at Pecan, a charity for the provision of training for the unemployed, make extremes of functional flexibility possible, where a staff member may be a receptionist one month and financial controller another. However, this can happen only with strong HRD. Likewise unusual forms of temporal flexibility are found in the NFP sector with complex combinations of working hours to suit a variety of voluntary and temporary staff, who may not always be able to access standard forms of off-the-job training and development. Managing an unpaid workforce also brings its own challenges for staff development, particularly when staff are driven by a personal commitment rather than a career.

The utilization of external human development consultants is one way in which charities can prepare themselves for these challenges. A distinctive feature of this service is the provision of support and information that can be tailor-made to suit a sector whose values are central to their mission, not grafted on as an additional policy or code of practice. Training and development needs to be provided in a way which is synergistic with both the nature of the changes, and the values, culture and ethos of the organizations themselves. Radical and innovative human resource management practices are widespread in the NFP area, one reason for this being the values present in the NFP sector itself.

Values and HRD in the NFP sector

The previous section described the NFP sector as a vibrant one with a challenging agenda for HRD. It was suggested that these organizations are built on strong value sets which have to be taken into account when providing development support to the sector to cope with the challenges. However, it is important to give these sets of values more thorough consideration.

First, social and caring values are perceived as dominant in the NFP sector. One way this can become problematic for an organization is when looking after its own front-line staff who are sorely stretched, yet desperately committed to their clients and service. In the context of the challenges above, this can lead to staff burnout. The role of the consultant can therefore be to help an organization deal with the developments outlined in Table 6.1 so as to avoid their staff becoming burnt out. Another way these social and caring values can be evident is in support for social justice which may underpin their campaigning activities, such as for Amnesty International, or in the services provided for example by organizations campaigning against homelessness.

Related to caring values are values to do with inclusion. One area where HRD can provide support and development to this sector is in user participation and consultation. The need to satisfy a complex set of stakeholders, such as trustees, members, volunteers and funding bodies leads to development needs in communication and stakeholder feedback. Although consultation with user groups is seen as good in principle, for small organizations this can mean that their time and resources can be severely stretched. One example here is the Lymphoma Association (see Littlejohns 2001) which in order to develop its strategy with relation to boundaries with other organizations (whether to merge or amalgamate, expand or contract), or in relation to which services to provide (whether to shift current services, keep them, or develop new ones such as campaigning, member support, lobbying, funding research) has engaged in a consultation exercise. This involved hundreds of members through a survey, focus groups with staff, and individual interviews with the trustees – a massive exercise, but an important one for a membership-based organization.

Value clashes within these organizations can occur in the context of the organizational changes mentioned above, and particularly with the introduction of more business-like practices. For example problems can arise between front-line staff committed to delivering a service on the one hand, and the board or management on the other, who may be more focused on financial considerations, particularly in a funding drought. The other frequently occurring area of value clash is between older and newer staff, particularly where the latter have been brought in after changes to the organization.

Another way the dominance of values in this sector can impact upon the work of the HRD consultant is in terms of value saturation. What is meant by this is that these organizations by their nature can attract people with both strongly held values, and a commitment to putting those values into action. Where too many value agendas are brought into the workplace, a situation of saturation can be the result, whereby an organization becomes top-heavy in values, and even paralysed by it. One example here is of a social housing collective, where a diverse group of over twenty people, had different agendas ranging from views on women and feminism, to Irish issues, race and class. An expectation existed within the organization of equal treatment, with all having the right to be heard, all had the right to attention, priority, affirmation and change. The agenda was too big, in the end the organization was destroyed.

The research approach

The research reported here is based on an empirical study of human resource and organizational development consultants and trainers working with the charity and voluntary sectors in the United Kingdom. The research aim was to identify issues around working with values in the NFP sector, to determine important themes for consultants in working with values, and to identify ways in which values can be put into practice. Although clearly not typical of all HR consultants, these consultants were seen to be particularly interesting from the view of exploring ethics and values, as they work largely alone or in very small groupings, and thus have considerable freedom in relation to how values and ethics are exhibited in their work. They also have chosen to work with sectors where values are prominent in the nature of the work. Although their own value sets are of interest to this work, of even more importance is the way in which these values are manifested in practice. So the principal research question was, how do these consultants live their values?

The research arose out of my interest in the charity sector, but discovery that there was little work available on how consultants worked in the NFP area, contrasted with the other two sectors. This was discussed in a one-day workshop that I gave in May 2000 to members of the Management Development Network (MDN), a network of consultants working in the UK NFP area. This day was facilitated by me with the aim of generating views and reflection on consultant ethics and values. The day resulted in enthusiasm for conducting a study in this area, utilizing members of the MDN. Essentially the research utilized a triangulation approach moving from the group discussion of the first workshop to individual interviews to group discussion at a second workshop at the end of the research, rather like a sandwich. There were nine semi-structured interviews with MDN consultants, as well as one interview with a consultant working in public, private and NFP sectors, and one interview with a consultant working predominantly with the private sector. The sample was a combination of self-selection and theoretical sampling, and being non random and too small cannot be said to be representative of consultants in general in this sector. However the data do uncover some practices that have relevance for our understanding of how some consultants work in the NFP sector, and provide us with different models to those practiced in the other sectors. It is likely that they are not typical of consultants who may work in larger practices, but their interest to us is in highlighting a value-based approach to working as an HRD consultant.

The interviews were semi-structured, utilizing a combination of open and closed questions about the values the participants perceived in the NFP sector, their own values and ways of working, as well as a scenario concerned with uncovering how as a consultant they would work with a specific NFP organization wishing to change its values. During the interviews the consultants were provided with a list of values drawn from codes of practice to rate their level of agreement (see Table 6.2). Typically each interview lasted ninety minutes, and there was time in the interview for consultants to spend time reflecting on their approach in real situations, and participants were encouraged to tell their own stories of putting values into practice. Most of the data were analysed inductively using a qualitative coding approach. Each participant was provided with a copy of their transcript to correct and validate. The interview findings were fed back to a one-day discussion workshop of MDN consultants in September 2001 as an opportunity to further validate the data and analysis.

This research was supplemented by action research at six charities to identify issues of change and development in the areas of strategy,

Table 6.2 List of values rated by consultants

Competence
- Not going beyond own expertise
- Responsibility to update and maintain own knowledge and competence
- Seek to achieve fullest possible development of others and encourage others to develop selves

Integrity
- Honesty, for example in reporting qualifications
- Acting lawfully and not encouraging or assisting unlawful conduct of others
- Accuracy of advice and information given
- Clarity in roles being performed
- Transparency over beliefs, values, ways of working and limitations
- Avoidance of conflicting relationships

Professional responsibility
- Clarify professional roles and obligations
- Accept responsibility for own behaviour
- Enhance the good standing and name of the profession

Respect of difference
- Adapt methods to needs of different populations
- Awareness of cultural, individual and role differences, including ones relating to age, gender, race etc.
- Accept different view of others, do not force own viewpoint upon others
- Not to knowingly condone unfair discriminatory practices, and promote non-discriminatory practice

Respect for others' rights and dignity
- Respect rights of others to privacy
- Confidentiality
- Self-determination
- Autonomy
- Voice, participation and a say in things that affect them

Concern for other's welfare/minimize harm to others
- Sensitive to and do not exploit power differentials
- Resolve conflicts in a way that avoids or minimizes harm

Social responsibility – to community, society, environment etc.
- Minimize adverse effect
- Advance sustainable future

operations, marketing, fundraising and HR, and to explore potential ways in which HRD or organizational development consultancy could support these changes. These charities included two organizations in the housing area, two in business support, one in health and one in training, and their activities covered service delivery and support, member support, information provision and campaigning. This work was conducted by MBA project students working with the author.

HRD consultants and their values

Sharing the values of the NFP sector

Unlike for other sectors, there is an assumption in the NFP sector that consultants will share the values of the client organization, and certainly most of the consultants interviewed expected to share these values, and may even turn work down if there was a significant value clash with their client:

> I am there because I want them to do well by the cause or the people they are helping. So there is a personal investment, and so I deal with my personal goals about a better society through the people I work with. So there needs to be a compatibility in a very broad sense between me and them. I have to feel at ease with them and want them to do the work well. I need to know that they are necessary, otherwise I might as well go and work with somebody else.

Most of the consultants had come to work with this sector because of the values.

Therefore it was not surprising that many of the values mentioned above were prominent. For example the value of caring extended to respectfulness and valuing each individual. Typical quotes here were:

> I must respect them and their experience.
>
> I value and respect their experience.
>
> The roundedness of human beings.

Social justice was also important to some consultants, and this was also extended to the way they would work, which linked with the value of inclusion for example by:

> Making sure the silent be heard.
>
> Including people – in a systematic and organized way.
>
> I would speak in a language that everyone can understand.

Many NFP organizations exist to make a difference in the area in which they work, and certainly the consultants were as equally committed. Their work was not done purely instrumentally, and the consultants were committed to 'Doing work which will result in a genuine improvement on something that is important, not playing politics, or doing it because it is fun.'

Codes of practice and the way a consultant works

Some of the consultants mentioned codes of practice which they felt supported and underpinned their practice, many of which were provided within directories of consultants in the NFP area. For example such codes included:

- Management Development Network (MDN) Briefing on choosing and briefing a management consultant or trainer.
- Chartered Institute for Personnel and Development (CIPD) codes of practice.
- Association of Consultants in Voluntary Organisations (ACVO) advice on using consultants.
- The Greater London Employer's Association documents on making the best use of a consultant.

Codes of practice also tend to suggest a formalized way of working, but in reality, most of the consultants interviewed worked in a highly informal way with their values, although a couple did write some down. Others would highlight their ethical principles and values and ways of working with the client at the beginning of the process. One reason for the informality may be that there are a number of sole practitioners working in the NFP sector, and it is likely that smaller organizations would work more informally than larger ones.

In discussing their values many of the typical items identified on professional codes would arise (see Table 6.2), for example reliability, safety, honesty and confidentiality:

> I like people to be able to rely on me, to know what we are doing.
>
> [from a trainer] Safety is important – any comment that is made, I don't shoot it down, I don't downgrade it, and although other people might, but then I might comment about that.
>
> Confidentiality – people should be able to feel that what they are saying and doing in the session is not going to be carried out of it into the workplace in a critical way.

On other values, the consultants would go even further than the codes. For example on the issue of 'being sensitive to and not exploiting power differentials', one consultant said she would:

> See it as my role to reduce, or equalize, for the period that I'm with them, the power differentials. So for example for a facilitated day, I would put a lot of energy into devising ways of them working together that do not allow what I call 'the big mouth' to dominate.

The research also drew attention to the shortcomings of codes. Some of the values identified in codes were not seen as straightforward issues in the NFP sector, take for example 'acting lawfully':

> I have no difficulty, you see, in supporting eco-warriors that break the law, but on the other hand, other things, I would be absolutely not be happy with.
>
> Obviously, I would always act lawfully, but what I will often say to them is here is what the law says you must do, but I know that you may well operate differently. And if you operate differently, you have to be aware you are breaking the law . . . Now I'm not encouraging them to break the law. For example in the case of recruiting a black man because they have an all-white female group, and they know that the funders are breathing down their necks on this one, and they want to balance the staff, and reflect the community. But I'm saying to them the reality is, in this particular case you may well choose to break the law, and if you are going to break the law, then do it knowingly.

It is not simply a case of taking the value and applying it, but one of dealing with more complex 'grey' areas. The work of Aragon and Hatcher (2001) is particularly useful in this regard as it develops more detailed case studies to enable a consultant to see how the values would work in practice. The difficulty of working with and through values is evident in the area of confidentiality. Although many consultants in the study recognized the importance of confidentiality, some also felt that an important part of their own support was being able to ring up a colleague or another consultant to discuss their experience of a difficult situation, or even just to let off steam – this also shows the importance of having support networks in place. The codes of practice are starting points only. To be useful they need to be discussed and worked with. There does seem to be evidence of the need for mentors or co-supervision to enable the ethical principles to be utilized, and to support individuals in difficult situations.

Another difficult area involving more than applying the code of practice is where values identified in codes clash or come into conflict in practice. It was suggested that the notion of 'hierarchies of values' is important:

> One example of a hierarchy of values is in mental health. Here there can be a clash between confidentiality and security. There are times when precise guidance is given on the need to break confidentiality for the need of security. For example a counsellor may break confidentiality with a client, when there is severe risk of harm to that person or someone else. However judgement is needed in interpreting this value hierarchy, and deep understanding is needed over the principles and values themselves.

Possible 'hierarchies of values' require explanation, training and clarity, and this may be one area of values work in which a consultant may get involved, but may also have to decide themselves, but in a way that is rarely supported through codes of practice.

Another potential problem with codes of practice is they almost always assume that the values can be grafted on to a consultant. For these consultants their values were deeply held beliefs that had been formed in childhood and crafted through experience – they were part of who they were and how they worked, not something they 'had' – a point made before on the difficulty of value change work by Woodall (1996). Three quotes in particular identify the depth and longevity of these values, and their role in acting as drivers to push consultants into working with the NFP sector:

> There was a kind of ethic in the family, that you would care for people and they always used to say 'if they lost me as a child, I would either be with a marine band or with a tramp', because I was keen on talking to people who were unusual in some way.

> I grew up in an environment where it was naturally assumed that, because we were quite lucky, that you gave back. We all ended up working with homelessness . . . The first thing my father did was take me along with him when he was working as a homelessness volunteer, and I was quite young. And my sister and I at 13, 14 went on to do voluntary work in the summer and things like that.

> There is a personal vindication to some degree, say with women and women's issues, but also people who are displaced in some way. And so I in some way deal with my pain, hurt around things not being right in our society, through helping those people who do that.

The last quote was of a consultant who was driven to repair the problems they had encountered as a child who had suffered at the hands of an alcoholic and abusive father. The depth of feeling over core values could lead them to work in this sector, although for some it was a mature career choice (for example following redundancy) or serendipity.

Other writers have drawn attention to the problems associated with ethical codes. For example Willmott (1998: 81, 85–87) states they do not give a firm ground for assessing competing claims, and they decontextualize them. Willmott gives the example of 'loyalty' – what if the person to whom one is supposed to be loyal is morally inappropriate? They also 'seek to establish their authority as an objective regime of truth', seeking to normalize some and marginalize others' values, particularly the personal values of employees. With relation to this study, the consultants worked in highly individualized and humanistic ways, which would make it even more difficult to regulate these values or fix them in a template, such as that presented by codes of practice. This may be one of the reasons the consultants worked alone and away from the private sector. In fact they were very sceptical of 'off-the-shelf' solutions and ways of working, with their approaches having been honed through years of experience and work in the NFP sector.

'Mavericks'

These consultants had developed personal and particularistic approaches to their work. They also mentioned their professional organizations and networks to which they belonged as important sources of advice and information in this area. However, these consultants are to some extent 'mavericks' (a term some used of themselves), because of their independent way of working, and their reluctance to formalize further codes of practice into more formal qualifications and quality 'kite-marks'. Rather than arguing for a formal route, many gained support from more informal arrangements. For example, this could include joint arrangements with other practitioners, which could range through involvement in

- support groups and networks (for example the seminars and workshop meetings organized by the MDN itself);
- action learning sets (where each meeting a different individual would have the opportunity to table their problems and issues on the agenda for discussion);
- mentoring (drawing on support and coaching from a more experienced consultant or professional mentor);
- co-supervision (where typically a pair of consultants would support and advise each other);
- joint-working (where consultants would deliberately work together to offer each other opportunities for mutual learning and support).

Perhaps because of their isolation due to working alone, there was evidence of many being 'reflective practitioners' (Hartog 2002; Schön 1983) where they would attempt to develop self-awareness and mindfulness, moving between action and reflection. They were attuned to working with emotion and emotional intelligence (possibly central in the work of organizational development practitioners). They would also actively seek out and give feedback, and promote power sharing and the engagement of the client and the staff in the client organization. They had a sense of their own moral agency and an ethics of care in their work.

An area which arose in the interviews was the need to value oneself, and that for the HRD consultants meant they had to find ways of looking after themselves. As well as formal and informal relationships, it did seem that many consultants struggled with work–life balance, and some had to put a lot of effort into maintaining their own energy levels. An example of their 'giving' approach to the work, even at the expense of their own health, is in the following quote:

> I'm not sure this is a value, but it certainly underpins how I work . . . [It] is this sense that when I'm with a group, I am with that group. My head or energy is not somewhere else. And even if I am three-quarters dead they won't know that. For example I smashed up my car going up the M11 [motorway], ended up with the car getting hit by a lorry, and being spun across the M11 and ending up in a tree. The car was a total write-off. And I went and did a full day's training after that.

Therefore supporting and looking after oneself, managing one's own boundaries, does seem to be an overlooked value for consultants in this area. As well as giving of time, it is common for consultants to give a percentage of their services free, and to engage in a lot of voluntary work themselves, without always being clear about where the boundary should be.

Keeping up-to date was one way of supporting oneself, and a value in some codes of practice. However there were a variety of ways in which people developed their knowledge base. As well as finding going on courses, reading certain books, and even writing books to be useful as a way of keeping up to date, informal forms of learning seemed important. For example one consultant learnt a lot through joint working with other consultants, or people from different specialisms.

As well as their autonomous and independent approach to work there is another reason why these consultants could be called 'mavericks'. This relates to their ability to work with and through their values. They prioritized

- respect for the client's experience
- valuing individuals
- unconditional positive regard
- inclusion of all and 'letting the silent be heard'
- doing a professional job and being a good consultant
- reliability
- honesty and integrity
- safety
- confidentiality
- transparency.

This is particularly evident in their work with organizational change, and working with values change.

Working with values

Where there were value differences between organizational members there were a number of hurdles the consultants felt they had to negotiate (and see Table 6.3). These meant they had to

- focus on the process and 'unknowing' rather than having views on what the content of change should be
- provide empathy rather than alignment
- be a catalyst rather than fixer
- be a surfacer, clarifier rather than change agent
- design processes for allowing participants to voice concerns
- provide relevant factual feedback.

Where strongly held values were prevalent in a consultancy or training situation, and these differed across groups, one consultant made the distinction of 'collusion' as opposed to 'alignment', where collusion meant that the consultant would 'affirm their value and their contribution and their right to a voice and to have certain experiences', but the consultant would not align with one group in agreeing that 'yes, you are right, the managers are bad' or 'yes they are out to get you'. Although the terminology differed (many would see this as 'empathy' rather than 'collusion'), this was an important aspect of the work. Not being used for 'hidden agendas' is a good example of that. For example where one group of staff saw the problem as being 'the chairperson' whom they wanted the consultant to expose as being to blame, the consultant thought it was particularly important not to align with one group against another. One way of doing this is not to 'be terribly active in the problem that the organization thinks it has got'.

Table 6.3 The role of the consultant in supporting value change in NFP organizations

- Providing *information, advice and training* to enable organizations to comply with legislation on diversity and equal opportunities, human rights and employment rights of the workforce, and also become knowledgeable about new laws, practices and ways of working.
- *Developing* staff to meet increasing expectations for continuous professional development, employability, as well as to have the skill and mindset to cope with transferable and flexible skill development, as well as core functional and managerial skills such as in areas of finance/accounting, marketing and sales, people management and client communication.
- Help with *managing change* to enable voluntary and employed staff to create, develop and cope with changing structures, practices and values and ethos, by
  - helping an organization to identify and *clarify* the changes to be made, developing transparency, and moving from the generalities of change, to the specifics of what will happen
  - *supporting* the organization to make the changes and develop
  - identifying *surfacing values clashes* that arise, where not all in the organization may support the change of direction and values, or alternatively identifying value clashes brought about by the difference between the old values and the new
  - changing overload, identifying pressure points of, for example, potential staff burnout and ensuring they are addressed.

This leads on to the difficult issue of how far a consultant will be a go-between or a voice for groups, rather than enabling groups and individuals to speak up for themselves. The preference was generally for the latter, but it seemed inevitable to most consultants, that their role was sometimes to be a vessel for voicing issues, as long as this did not compromise their sense of independence and non-alignment. Most saw the consultant as a catalyst, rather than as a fixer, where the responsibility had to be kept with the client. One consultant said:

> One of the things that I learned years ago was that nothing is so awful that once you turn the light on, it doesn't feel a bit better. It's the thing about shadows when you are in the dark – I remember as a child lying in bed and being frightened when there were shadows on the wall, and somebody turns the light on, and you are all right then.

In this way the consultant's focus seemed to be on process, on surfacing issues in a safe way, clarifying these, sharing them, and helping people deal with them, rather than someone who comes in with a template for change which is put into action. In the perception of these consultants, this was where they felt they differed significantly from consultants working within large consultancies operating for private sector clients.

To work with the process required a confidence in being able to cope with not knowing what the outcome of the work might be, and a confidence that something would emerge from sessions. There was an element of intuitiveness about the work, where some were drawn instinctively to where the energy or heat was. Some talked about the 'aha' moment when something clicks inside the participants at facilitated sessions, that would then move the process on. Important issues were not just drawn from a consultant's toolkit, they would emerge from processes designed to allow participants from the organization to give voice to their concerns. However this did not mean that consultants withheld relevant knowledge and skills, so for example if a consultant had expertise on law, structures, roles and responsibilities, finance and IT systems, or fundraising, then they would provide input to these issues. In one case putting various roles and structures in place could be made a requirement of the consultant taking on the work. The balance between these different processes differed from consultant to consultant, with some giving more emphasis on process and voice, and others on information and expertise. Some were more diagnostic, others were more of a facilitator and catalyst.

Consultants were sometimes very innovative in their approach to surfacing issues, and also then consolidating this, so that learning was not dissipated on return to the workplace. One consultant for example 'fixed' the learning from facilitated sessions by using information they had gathered in a 'magpie' or 'jackdaw' way. The consultant collected useful quotes from newspapers like 'good management is like hidden wiring' and then store these on postcards, which would be used at the end of sessions, where people would chose a picture and talk about the quote and how it related to what they had learnt, as a way of consolidating the learning. Alternatively, at the end of a session, another gave participants chocolates which had congratulatory messages in the wrapping, and participants were asked to read them out and say how they related to the changes they were making. Others drew on therapeutic models of change such as the Gestalt cycle of change and paradox of change. One even utilized genetic and biological models of change, exploring ideas of evolution and mutation. Another worked with imagery, utilizing the idea of 'weaving' tapestries of the organization and changes that were happening and ones which challenged the formal view of the organization. Consultants also drew from mainstream organizational development.

Conclusion

This chapter has suggested that there are many innovative practices in evidence in both the NFP sector and among the HRD consultants working in it, and these are an under-researched and less visible area of the literature compared to the templates and models offered within the private sector and elsewhere. We have shown that the NFP sector in the United Kingdom is an expanding one, with many challenges for HRD consultants to help organizations to face. Due to size, financial and resource pressures, many of these organizations do not have the internal capability or expertise to develop their own human resources, and so utilize consultants. The consultants are seen as 'mavericks', not fitting into conventional consultancy models and prescriptions. Values play a strong underpinning role in the aims and objectives of NFP organizations, and also are important to consultants working within this sector. Further, a number of consultants would claim that value congruence with their clients was essential to their way of working. These values are not lightly held. They are deeply embedded in both the client organizations and the consultants and their way of working. Codes of conduct and practice therefore, although they may be useful to surface some value and ethical issues, are not particularly helpful in developing value change. The values are deeply held, and are to do with what a person 'is' rather than 'has'. Codes of conduct can also mask some contradictions – such as between different values. They also do not fully capture the spirit of the values nor are they particularly helpful in enabling a practitioner to put them into place. This chapter has suggested some other ways of supporting HRD consultants in this area, for example through co-supervision and action learning sets. Finally the chapter explained in more detail ways in which these consultants may work with value change in their client organizations.

References

Adirondack, S. (1998) *Just about Managing*, 3rd edn, London: London Voluntary Service Council.

Aragon, S. and Hatcher, T. (2001) 'Ethics and integrity in HRD: case studies in research and practice', special issue of *Advances in Developing Human Resources*, 3, 1, February.

Beattie, R. and McDougall, M. (2000) 'Ethical issues in HRD research', in J. McGoldrick, J. Stewart and S. Watson (eds) *Researching HRD*, London: Routledge.

Charities Digest (2003) *Charities Digest*, London: Waterlow Professional (compiled by Claudio Rios).

Connors, T. D. (2001) *The Nonprofit Handbook*, New York: John Wiley.

Drucker, P. (1990) *Managing the Non-Profit Organization: Practices and Principles*, New York: HarperCollins.

Fisher, C. and Lovell, A. (2003) *Business Ethics and Values*, Harlow: FT Prentice Hall, Pearson.

Handy, C. (1988) *Understanding Voluntary Organizations*, London: Penguin.

Hartog, M. (2002) 'Becoming a reflective practitioner: a continuing professional development strategy through humanistic action research', *Business Ethics: A European Review*, 11, 3: 233–243.

Hatcher, T. (2002) *Ethics and HRD: A New Approach to Leading Responsible Organizations*, Cambridge, MA: Perseus.

Hudson, M. (1999) *Managing without Profit*, 2nd edn, London: Penguin.

Johnson, K. (ed.) (1997) *Charities: Key Note Market Report*, 5th edn, Hampton, Middlesex: Key Note Ltd.

Key Note (2001) *Charity Funding: Key Note Market Assessment Report*, Hampton, Middlesex: Key Note Ltd.

Littlejohns, M. (2001) *A Strategic Review of the Lymphoma Association*, London: Imperial College Business School MBA Project, Imperial College, University of London.

McEwan, T. (2001) *Managing Values and Beliefs in Organisations*, Harlow: FT Prentice Hall, Pearson.

McLagan, P. A. (1989) *Models for HRD Practice: A Manager's Guide*, Alexandria, VA: American Society for Training and Development.

Mintel (2001) *Charities Report*, August 2001, London: Mintel.

Schön, D. (1983) *The Reflective Practitioner: How Professionals Think in Action*, New York: Basic Books.

Wilbur, R. H. (ed.) (2000) *The Complete Guide to Non Profit Management*, Smith Bucklin and Associates, Inc., New York: John Wiley.

Willmott, H. (1998) 'Towards a new ethics? The contribution of poststructuralism and post humanism', in M. Parker (ed.) *Ethics and Organisations*, London: Sage.

Woodall, J. (1996) 'Managing culture change: can it ever be ethical?', *Personnel Review*, 25, 6: 26–40.

Woodall, J. and Douglas, D. (2000) 'Winning hearts and minds: ethical issues in human resource development', in D. Winstanley and J. Woodall (eds) *Ethical Issues in Contemporary Human Resource Management*, London: Macmillan.

7 The relationship between professional learning and continuing professional development in the United Kingdom

A critical review of the literature

Jean Woodall and Stephen Gourlay

Introduction

This chapter seeks to provide a critical review of the theorizing of learning processes in which business professionals engage after they have qualified and are in professional practice. The focus upon business professionals has been chosen because, along with other high-performance knowledge workers, professionals are the fastest growing group in the UK workforce, and within this category, the growth in the number of business professionals is particularly marked. However, in examining the pressures for this group to engage in continuing professional development (CPD) it becomes immediately obvious that implicit assumptions about professional learning, and the learning contexts and processes in which business professionals might participate, lie uneasily beside the conditions of business professional practice. This chapter addresses this issue firstly by revisiting current assumptions about the learning of professionals held by both scholars and professional bodies. It then moves on to evaluate these assumptions in terms of the developments in the context of business professional practice in three areas: human resource management, accountancy and marketing. Finally, it engages with current debates within sociocultural theory and situated learning and cognition, before arriving at a series of recommendations for future research in CPD.

Defining continuous professional development

CPD has been defined as: 'The maintenance and enhancement of the knowledge, expertise and competence of professionals throughout their careers, according to a plan formulated with regard to the needs of the professional, their employer, and society' (Madden and Mitchell 1993: 12). It has been presented as having three main functions: updating knowledge and skills in existing and new areas of practice, preparation for a changing role in the organization, new responsibilities and promotion, and increasing competence in a wider context with benefits to both professional and personal roles.

However, there is a danger in searching for general definitions. When it comes to what is acceptable CPD activity among UK business professions, it is true that professional body policies do exhibit some common features such as the development of obligatory (and sometimes mandatory) structured CPD frameworks, the provision of more individual support and guidance, and the requirement for individual members to produce evidence of learning and CPD plans increasingly based on learning outcomes and competencies, rather than inputs (especially the Chartered Institute of Personnel and Development, the Institute of Chartered Secretaries and the Chartered Institute of Marketing). Yet, business professional bodies can differ considerably in many respects. Some have moved to competence schemes. The Institute of Chartered Secretaries and Administrators (ICSA) and all the accountancy bodies not only have 'mandatory' CPD schemes which define what constitutes acceptable 'structured' CPD activities, for those who wish to retain their licence to practise, but also prescribe preferred providers of these. This is not the case in human resource management or marketing. Similarly, the Institute of Chartered Accountants for England and Wales excludes activities that relate to 'normal working activities' from contributing to CPD. In contrast, the Chartered Institute of Personnel and Development (CIPD) appears to be unique in avoiding specification of preferred provision of CPD activity, and along with the Chartered Institute of Management Accountants (CIMA) and the Chartered Institute of Marketing (CIM), emphasizes self-directed learning and learning from workplace activities.

However, when we move from a consideration of formal CPD policy to a consideration of how it is undertaken by individual professionals, the confusion becomes greater. The debate around CPD becomes swallowed up within a wider discussion about lifelong learning, the knowledge society, organizational learning and work-based learning, so that a clear understanding of what is specifically *professional* about the process of learning is lost. Furthermore, the development of professional knowledge and expertise is conceptualized as an essentially individually driven, cognitive, problem-solving activity. Finally, there is a tendency to generalize across all groups of professionals and to disregard whether professional learning and engagement with CPD is context-specific according to professional body membership and site of professional practice (Galloway 2000). Thus is it important to start with a review of current theoretical assumptions that underpin professional learning.

Current theoretical assumptions about the learning of professionals

There are a number of different theoretical assumptions about how professionals *do* and *should* learn that are held by scholars researching CPD on the one hand and by professional bodies on the other. The main developments in theorizing around professional learning have been led by adult educators in the United Kingdom and United States. A long tradition stretching back to the work of John Dewey and Mary Parker Follett stressed the importance of learning taking place through individual experience, the informal nature of this learning, and the role of critical reflection. The andragogic model developed originally by Edward C. Lindeman, and later Malcolm Knowles, has dominated research and theory. However, the strongly humanistic values that underpin adult learning theory (Knowles 1989), and which emphasize the centrality of human agency and personal fulfilment, marginalize the significance of situation and context on learning. This is the case no matter the importance conceded to 'critical reflection' through which individuals are enabled to challenge the assumptions underpinning their pre-existing frames of reference. Attention is focused upon *individual* learning processes and attendant interventions to assist *individuals* to engage in critical reflection and optimize the use of informal and incidental learning. There is also an implicit assumption that an adult educator will be present to guide the individual learner. Brookfield (1987) and Mezirow (1991) are able to identify a range of techniques to be used in a classroom situation to encourage critical reflection such as critical questioning, critical incident exercises, criteria analysis, role play, crisis simulation, brainstorming and scenario building, and Wood-Daudelin (1996) shows that one-to-one counselling followed by group facilitation is more effective for learning than solitary reflection. The work of Reynolds (1998) on critical reflection as a way of dealing with political and social problems at work, and Vince's (2002) ideas on reflection as an organizing rather than individual process take the concept of reflection into the workplace. However, the conditions under which critical reflection might be encouraged or impeded in everyday professional practice has been overlooked. Thus most research on CPD is heavily influenced by its adult learning theory antecedents and emphasis upon formal or informally facilitated learning mainly in class rooms.

Inasmuch as adult learning theory addresses the workplace, the main theme has been supporting the notion of 'informal and incidental' learning (Marsick and Watkins 1990) which occurs naturally as managers go about their daily work. This type of learning arises out of trial and error in their tasks, and from their interactions with their own managers, peers and customers. Informal learning is predominantly experiential and non-institutional, while incidental learning is unintentional or the by-product of a different activity (Cseh *et al.* 1998). Both these forms of learning occur in a haphazard manner, and are often triggered by disconcerting or challenging experiences (Marsick and Volpe 1999). Marsick (1987) estimated that more than 80 per cent of professional learning occurs in this way, and Marsick and Watkins (1990) provided evidence that professionals were more likely to learn from their peers (either as co-workers or mentors), a point that was reaffirmed by Eraut *et al.* (1998). Baskett *et al.* (1992) have argued that it is fallacious to assume both that professional learning occurs in isolation from others, and that learning is a purely cognitive experience. They have also shown how organizations can deliberately encourage informal learning through techniques such as action learning, peer-assisted learning, practice-based learning, individual learning contracts and mentors, 'cognitive apprenticeship' and workplace partnerships, which echoes Vince's (2002) findings. They also show how such techniques have furthered the learning among different professional groups. Others (Woodall and Winstanley 1998; Maister 1997) would argue that networking, mentoring, role-modelling and participation in task forces and working parties also create favourable conditions for such informal learning to take place.

There has, however, been another strand that has influenced scholarly assumptions around the learning of professionals. This tends to view it as something discrete, highly contextualized and work related, in contrast to the undifferentiated nature of adult learning. Schön's (1983) landmark study of the 'reflective practitioner' has been hailed as both an anti-positivist and anti-technicist view of professional knowledge, and a celebration of the 'artistry' of professional practitioners (Eraut 1994). Schön drew attention to the importance of tacit knowledge and the transformation of this 'knowing in action' into knowledge that goes beyond the propositional knowledge base and concepts of the professional discipline. He has been criticized by Eraut (1994:145) for an over-focus upon instances of professional creativity rather than everyday routine professional practice, and for lack of clarity over what he meant by 'reflection-in-action'. This is presented as a series of overlapping attributes, which are contingent upon a situation, but it is unclear as to what might influence individual professionals to engage in 'reflection-in-action' or 'reflection-upon-action' in specific circumstances. This 'rosy' view of professional learning may well be wide of the mark as left to themselves, many professionals (and business professionals in particular), are likely to indulge in unreflective action (Starbuck 1993) given the many demands upon their time. Conversely, perhaps Schön's (1983) ideas are relevant to certain types of professionals, and can function as an ideal type against which to compare professionals working in a business context. It is not necessarily an attribute of business professionals as such that they do not engage in reflective practice, but of certain types of professionals who work in certain kinds of environments. Despite these shortcomings, however, Schön's work has drawn attention to the centrality of professional learning through everyday work. The implications of the preceding discussion are that traditional theories of adult and professional learning draw attention to the importance of intuitive, tacit and social learning, but that they stop short of explaining relationships between this and specific organizational and occupational contexts.

While this debate and research on professional learning has been taking place the practice of most UK professional bodies has largely remained unaffected by it. Practice has tended to draw on the concept of 'managerial learning style' apropos the model established by Kolb (1984) and popularized by Honey and Mumford (1992). This model remains surprisingly resilient in the face of trenchant criticizm for its over-simplicity, excessive cognitive focus, preoccupation with problem-*solving* rather than problem-*setting* and over-focus on the individual and disregard of the socially constructed and situated nature of learning (Jarvis 1995; Reynolds 1997; Holman *et al.* 1997).

As a result professional body CPD policies and practice give little consideration to current thinking around managerial and professional learning. The accountancy bodies place particular emphasis upon professional course attendance, and possibly because they run short course units that earn considerable revenue, they have an ambivalent attitude towards the role of higher education within CPD. Also, work-based learning is conceived of as occurring in an individually driven manner, with little recognition of the potential for social learning. There is glancing reference to the power of secondments and shadowing (CIMA) and mentoring (CIM), and some encouragement for peer mentoring and the creation of smaller networks and learning sets (CIPD). Also, while lip-service is given to self-directed learning (Sadler-Smith and Badger 1998) there is evidence that conflict between individual cognitive style and learning preferences might impede its take-up (Sadler-Smith *et al.* 2000). There is evidence that professionals who are members of the CIPD may well support the principles of lifelong learning, and prefer job-related learning opportunities, and informal self-directed development, but strongly dislike formal monitoring and recording requirements (Jones and Fear 1994; Sadler-Smith and Badger 1998). Several authors are now drawing attention to the importance of context as it relates to informal learning (Eraut *et al.* 1998); this is discussed at some length by Ellinger (2003), who quotes Watkins and Cerverro: 'there is some evidence in the larger field of human resource development that a focus on the learning of individuals is less significant than a focus on the organisation as a context for learning' (Watkins and Cervero 2000: 193). Also, because CPD schemes appear to focus upon individual effort and rely upon the individual bearing the costs of formal instruction, and loss of earnings for time off work, professional bodies are either not aware of or choose not to acknowledge the evidence of adult and professional learning, and often CPD is dominated by formal education provision that introduces a new syllabus rather than providing opportunities for reformulating existing theories of practice (Eraut 1994). However, while there is some acknowledgement of the importance of organizational contexts, this does not yet go far enough in answering a number of questions concerning what influences the learning of different types of business professionals operating in different organizational context. This can be illustrated by looking at developments in the work of business professionals.

Developments in business professional practice

Research into the sociology of professions has a long history, and, at the risk of simplifying a very rich debate, the main research questions have moved beyond defining and comparing the 'traits' of various professions, towards exploring the differences in the history, development, culture and types of professional work (the processes of professionalization) and the perceived fluctuations in professional 'power' and 'status' relative to other employee groups. The process of professionalization can thus be seen as a battle for occupational closure and jurisdiction between different professional bodies (Abbott 1988; Witz 1992). The business professions under consideration here are human resource management, accountancy and marketing where there has been a spectacular growth in professional employment in the United Kingdom since the early 1980s. Professional bodies in accountancy, human resource management and the law have consolidated their professional power and status some time ago (Armstrong 1993; Hanlon 1997; Hanlon and Shapland 1997), while elsewhere, as in marketing, they have only recently mapped out their territory.

A Weberian preoccupation with the dichotomous relationship between management and professional workers still persists in the assumption that there is more that unites the increasing numbers and types of professionals than divides them. Such a view has certainly influenced research on CPD. While common features of professionalism and professionalization may still be traced, many contemporary developments involve fragmentation and the emergence of differences within and between professional groups. We witness the appearance of specialist interest groups, the emergence of new professional associations, and changes in membership profiles to include more young women and ethnic minorities and those on flexible contracts, as characteristics of professional occupations in the field of business management in the United Kingdom. Within business management itself the conduct of professional practice has not remained static. The growing demand for professional work has been accompanied by changes in the professional division of labour, the location of professional work, the content of professional skills and the relationship between professionals and clients (Watkins 1999). Changes in the division of labour have accompanied increasing price competition and globalization, and developments in new technology. On the one hand these have led to the growth of para-professional roles in fields such as accountancy and legal practice, thereby enabling the delegation of routine work such as company audit or conveyancing of property, and on the other to specialization based upon firm size, type of work done, source of revenue and client size. In addition, the growth of the professional services firm which provides multiple professional services has added further diversity to both the content, and the location of professional practice away from individual partnerships (especially in law and accountancy) or specialist units in corporate organizations, to a growth in specialist consultancies (such as in personnel management and marketing). In many cases this has been accompanied by a broadening of the individual professional skill base into other areas of business practice, and especially wider commercial and interpersonal skills (Hanlon and Shapland 1997; Hanlon 1997).

While all these changes must, in principle, have some impact on the demand for and nature of relevant CPD, some changes are already directly affecting its provision. In the case of accountancy, for example, business-driven pressures from the 'Big Five' ('Big Four' since the demise of Arthur Andersen) UK firms have placed demands upon the main professional bodies for changes in the curriculum of initial professional development and CPD. This creates tension between meeting these new challenges of specialization while retaining the core identity of the professional knowledge base (Hoskin and Anderson-Gough 2000). In addition we find that public policy pressure for accountability to the public and clients, and for quality assurance have resulted in efforts to demonstrate a greater transparency of professional transactions, and in turn led professional bodies to seek to ensure their members' knowledge is formally up to date. Thus the 1991 UK Government Regulations on Company Audit appear to have been a very significant stimulus for CPD in the UK accountancy professions (Woodall 2000).

This is the context in which debate about the form, significance and purpose of CPD in the United Kingdom becomes an important issue in the process of professionalization. Its significance has grown in association with the pressure for growing regulation, accountability and quality assurance of professional practice, and as a means for enhancing professional status. Some bodies, such as the Chartered Institute of Marketing and the Chartered Institute of Personnel and Development, have had formal but voluntary CPD policies since the mid-1990s. They tend to promote CPD in terms of lifelong learning, which is more broadly conceived as including self-development and career development. This is endorsed to a certain extent by two of the finance professional bodies – the Institute of Chartered Secretaries and Administrators (ICSA) and the Association of Chartered Certified Accountants (ACCA). On the other hand, some of the other UK accountancy professional bodies now appear to be seeing CPD as a means of enforcing their members' updating of knowledge on, for example, new standards and practice. Yet since their members now come from more diverse backgrounds than previously, and consequently have very different and varied developmental needs, such 'one size fits all' approaches may not fit their members' needs.

The ongoing processes of professionalization of business groups like human resource management, accountancy, marketing and legal professionals, as well as the wider context of work and business affecting professionalization itself, clearly has implications for research into CPD. Such research needs to consider the changes in the professional division of labour, including the growth of para-professionals and the division between practice in routine or innovative work, or between general and specialist work. It needs to ask questions not only about the implications for the *content* of CPD, but also about *how* different professionals will *learn* in such circumstances. It also needs to address the organizational context in which professionals work: the professional services firm versus the small partnership; the private, public or not-for-profit corporate sector or the sole practice and consultancy. It also needs to address the career stage of professionals; the early career professional who has recently emerged from a professional training in higher education and the mid or late career professional. Above all, there needs to be more account taken of the contextual and social aspects of learning.

Incorporating a sociocultural perspective into professional learning

Reference to the social dimension of learning has recently become fashionable. However, acknowledgment is often made in passing without full discussion of the differing perspectives and contributions. Perhaps the most oft-cited notion is that of 'community of practice' (Brown and Duguid 1991; Lave and Wenger 1991) to illustrate how novices move through a process of 'legitimate peripheral participation' in work settings to become experts. The main point is that learning occurs in a context (situation) that critically influences what is actually learned, and is interactive, informal and tacit. Thus, for example, 'war stories' may be used in communities of practice to teach newcomers rather than formal instruction designed to transmit propositional knowledge to passive individual learners.

This approach is one of several (see Granott 1998) that have evolved out of activity theory inspired by Lev Vygotsky's ideas suggesting that human mental functioning evolves from the negotiation of meaning within a community of learners, and where the internal construction of reality is the result of interactions with adults, tools and more capable peers. Vygotsky's ideas were focused mainly upon childhood learning, with most research carried out in US grade twelve classrooms. However, Bonk and Kim (1998) have shown that the six key sociocultural concepts (zone of proximal development, internalization, scaffolding, intersubjectivity, cognitive apprenticeship and assisted learning) can be applied to adults, and through combining the six teaching methods that are to be found in cognitive apprenticeship with seven forms of learning assistance, ten socioculturally based teaching techniques can be generated (modelling, coaching, scaffolding and fading, questioning, encouraging articulation, encouraging exploration, fostering reflection and self-awareness, providing cognitive task structuring, providing feedback on performance and direct instruction). They argue that the sociocultural opportunities that flourish in informal adult learning settings in terms of both cultural institutions and artefacts are immense, but present a considerable challenge in working with adult learners who are accustomed to more traditional teacher-centred instruction, a point of considerable relevance to considerations of CPD. Business professionals who are likely to have acquired their initial professional education in a structured higher educational environment, are left to make their own decisions about how and when they undertake CPD, and their different experiences of the work context may well heavily influence their orientations towards learning.

These ideas are valuable in drawing attention to the socially situated nature of learning and in providing an intellectual challenge to the subject–object dualism inherent in cognitive approaches. However, they are not without problems, including a tendency towards reductionism (Bredo 1994) whereby the processes of 'internalization' of learning within the individual are ignored, and intelligence becomes an unreflective practice that just happens. In addition, the distinction between novice and expert can become problematic where individuals are moving in and out of a variety of communities of practice, as, indeed, can the issue of community of practice itself. If professionals are moving between organizations, departments or changing their basis of employment to sole practitioner or consultant, the notion of the novice learning from the practitioner breaks down. Also, the definition of professional knowledge as something distinct from basic knowledge becomes fuzzy as individuals progress through a career which may take them out of their purely professional practice. It might be tempting to equate communities of practice with professional and/or occupational groups and their associated role in shaping individual identity. But professionals in employing organizations are also employees, managers, peers, supervisors, colleagues and competitors, and may have little to do with their occupational group as such. (This statement obviously has to be treated differently with respect to different professionals – some professions may virtually enforce the maintenance of stronger occupational links than others.) Finally, the issues of professional power and status including willingness to share expertise and the role of formal teaching and instruction become unclear. To some extent this is acknowledged by some of the main proponents of situated learning theory (Greeno *et al.* 1999) and researchers in the field of HRD (Torraco 1999). But while providing an interesting new insight into how professionals might learn, situated learning theory simultaneously raises problems, especially around understanding how individuals learn when they are acting across organizational contexts, and moving flexibly in and out of job roles (Triche and St Julien 1995).

Scribner (1986) provided an insight into how this might occur. She developed the notion of 'practical thinking' based upon studies of job tasks that are routine parts of everyday activities to demonstrate how even those with little formal education such as dairy workers, become engaged in complex thought processes displaying considerable flexibility and ingenuity to both solve and set problems in their work activity. Her results provided evidence that challenged conventional cognitive assumptions about learning and in particular the movement from the abstract to the concrete. Scribner (1986) was apparently keen to dissociate her work from those working on 'situated cognition', because she emphasized *activity* (an integrated function of thought and setting) as the defining event for practical intellectual activity, and developed a research design combining observation and in-depth interviews and experimentation (Martin 1995). Engeström and Middleton (1998: 1) who examined 'mindful practices and communicative interaction as situated issues in the reproduction of communities of practice' also challenged traditional cognitive psychology to show that cognition is distributed between individuals and between human beings and their artefacts, so that 'work practices are ineluctably communicative practices' (1998: 4). In doing so they openly acknowledge their debt to the sociologists of the Chicago School such as Howard Becker, Barney Glaser and Anselm Strauss, as well as the pragmatist philosophical tradition associated with John Dewey and George Herbert Mead. Indeed, one of the contributors to their collection, Susan Leigh-Star (1998), also demonstrates the contribution of American symbolic interactionism to activity theory's understanding of the relation between work and practice. However, while this opens up a new perspective on how the learning of qualified professionals might take place, it is still problematic. The main problem for sociocultural theory is the specification of the social unit within which 'mindful practices and communicative interaction' or 'practical thinking' take place, and which can be examined in experiments without constraining and excluding the activity being studied. Granott (1998) has gone some way towards this with her notion of the 'ensemble' as a unit of analysis defined as the smallest group of people who co-construct knowledge through interaction. Nonetheless, the problems for data collection associated with this approach are enormous.

Such ideas have considerable implications for CPD. In particular, the current professional body emphasis upon individual learning, and also the preference of some for formal instruction by prescribed providers displays an ignorance of the sociocultural dimension of learning. This overlooks the fact that professionals can learn collectively from their professional interactions, and that the different 'cultural milieux' including different types of workplaces (for example the professional services firm versus small firm partnership or freelance consultancy) and artefacts (such as access to various forms of ICT, the jargon of professional expertise, or the location of professional offices – from big open-plan offices to 'virtual' offices for those who 'hot desk' or work remotely) also influence the learning that takes place. It also raises questions about the support provided both by professional bodies and by other trainers within organizations, and whether they have sufficient expertise in the ten 'socioculturally based teaching techniques' identified by Bonk and Kim (1998).

Conclusion: towards new agendas for research into CPD

There are a number of major findings from this review of literature around professional learning. First, an essentialist definition of *professional* learning as distinct from *managerial* or *adult* learning is questionable. The search for generic definitions and understanding may be misplaced. Second, it is argued that professional learning needs to be studied in the context of specific professions, if the discussion is to progress beyond simple reporting, classification, and prescription of learning strategies. Third, notwithstanding this point, the weakness of the highly individualistic approach to learning that underpins both professional body assumptions and scholarly research about CPD demands attention to the social dimension of learning. Finally, the sociocultural approach to professional learning reinforces the importance of attention to the professional context, but is not without conceptual fuzziness over the unit of analysis to be studied. Thus a limited set of research questions have been identified for further study:

- To what extent does the context of professional socialization influence orientations towards learning and participation in CPD?
- To what extent does the context of professional practice (location, firm structure and size, type of work, client size, source of revenue etc.) influence participation in CPD and the learning strategies adopted?
- What balance do individuals perceive they strike between individual and social dimensions of learning, and what are the main techniques by which this is achieved?
- How do individuals manage their learning when they are moving across organizational contexts and between different job roles in their professional practice?

These are challenging questions that present considerable problems in terms of research design and data collection in particular. Simple cross-sectional surveys based upon self-report questionnaires are unlikely to be suitable. Equally, semi-structured interviews with purposive samples of respondents are unlikely to be a satisfactory means of going beyond a superficial investigation. More sophisticated data collection instruments are needed for a research design that will need to be both interpretative and longitudinal, and above all, contextual and situated.

References

Abbott, A. (1988) *The System of Professions: An Essay in the Division of Expert Labour*, Chicago: University of Chicago Press.

Armstrong, P. (1993) 'Professional knowledge and social mobility: postwar changes in the knowledge base of management accounting', *Work, Employment and Society*, 7, 1: 1–21.

Baskett, H. K. M., Marsick, V. J. and Cervero, R. M. (1992) 'Putting theory to practice and practice to theory', in H. K. M. Baskett and V. J. Marsick (eds) *Professionals' Ways of Knowing: New Findings and How to Improve Professional Education*, San Francisco, CA: Jossey-Bass.

Bonk, C. J. and Kim, K. A. (1998) 'Extending socio-cultural theory to adult learning', in M. C. Smith and T. Porchot (eds) *Adult Learning and Developmental Perspectives from Education Psychology*, Hillsdale, NJ: Lawrence Erlbaum.

Bredo, E. (1994) 'Cognitivism, situated cognitivism and Deweyian pragmatism', *Philosophy of Education Yearbook*, Urbana-Champaign, IL: Philosophy of Education Society.

Brookfield, S. D. (1987) *Developing Critical Thinkers: Challenging Adults to Explore Alternative Ways of Thinking and Acting*, Milton Keynes: Open University Press.

Brown, J. S. and Duguid, P. (1991) 'Organizational learning and communities of practice: towards a unified view of working, learning and innovation', *Organizational Science*, 2, 1: 40–57.

Cseh, M., Watkins, K. and Marsick, V. (1998) 'Informal and incidental learning in the workplace', in R. J. Torraco (ed.) *Proceedings of the Annual Conference of the Academy of Human Resource Development*, Baton Rouge, LA: AHRD.

Ellinger, A. D. (2003) 'Contextual factors and informal learning: the case of "reinventing itself company"', *Conference Proceedings of the Academy of Human Resource Development*, Minneapolis, MN: AHRD.

Engeström, Y. and Middleton, D. (1998) 'Introduction: studying work as mindful practice', in Y. Engeström and D. Middleton (eds) *Cognition and Communication at Work*, Cambridge: Cambridge University Press.

Eraut, M. (1994) *Developing Professional Knowledge and Competence*, London: Falmer Press.

Eraut, M., Alderton, J., Cole, G. and Senker, P. (1998) 'Learning from other people at work', in F. Coffield (ed.) *Learning at Work*, Bristol: Policy Press.

Galloway, S. (2000) 'Issues and challenges in CPD', paper presented at *SKOPE Symposium Continuing Professional Development: Looking Ahead*, Pembroke College, Oxford, May.

Granott, N. (1998) 'Unit of analysis in transit: from the individual's knowledge to the ensemble process', *Mind, Culture and Activity*, 5, 1: 42–66.

Greeno, J. G., Eckert, P., Stucky, S. U., Sachs, P. and Wenger, E. (1999) 'Learning in and for participation in work and society', *How Adults Learn*, September (online).

Hanlon, G. (1997) 'A shifting professionalism: an examination of accountancy', in J. Broadbent, M. Dietrich and J. Roberts (eds) *The End of the Professions? The Restructuring of Professional Work*, London: Routledge

Hanlon, G. and Shapland, J. (1997) 'Professional disintegration? The case of law', in J. Broadbent, M. Dietrich and J. Roberts (eds) *The End of the Professions? The Restructuring of Professional Work*, London: Routledge.

Holman, D., Pavlica, K. and Thorpe, R. (1997) 'Rethinking Kolb's theory of experiential learning in management education: the contribution of social constructionism and activity theory', *Management Learning*, 28, 2: 135–148.

Honey, P. and Mumford, A. (1992) *Manual of Learning Styles*, 3rd edn: Maidenhead: Peter Honey.

Hoskin, K. and Anderson-Gough, F. (2000) 'From accountant to added-value business advisor: training professionals for a changing world', paper presented at *SKOPE Symposium Continuing Professional Development: Looking Ahead*, Pembroke College, Oxford, May.

Jarvis, P. (1995) *Adult and Continuing Education*, London: Routledge.

Jones, N. and Fear, N. (1994) 'Continuing professional development: perspectives from human resource professionals', *Personnel Review*, 23, 8: 49–60.

Knowles, M. (1989) *The Adult Learner: A Neglected Species*, Houston, TX: Gulf.

Kolb, D. (1984) *Experiential Learning*, Englewood Cliffs, NJ: Prentice Hall.

Lave, J. and Wenger, E. (1991) *Situated Learning*, Cambridge: Cambridge University Press.

Leigh-Star, S. (1998) 'Working together: symbolic interactionism, activity theory and information systems', in Y. Engeström and D. Middleton (eds) *Cognition and Communication at Work*, Cambridge: Cambridge University Press.

Madden, C. A. and Mitchell, V. A. (1993) *Professions, Standards, and Competence: A Survey of Continuing Education for the Professions*, Bristol: University of Bristol.

Maister, D. (1997) *Managing the Professional Services Firm*, New York: The Free Press.

Marsick, V. (1987) *Learning in the Workplace*, London: Croom Helm.

Marsick, V. J. and Volpe, M. (eds) (1999) *Informal Learning on the Job, Advances in Developing Human Resources*, 2, San Francisco, CA: Berrett-Koehler.

Marsick, V. J. and Watkins, K. (1990) *Informal and Incidental Learning in the Workplace*, London: Routledge.

Martin, L. M. W. (1995) 'Linking through and setting in the study of work and learning', in L. M. W. Martin, K. Nelson and E. Tobach (eds) *Socio-Cultural Psychology*, Cambridge: Cambridge University Press.

Mezirow, J. (1991) *Transformational Dimensions of Adult Learning*, San Francisco, CA: Jossey Bass.

Reynolds, M. (1997) 'Learning styles: a critique', *Management Learning*, 28, 2: 115–133.

Reynolds, M. (1998) 'Reflection and critical reflection in management learning', *Management Learning*, 29, 2: 183–200.

Sadler-Smith, E. and Badger, B. (1998) 'The HR practitioner's perspective on continuing professional development', *Human Resource Management Journal*, 8, 4: 66–75.

Sadler-Smith, E., Allinson, C. W. and Hayes, J. (2000) 'Learning preferences and cognitive style: some implications for continuing professional development', *Management Learning*, 31, 2: 239–256.

Schön, D. A. (1983) *The Reflective Practitioner: How Professionals Think in Action*, New York: Basic Books.

Scribner, S. (1986) 'Thinking in action: some characteristics of practical thought', in R. J. Sternberg and R. K. Wagner (eds) *Practical Intelligence: Nature and Origins of Competence in the Everyday World*, Cambridge: Cambridge University Press.

Starbuck, W. H. (1993) 'Keeping a butterfly and an elephant in a house of cards: the elements of exceptional success', *Journal of Management Studies*, 30, 6: 885–922.

Torraco, R. J. (1999) 'Integrating learning with working: a reconception of the role of workplace learning', *Human Resource Development Quarterly*, 10, 3: 249–271.

Triche, S. and St Julien, J. (1995) 'Reconceptualizing educational psychology: a pragmatic approach to developments in cognitive science', *Philosophy of Education Yearbook*, Urbana-Champaign, IL: Philosophy of Education Society.

Vince, R. (2002) 'Organising reflection', *Management Learning*, 33, 1: 63–78.

Watkins, J. (1999) 'UK professional associations and continuing professional development: a new direction', *International Journal of Lifelong Education*, 18, 1: 61–75.

Watkins, K. E. and Cervero, R. M. (2000) 'Organizations as contexts for learning: a case study in certified public accountancy', *Journal of Workplace Learning*, 12, 3: 187–194.

Witz, A. (1992) *Professions and Patriarchy*, London: Routledge.

Wood-Daudelin, M. (1996) 'Learning from experience through reflection', *Organizational Dynamics*, 24, 3: 36–49.

Woodall, J. (2000) 'Continuing professional development and approaches to learning within the business professions', working paper no. 2, Kingston Business School, Kingston upon Thames.

Woodall, J. and Winstanley, D. (1998) *Management Development: Strategy and Practice*, Oxford: Blackwell.

Part III

Developments in the organizational orientation of HRD

8 Project-based learning in work organizations

Strategies used by employees, managers and HRD professionals

Rob F. Poell

Introduction

The notion of a project has long been recognized in adult learning theory. It has also been applied to learning in work and organizational settings (see, for instance, Tough 1978; Argyris and Schön 1978). The concept of 'project' expresses a desire to focus people's energy on a common goal to be reached over a limited period of time. It serves to make rather intangible processes such as learning manageable, or at least to give those concerned the idea that they can actually be managed. From an organizational perspective this may be a helpful construct, because projects can be identified, deployed strategically, measured and evaluated. However, from the perspective of the project participants, the process may not be so clear cut. Hidden agendas, different interests and power games are as much part of organizational reality in projects as elsewhere. Adult learning theory has never been very comfortable with facing this 'political side' of work organizations, preferring instead to focus on collaboration, joint effort and learning from each other. What exactly do we see when we apply the notion of a project to the field of adult learning in organizations?

This chapter explores the concept of project-based learning in work organizations, using an actor perspective. In the first section the educational and organizational literature on projects is summarized and evaluated. The second section introduces the learning network theory as an alternative, actor-based perspective on learning in organizations. In the third section this actor perspective is applied to project-based learning by focusing on the various strategies that employees, managers and HRD professionals use to organize work-related learning projects. The final section deals with the implications of this approach for adult learning theory, practice and research.

Projects, project-based work and project-based learning

The concept of a project is well known in the educational literature. This literature shows numerous references to project methods, usually in connection with cooperative learning. Although these do refer to learning, they focus mainly on didactic methods used for pupils in schools (see, for example, Sharan and Sharan 1992; Wolk 1994; Bonnet 1994; Kolmos 1996). Wade *et al.* (1995) provided an overview of 926 book and article references about cooperative learning efforts, almost all of which focus on primary and secondary education. The short section about higher and adult education contained a few references to learning groups of employees in work organizations, with an additional few in the teacher training section. There are additional references to educational projects conducted by professionals, however their efforts are usually part of graduate degree programmes (Lynn and Taylor 1993; Dunne 1993; Gross 1994; Peterson and Myer 1995; Gasen and Preece 1996; Kolenko *et al.* 1996; Dowling and Coppens 1996; Hubbe *et al.* 1996).

The organization theory literature features a growing body of knowledge about project-based work, about project organizations, and about innovation projects, sometimes even with a view to (organizational) learning from projects (Nevison 1994; Ayas 1996; Peters and Homer 1996; Pellegrinelli 1997). In these references, though, employee learning is viewed only as a secondary goal, the main goal being organizational innovation.

In the HRD literature formal training arrangements remain dominant over project-based learning. Interestingly, the occasional references to project-based learning are mostly directed at management instead of employee development (O'Neil and Watkins 1994; Raelin 1994; Smith and Dodds 1997). In addition, they usually prescribe highly prestructured instead of more open projects (Frey 1993; Freimuth and Hoets 1996; Oberscheider 1996).

Work-related learning projects

I have introduced elsewhere the notion of a work-related learning project as a way for organizational actors to systematically organize learning activities in a group (Poell and Van der Krogt 1997; Poell *et al.* 2001). In this notion, a work-related learning project is organized by a group of employees who participate in a coherent set of activities centred on a work-related theme or problem, with a specific intention to learn and to improve work at the same time. The activities can include various kinds of learning situations, both on and off-the-job, self-organized and facilitator-directed, action-based and reflection-based, group-focused and individual-oriented, externally and internally inspired, highly prestructured and more open-ended situations. The activities are bound together by the fact that they all focus on the core theme or problem. Some examples of possible problems or themes for learning projects include increasing client-centredness, operating Windows 98, improving the work climate, investigating a new treatment or introducing team-based working.

Although learning projects can be found at every level of an organization, the focus in this chapter is on the operating core at the shop floor (Mintzberg 1979). These employees perform a key role in the learning project, but usually managers, HRD consultants, trainers and other (external) actors also participate. To learn something new by investigating a work-related problem should be the most important goal for a learning project to take place. Secondary goals of the participants could be to develop a new product, increase employee motivation or job satisfaction, change the organization structure, develop an innovative culture, to name just a few possibilities.

This concept of a work-related learning project draws on ideas from existing literature, but it is different from those ideas in a number of ways. First, the thematic element linking all learning activities together is clearly derived from educational thinking about project education (see, for instance, Sharan 1994). However, this is less a didactic measure undertaken by a training professional for the employees than it is an organizing principle for all activities undertaken by the project group.

Second, the combination of learning with work improvement activities is encountered more often in the organizational literature (see, for example, De Lange-Ros 1999). In a work-related learning project, however, it is crucial for employee learning or development to be the primary goal. Work and its improvement do constitute a very important context for learning, usually providing many opportunities for employee development. It should nevertheless be taken into account that some kinds of work offer more and different learning opportunities than others.

Third, the group aspect of learning so central to the notion of a work-related learning project is often emphasized in the HRD literature (see, for instance, Wenger and Snyder 2000). It is probably true that people can learn a lot from each other and that therefore groups can make powerful contexts for learning. This does not mean, however, that all members belonging to a group necessarily share the same ideas or cannot have legitimate conflicts of interest. In my view groups can also be regarded as arenas, in which alliances between various parties are made and broken as the project progresses.

The next section describes the theoretical framework of the actor perspective underlying these notions about work-related learning projects.

An actor perspective on project-based learning

I have previously criticized existing theories about learning in work organizations for a number of reasons (Poell *et al.* 2000). First, although the importance of continuous learning for work is increasingly stressed, what seems to be forgotten is that most employees do already learn a lot at work. However, they are not always aware of this, the learning often goes unrecognized and, more fundamentally, what employees (want to) learn need not be in line with what the organization (that is, management) thinks they should be learning. Related to that is a second criticism, namely learning is too often seen only as functional for work and as a tool of management.

The idea that work and organization can also be adapted to people's characteristics instead of the other way around is not very common in the literature. Third, learning is usually referred to in terms of the activities of HRD consultants or trainers, who organize programmes for employees by order of management and in line with corporate policy. The strategies that employees themselves use to learn at work are either not mentioned or regarded only in connection with reaching corporate goals. A final criticism concerns the tendency to focus on learning in only a few types of work and organization, notably Taylorist work in a machine organization. Since this context is becoming rather unpopular (in normative theory, if not practice), apparently the only alternative available is team-based work in an organic, learning organization. Self-managed work and professional organizations, for instance, are much less frequently mentioned as viable alternative contexts for learning. Instead of replacing one dominant organizational model with a different one that is equally uniform, it seems more fruitful to take the diverse and constantly dynamic nature of work into account.

The actor perspective on organizing work-related learning aims to meet the need for an alternative theoretical framework, in view of the criticisms raised earlier. It regards employees as core actors co-organizing learning according to their ideas and interests. It recognizes diverse ways of organizing learning as a product of the different strategies that actors use. It focuses on the inherent tensions between employee development and work performance, thereby avoiding pure functionalism. It acknowledges that people can adapt work to their competencies as well as learn in order to adjust to work innovations.

Basic ideas

The basic idea of the learning network theory is that learning is organized by different actors (such as employees, managers, HRD consultants, trainers and so forth), who together constitute a learning network through their interaction (Van der Krogt 1998). Applied to project-based learning, the learning network takes the shape of a work-related learning-project group. This group can be regarded as a small temporary learning network at the shop-floor level of an organization.

A work-related learning project is created through the activities of its members. They organize the learning activities around a common theme or work problem. The different actors within the group have their own policies, their own agendas, their own theories and their own interests. These become manifest as the different parties interact in the learning project. Since actors are expected to use different strategies, their interactions in learning processes are crucial in organizing the learning project. Employees, managers, HRD professionals and other actors develop a policy and execute a programme within the learning project.

Gradually, their interactions become part of certain structural arrange-

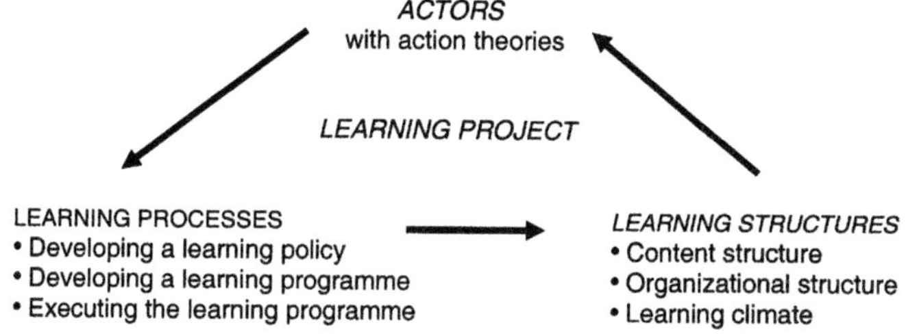

Figure 8.1 Organizing a learning project viewed from an actor perspective.

ments with regard to content, organization and climate. These learning structures in turn influence the strategies that actors use, but they do not necessarily determine them. This is the basic organization of a learning project viewed as a network, as Figure 8.1 summarizes.

This actor perspective on the organization of a learning project is familiar to Giddens' (1984) structuration theory in its proposed relationship between actors and structures. The learning network theory (LNT) assumes that people are competent actors who interact with each other on the basis of their own theories and interests. Thus, they create learning processes that evolve into structures over time. These structural arrangements, which provide the context for organization members to act, in turn influence people's actions but do not necessarily determine them. Actors have choices, within certain limits. The LNT thematizes this tension between actors' choices and their self-created structural context, or between agency and structure (Giddens 1984). It tries to avoid both an over-reliance on structural determinism (Donaldson 1996) and a somewhat naive and context-independent action focus (Argyris and Schön 1978).

Four theoretical types of learning projects

Learning network theory distinguishes four theoretical learning project types that actors can organize to learn and to solve work-related problems. These four learning project types are summarized in Table 8.1.

First is a liberal learning project, in which individual employees organize learning activities they deem necessary to deal with their own work-related problems. They team up with people who experience similar problems to learn from each other for their individual benefit. This liberal type capitalizes on the self-directed learning capacities of individual group members (Brookfield 1986). The group context serves to facilitate and enrich the individual learning processes of each member, for which everyone takes their own responsibility (Candy 1991).

The second type is a vertical learning project, in which HRD professionals and managers organize learning activities and accompanying work measures

Table 8.1 Four theoretical types of learning project in terms of their structural arrangements

	Liberal	*Vertical*	*Horizontal*	*External*
Dominant actor	Individual learners	HRD professionals and managers	Learners as a group	Professional associations
Organization of learning activities	Isolated activities	Linear planning	Organic	Externally co-ordinated
Resulting content structure (profile)	Unstructured	Task or function oriented	Problem or organization oriented	Profession oriented
Resulting organization structure	Loosely coupled	Centralized	Egalitarian	Externally inspired

for employees. The latter take part in delivery but contribute only moderately to learning policy and programme development. This vertical type is similar to the training-for-impact approach described by Robinson and Robinson (1989) and the structured on-the-job training approach of Jacobs and Jones (1995). A highly prestructured way of organizing formal off-the-job training is supported here by a set of transfer-enhancing measures (Broad and Newstrom 1992).

Third is a horizontal learning project, in which employees as a group systematically tackle work-related problems and reflect on their actions in order to learn. This horizontal type was inspired by the early work on organizational learning by Argyris and Schön (1978). It was popularized in the 1990s through the ideas around learning organizations (Senge 1990). A reference point for this type of learning is the literature on communities of practice (Wenger 1998). The horizontal type focuses on the use of collaborative everyday problem-solving as an opportunity to integrate learning with daily work, which is in line with the ideas of these authors.

The fourth type is an external learning project, in which professionals acquire new working methods by participating in continuing professional development to keep abreast of recent insights developed within, for example, professional bodies. They adapt their work to incorporate these new methods. In this external type, it is assumed that professionals are reflective learners (Schön 1983), who need to continually develop their expertise within their professional peer group (Daley 1999). This type focuses on the incorporation by professionals of new methods in their daily work routine.

The relationship between learning project and work types

Organizations provide the context for learning projects and for work. Organizations can, according to Mintzberg, take various forms, ranging from a machine bureaucracy to a professional bureaucracy, from an entrepreneurial organization to an adhocracy (Mintzberg 1979). Work is organized in various ways as well, ranging from Taylorist to professional work, from entrepreneurial to adhocratic-group work. Differences in work type are reflected in different work contents and different power relations regarding work.

Within learning network theory, learning projects are expected to have a certain relationship with these various work types. The activities within learning projects are strongly work related, because they centre around a theme or problem that is relevant for work. Moreover, many of these learning activities take place in actual work situations. Some actors may treat learning projects as functional for work, meaning that they are sophisticated ways to adapt employee qualifications to the work requirements. Other actors will use a learning project to try and adjust their work to newly acquired qualifications. Most learning projects feature both approaches at the same time, in that, by addressing work-related themes or trying to solve problems that are relevant for work, actors develop their competencies as well as improve their work. Exactly how the learning project is organized depends on the interactions between the actors. Work actors with power are in a position to dominate the learning project and organize it according to their own views and interests. The power relations are likely to be related to the type of work in which the learning project takes place. On the other hand, the actor perspective points to the observation that the power relations with respect to learning are usually different from those regarding work. So, the type of learning project is likely to be related to the type of work in which it occurs, but it is not an exact one-to-one relation that is expected.

Table 8.2 summarizes the expected relationships between learning projects and work types. The X-marks on the diagonal indicate the learning projects that correspond, theoretically, with their work context. The question marks off the diagonal refer to discrepancies, that is learning projects exhibiting characteristics that do not correspond with their work context. Learning groups produce their own dynamics, because actors develop their own learning patterns together. Thus learning groups and projects can come into being that are specific to this set of actors and exhibit discrepancies with the context.

Table 8.2 The relationship between learning project and work types

	Learning project type			
Work type	*Liberal*	*Vertical*	*Horizontal*	*External*
Entrepreneurial work	X	?	?	?
Taylorist work	?	X	?	?
Adhocratic-group work	?	?	X	?
Professional work	?	?	?	X

Table 8.3 Four empirically based learning project types in terms of the strategies used by the actors

Actor	*Process*	*Direct representation*	*Continuous adaptation*	*Professional innovation*	*Individual negotiation*
Employees	*Learning policy development*	(Have representatives) raise ideas for work improvement and learning group activities; (dis)approve of what is planned	Consider the why and how of the learning group together from the very beginning; look for common meaning in learning experiences	Be inspired by a methodology developed externally; look for adjustments with fellow practitioners by publications and conferences	Monitor the coherence in the individual activities; focus on their own learning needs; balance investment costs and learning gain
	Learning programme development	Provide the manager with information about personal goals and learning style; give feedback on learning programme proposals; plan activities by a fixed method	Hold group brainstorm sessions about the learning theme; invent new activities on the way	Use external knowledge and expertise to create a specific approach to adapting work	Look for solutions to work problems within the boundaries set by the manager; arrange for an individual learning programme with the manager
	Learning programme execution	Enroll in the learning programme; indicate whether it works; carry out practical assignments and evaluate them together; ask the manager to help	Discuss and reinterpret work problems; challenge assumptions; share ideas with the learning group; conduct and reflect upon practical work improvement experiments	Investigate a new working method; reflect upon these experiences with colleagues; visit fellow organizations	Improve work individually and discuss learning progress with the manager; address other individuals to talk or read about mutual problems and possible solutions
Managers	*Learning policy development*	Formulate and monitor project goals and method after consultation with employees' representatives; offer them alternatives	Engage in brainstorm sessions about the learning theme with employees; reflect with them upon the course of the project continuously	Follow the learning group from a distance; stress its importance to the organization; provide coordination and favourable conditions	Set boundaries for individual employees to solve work problems; stress the importance and encourage participation
	Learning programme development	Translate new insights into work procedures; create a learning plan for employees with consultants; prepare learning group meetings	Conduct a range of small-scale work improvement activities with employees; prepare learning group meetings; keep looking for the best project approach	Encourage professional consultation sessions and evaluation of practical cases	Monitor individual employees' planning of work improvement activities; resolve conflicts between individual learners

Table 8.3 continued

Actor	*Process*	*Direct representation*	*Continuous adaptation*	*Professional innovation*	*Individual negotiation*
	Learning programme execution	Inform employees about work changes; answer questions about the project approach; act as a model figure	Support the practical experiments and learning process of employees; discuss and reflect upon differences of opinion	Encourage employees to develop themselves professionally and provide facilities for this	Assist individual employees to practise new ways of working and to see the bigger picture of their learning progress
HRD consultants	*Learning policy development*	Advise the manager about the project approach; transfer the manager's vision to the employees; monitor the design during the course of the project	Consider with the learning group the course of the project; challenge their assumptions about it; make sure that everyone can participate	Suggest thematic approaches to extending professional expertise; help employees translate external insights to a specific approach	Offer employees a framework to conduct individual learning activities; help them monitor the course and coherence
	Learning programme development	Specify learning objectives; design learning activities for employees by order of the manager; prepare learning group meetings; answer questions about the project approach	Give feedback to the learning group about their progress; offer alternative suggestions for learning activities; build their ideas into the learning programme	Assist employees in adapting their work to the newly acquired methodology; suggest possible activities to accomplish this	Enable individual employees to elaborate a learning theme; advise employees and the manager about the individual learning plan and mediate between them
	Learning programme execution	Deliver training sessions; transfer theory; explain and monitor the learning method; give practical assignments to employees; provide practical support	Help the learning group reflect upon work problems; let them exchange experiences; guide them through the collective learning process	Assist employees in systematically comparing their experiences to an external model	Direct employees to knowledge carriers; guide their self-study and other activities; advise them about building in learning activities into daily work

Project-based learning strategies of employees, managers and HRD consultants

In the actor perspective, organizing is not regarded as the training department designing and implementing structured learning arrangements. Instead, a broader concept of organizing is used, which refers to systematizing action. Organizing is explicitly viewed as the ensemble of strategies of the different actors with respect to learning. Strategies are action patterns influenced by the action theories and interests of the actors.

Four theoretical models of learning-project strategies have been distinguished and elaborated from learning network theory. Whereas the liberal, vertical, horizontal and external types of Table 8.1 referred to structural aspects of project-based learning, Table 8.3 summarizes the action strategies that actors can use to organize project-based learning. In an individual negotiation strategy (leading to a liberal structure), individual employees come together to enrich their own work improvement and learning programmes with group reflection on their experiences. All group members thus create their own individual learning project. In a direct representation strategy (leading to a vertical structure), management decide on new work policies, work-design staff translate these into work programmes, and HRD professionals design a learning programme in which the learning group takes part. In a continuous adaptation strategy (leading to a horizontal structure), the learning group sets out to solve complex work problems by reflecting on experiences, developing joint action theories, and bringing these into practice in an investigative manner. In a professional innovation strategy (leading to an external structure), the learning group is inspired by action theories developed outside their organization (e.g. by new work methods developed by professional associations). The employees in the learning group adjust their work to the new externally acquired action theories.

These models of learning-project strategies were developed through alternating theoretical and empirical work. Poell *et al.* (2001) provide a detailed account of this development process. First, the cells of the matrix were derived from the categories of the learning network theory. Next, a three-round iterative process involving sixteen learning-project case studies was conducted to operationalize the content of the matrix until all cells reached their current shape. Each round involved labelling activities as described in interview excerpts according to actor, core process, and learning project type. The descriptions in each cell of the matrix were generalized to an intermediate level of abstraction and then used as input for the next round of operationalization. Finally, after three rounds all cells of the matrix contained empirical illustrations of activities carried out by various learning-project actors in three core processes of four learning project types. With a view to broad application, references to particular organizations and situations were of course not included (see Table 8.3).

The result is an overview of actual strategies used by employees, managers and HRD consultants to organize the core processes of a variety of learning project types. For example, the learning policy development activities of a manager in a direct representation strategy include advising the manager about the project approach, transferring the manager's vision to the employees and monitoring the design during the course of the project. In a continuous adaptation strategy for the execution of a learning programme, employees discuss and reinterpret work problems, challenge assumptions, share ideas with the learning group and conduct and reflect upon practical work improvement experiments. For a third example, the activities of managers using a professional innovation strategy to learning programme development are mainly encouraging professional consultation sessions and the evaluation of practical cases by the employees. Finally, HRD consultants operating from an individual negotiation strategy to learning-programme execution direct employees to knowledge carriers, guide their self-study and other activities and advise them about building in learning activities into daily work.

This, in brief, is the actor perspective on project-based learning in work organizations. It regards work-related learning projects as arenas for organizational actors to combine learning and work improvement according to the various views and interests of the parties concerned (see Figure 8.1). It takes into account the fact that everyday learning by employees at work can provide a basis for more systematic project-based learning (see Table 8.2). It differentiates between various work types associated with different learning opportunities and power relations (see Table 8.1). It offers employees, managers and HRD consultants concrete action patterns to set up learning policies and execute learning programmes within their own group projects (see Table 8.3).

Conclusion: implications for adult learning theory, practice and research

An important implication of the actor perspective for adult learning theory is that theory has to take into account the fact that the work context (i.e. both the work content and the power relations concerned) influences the way employee learning is organized. And since a number of various work types can be distinguished and work is dynamic in nature, adult learning theory could pay more attention to this relationship between learning and work. It could help us understand, for instance, why management in professional organizations tend to have a hard time getting professionals in line with corporate policies (Pettigrew *et al.* 1992), or why innovative ideas about encouraging self-directed employee learning fail (Brookfield 1986) to inspire real changes in basically still Taylorist organizations. Or why Argyris and Schön's (1978) model II behaviour, while a beautiful idea in practice, is hardly encountered in organizational reality. In this connection, the actor perspective also rebalances the widespread attention to management development (see, for example, Marsick and Watkins 1999; Mumford 1997) by focusing on learning by employees at the shop-floor level.

For adult learning practice, using the learning network theory can help tune employee learning efforts to the context of work and to the other actors involved. It provides ideas about which project-based learning strategy is most likely to succeed in a given work type. Employees, managers and HRD consultants can use the various strategies to find out which one suits their purposes best. The models can also be used to describe how various actors employ different strategies and to explain how this affects progress in project-based learning. Finally, the actor perspective gives to all these actors (not just the HRD specialist) a language of learning, a way to communicate about often intangible processes that people tend to remain unaware of.

Adult learning research from this perspective will benefit from using a constructivist rather than a (post-)positivist research paradigm. Organizational actors are not necessarily helped by specific guidelines for action derived from some 'grand' theory. 'Local' frames of reference (action theories), with which to confront their own views, can be more worthwhile to guide their learning actions. Local theories are by definition hard to measure using standardized instruments. The four models of actor strategies described in Table 8.3 could probably be further operationalized into a questionnaire to be administered to learning project participants. But actor strategies are so context dependent that to develop a standardized questionnaire in order to measure them would not be sensible. This would result in either an instrument that can be used in certain work contexts only, or one using such context-independent items that participants would not know how to relate them to their specific learning project activities. It seems more worthwhile to develop protocols for actors to use learning project models in order to make sense of their own learning activities. The methodological approach known as action research can be useful in this respect (Toulmin and Gustavsen 1996; Hendry 1996; Easterby-Smith 1997). It implies that the researcher sets out to gradually develop local concepts in cooperation with the field of practice. This means an iterative research process in which practical experiments are conducted and constantly alternated with the further elaboration of local theoretical models. Both the participants and the researcher learn during such processes as they try and make sense out of their situation and progress. Actors can frame their own actions within a number of learning project models, discuss the differences between them, engage in further action and reflection, adapt their current theories, try out new ways of learning and working, adjust their frames of reference accordingly, and so forth. In context-dependent counselling of such processes lies a potential new role for HRD professionals operating as action researchers. Learning network theory can be applied as a descriptive framework in order to ensure the comparability of the various learning project cases and thus improve the generalizability of the conclusions that are drawn.

References

Argyris, C. and Schön, D. A. (1978) *Organizational Learning: A Theory of Action Perspective*, Reading, MA: Addison-Wesley.

Ayas, K. (1996) *Design for Learning for Innovation*, Delft: Eburon.

Bonnet, J. (1994) 'Atouts et limites de la démarche de projet dans les processus d'apprentissage' [Advantages and limits of the project approach in the learning process], *Education Permanente*, 119: 155–164.

Broad, M. L. and Newstrom, J. W. (1992) *Transfer of Training: Action-packed Strategies to Ensure High Pay-off from Training Investments*, San Francisco, CA: Addison-Wesley.

Brookfield, S. D. (1986) *Understanding and Facilitating Adult Learning: A Comprehensive Analysis of Principles and Effective Practices*, Milton Keynes: Open University Press.

Candy, P. C. (1991) *Self-direction for Lifelong Learning: A Comprehensive Guide to Theory and Practice*, San Francisco, CA: Jossey-Bass.

Daley, B. J. (1999) 'Novice to expert: an exploration of how professionals learn', *Adult Education Quarterly*, 49, 4: 133–147.

De Lange-Ros, D. J. (1999) *Continuous Improvement in Teams: The (Mis)fit between Improvement and Operational Activities of Improvement Teams*, Enschede: Twente University.

Donaldson, L. (1996) *For Positivist Organisation Theory: Proving the Hard Core*, London: Sage.

Dowling, J. S. and Coppens, N. M. (1996) 'Understanding culture and health practices through an experiential learning project', *Nurse Educator*, 21, 6: 43–46.

Dunne, F. P. E. (1993) 'A project-based learning approach for computer-integrated design and manufacture', *European Journal of Engineering Education*, 18, 3: 269–276.

Easterby-Smith, M. (1997) 'Disciplines of organisational learning: contributions and critiques', *Human Relations*, 50, 9: 1085–1113.

Freimuth, J. and Hoets, A. (1996) Projektlernen [Project learning], in S. Grief and H.-J. Kurtz (eds) *Handbuch selbstorganisiertes Lernen* [Handbook of self-organized learning], Göttingen: Verlag für Angewandte Pychologie.

Frey, K. (1993) *Die Projektmethode* [The project method], Basel: Beltz.

Gasen, J. B. and Preece, J. (1996) 'Collaborative team projects: key issues for effective learning', *Journal of Educational Technology Systems*, 24, 4: 381–394.

Giddens, A. (1984) *The Constitution of Society: Outline of the Theory of Structuration*, Oxford: Blackwell.

Gross, J. W. (1994) 'Learning nursing process: a group project', *Nursing Outlook*, 42, 6: 279–283.

Hendry, C. (1996) 'Understanding and creating whole organisational change through learning theory', *Human Relations*, 49, 5: 621–641.

Hubbe, J., Cearlock, D. M. and Etynre-Zacher, P. (1996) 'Project based learning for the articulating clinical laboratory technician', *Clinical Laboratory Science*, 9, 5: 305–309.

Jacobs, R. L. and Jones, M. J. (1995) *Structured On-the-job Training: Unleashing Employee Expertise in the Workplace*, San Francisco, CA: Berrett-Koehler.

Kolenko, T. A., Porter, G., Wheatley, W. and Colby, M. (1996) 'A critique of service learning projects in management education: pedagogical foundations, barriers, and guidelines', *Journal of Business Ethics*, 15, 1: 133–142.

Kolmos, A. (1996) 'Reflections on project work and problem-based learning', *European Journal of Engineering Education*, 21, 2: 141–148.

Lynn, N. and Taylor, J. E. (1993) 'Personal and business skills development: a project-based approach at the University of Salford', *Studies in Higher Education*, 18, 2: 137–150.

Marsick, V. J. and Watkins, K. E. (1999) *Facilitating Learning Organisations: Making Learning Count*, Aldershot: Gower.

Mintzberg, H. (1979) *The Structuring of Organizations*, Englewood Cliffs, NJ: Prentice Hall.

Mumford, A. (ed.) (1997) *Action Learning at Work*, Aldershot: Gower.

Nevison, J. M. (1994) 'What can we learn about learning on projects?', *Project Management Network*, 8, 6: 6–8.

Oberscheider, S. (1996) *Individuum und Organisation: Zum Ansatz einer organisationsorientierten Weiterbildung* [Individual and organization: towards an organization-oriented continuing education], Frankfurt: Lang.

O'Neil, J. and Watkins, V. J. (1994) 'Becoming critically reflective through action reflection learning', in A. Brooks and K. E. Watkins (eds) *The Emerging Power of Action Inquiry Technologies*, New Directions for Adult and Continuing Education, 63, San Francisco, CA: Jossey-Bass.

Pellegrinelli, S. (1997) 'Programme management: organising project-based change', *International Journal of Project Management*, 15, 3: 141–149.

Peters, L. A. and Homer, J. (1996) 'Learning to lead, to create quality, to influence change in projects', *Project Management Journal*, 27, 1: 5–11.

Peterson, S. E. and Myer, R. A. (1995) 'The use of collaborative project-based learning in counselor education', *Counselor Education and Supervision*, 35, 2: 150–158.

Pettigrew, A., Ferlie, E. and McKee, L. (1992) *Shaping Strategic Change: Making Change in Large Organisations – The Case of the National Health Service*, London: Sage.

Poell, R. F. and Van der Krogt, F. J. (1997) 'Organising work-related learning projects', *International Journal of Training and Development*, 1, 3: 181–190.

Poell, R. F., Chivers, G. E., Van der Krogt, F. J. and Wildemeersch, D. A. (2000) 'Learning-network theory: organising the dynamic relationships between learning and work', *Management Learning*, 31, 1: 25–49.

Poell, R. F., Van der Krogt, F. J. and Wildemeersch, D. A. (2001) 'Constructing a research methodology to develop models for work-related learning: social science in action', *International Journal of Qualitative Studies in Education*, 14, 1: 55–70.

Raelin, J. A. (1994) 'Whither management education? Professional education, action learning and beyond', *Management Learning*, 25, 2: 301–317.

Robinson, D. G. and Robinson, J. C. (1989) *Training for Impact: How to Link Training to Business Needs and Measure the Results*, San Francisco, CA: Jossey-Bass.

Schön, D. A. (1983) *The Reflective Practitioner: How Professionals Think in Action*, London: Temple Smith.

Senge, P. M. (1990) *The Fifth Discipline: The Art and Practice of the Learning Organization*, London: Century Business.

Sharan, S. (ed.) (1994) *Handbook of Cooperative Learning Methods*, Westport, CT: Greenwood Press.

Sharan, Y. and Sharan, S. (1992) *Expanding Cooperative Learning through Group Investigation*, New York: Teachers College, Columbia University.

Smith, B. and Dodds, B. (1997) *Developing Managers through Project-based Learning*, Aldershot: Gower.

Tough, A. (1978) 'Major learning efforts: recent research and future directions', *Adult Education*, 28, 4: 250–263.

Toulmin, S. E. and Gustavsen, B. (eds) (1996) *Beyond Theory: Changing Organizations through Participation*, Philadelphia, PA: Benjamins.

Van der Krogt, F. J. (1998) 'Learning network theory: the tension between learning systems and work systems in organisations', *Human Resource Development Quarterly*, 9, 2: 157–177.

Wade, A., Abrami, P. C., Poulsen, C. and Chambers, B. (1995) *Current Resources in Cooperative Learning*, Lanham, MD: University Press of America.

Wenger, E. (1998) *Communities of Practice: Learning, Meaning, and Identity*, New York: Cambridge University Press.

Wenger, E. and Snyder, W. M. (2000) 'Communities of practice: the organizational frontier', *Harvard Business Review*, 78, 1: 139–146.

Wolk, S. (1994) 'Project-based learning: pursuits with a purpose', *Educational Leadership*, 52, 3: 42–45.

9 Emotion, politics and learning

Towards an organizational orientation in HRD

Russ Vince

Introduction

In this chapter I argue that common practices that are used to implement learning in organizations have emphasized the development of individuals. The effect of such an approach has been to limit the ability of individuals and collectives to understand the many social, emotional and political issues that impact on learning and organizing. To put this more directly, the individual orientation of much HRD practice can be an obstacle to strategic learning. I outline the thinking and action that might inform initiatives designed to explore the relationship between emotions, politics and learning. I ask what learning methods might best promote an understanding of this relationship as well as suggesting some of the implications of this approach for rethinking the implementation of HRD. An assumption that informs my discussion is that an exploration of the different emphasis between individual and organizational learning is a key issue in both developing the theory and application of strategic learning as well as the components of an emerging 'critical' practice of HRD (see Vince 2004).

Towards the end of the chapter, I link my reflections to the three main themes of HRD. McGoldrick *et al.* (2002: 396) have described what these are. First, 'HRD has a central focus on and concern with learning'. Second, HRD is likely to have a wider constituency and purpose than organizational success, which suggests that HRD practice has a broader accountability than performance. Third, 'HRD is clearly a political activity', it is central to power and control processes. I therefore provide elements of a revised approach to HRD, an approach that attempts to be more critically reflective, collectively focussed and more politically and emotionally astute than many of the current ideas that inform HRD and the resultant practices.

A key aspect of my understanding is that there is a difference between 'individual learning in an organization' and 'organizational learning'. The sum of individuals' learning in an organization is frequently assumed to equate with organizational learning. Such an interpretation is based on the idea that the combined impact of individuals' applied learning in an organization probably means that organizational learning (or change) will take place. Organizational learning does not mean that an organization is learning, but it does imply that learning and organizing are related. Efforts to understand organizational learning have been assisted in recent years by the general shift of interest away from organizations and towards organization and organizing (Clegg *et al.* 1996). An increasing focus on collective learning, situated learning, communities of practice, and on politics, power relations and learning have helped to shift the academic study of organizational learning away from individual learning, towards social, political and relational interpretations of learning and organizing (see Gherardi *et al.* 1998; Easterby-Smith *et al.* 1999).

Lipshitz and Popper (2000) have attempted to 'solve the problematic link' between individual learning in an organization and organizational learning. They have proposed a conceptual framework whereby 'organizational learning mechanisms' can be identified, emerging from the experience of organizational members, but ultimately becoming the 'property of the entire organization, either through distribution of lessons learned to relevant units or through changes in standard operating procedures' (Lipshitz and Popper 2000: 347). They make the distinction between 'learning-in organizations' and 'learning-by organizations'. The first implies learning that is directed at improving the proficiency of organizational members, the second has organizational level outputs, which implies changes in informal norms and procedures. The research by Lipshitz and Popper (2000) is useful because it provides both a critique of the idea of a learning organization, as well as describing aspects of the difference between the development of individual cognitive processes and the social processes that underpin organizing. However, their research was not concerned with describing key components of these social processes, the emotional or unconscious dynamics and the politics that shape organizational behaviour and design.

In-use HRD strategies and organizational approaches to management education and development still focus primarily on the knowledge and learning of individual organizational members (Vince and Broussine 2000). The ubiquity of programmes of individual appraisal, self-managed learning, personal qualification development and skill-based training have done little to assist an understanding of the subtle connections between learning and organizing and the role of individuals and collectives in creating the emotions and politics that characterize and limit organizational behaviour and design. Similarly, programmes of mentoring and role shadowing and/or exchange have focussed on individuals gaining new insights from or with other individuals rather than on the power relations that characterize roles in context, or the emotions generated within or by them. There has been relatively little reflection on the implementation of an approach to learning that enables organizational members, both individually and collectively, to better understand what organizational designs are being constructed through simultaneous attempts both to learn and to organize. In this chapter I try to address this issue and (at least begin) to answer the question – what approaches to management education and in-company HRD can assist in developing a better understanding of the relationship between learning and organizing?

At the heart of my understanding of organizational learning is the interplay between emotions, politics and learning. I am interested in the way that emotions and politics combine: to create organizational structures or processes that then limit, for example, knowing, feeling, sensemaking; to reinforce existing organizational designs or power relations; and to inhibit the organization of learning and change. One way to express this would be to say that I am concerned about the ways in which emotional responses become political, which means how they help to maintain or challenge existing power relations.

I can clarify this with a common example from experience in organizations. Most people in organizations have at some point experienced the weight of 'expectations from above'. Where these are powerfully felt they can produce cautious and self-protective behaviour, the result of fears about problems arising or of getting things wrong. Caution and self-protection stimulate a tendency to deny or to blame others for problems that arise. As blame becomes a habitual individual response it starts to have an impact on organizational processes, for example, how reflection is both undertaken and avoided. Reflection is undertaken in isolation from others (if at all) and becomes focussed on 'looking back' at actions. Blame undermines the ability of managers to reflect with others, out loud or in public. The individual feels too anxious and is therefore too 'busy' to reflect, and the collective is not to be trusted, because decisions are an individual responsibility. Ambivalence about engaging in collective, public and strategic reflection reinforces difficulties of communication across organizational subsystems. From a relatively simple and common emotional reaction (caution in the face of expectations) has emerged an organizational process or 'structure' that limits learning and change. Examples like this of the relationship between emotion, politics and organizing suggest that it is unlikely that organizational learning will be meaningful in practice, unless in addition to examining the knowledge in the minds of organizational members, we also explore the organizational dynamics that impact on knowledge and that construct it in practice.

The exploration of organizational dynamics inevitably involves engagement with emotions that are generated through organizing. Emotion is knowledge, often 'uncomfortable knowledge' (Fineman 1993) about learning and organizing in both manageable and unmanageable forms. The individual and collective reaction to emotions mobilized through organizing (i.e. what is done to try to prevent things from feeling uncomfortable) is political. Defending against emotion takes up a lot of managerial time and effort and, over time, is integrated into enactments of role, authority and responsibility. The relationship between emotion and politics is an everyday aspect of organizing. My interest in how individual and collective emotional responses become organizational politics and designs is linked to an acknowledgement of knowledge, learning and development as *emergent* concepts (Lee 2001).

Knowledge that informs HRD as practice is also linked to and constructed from the emotional and political dynamics of organizing. This may be one reason why many interventions aimed at development can reinforce the control processes of the current organization more than they help to imagine and underpin processes of change. There is currently very little attempt to include appreciations of underlying emotional and political dynamics in understanding HRD, something that this chapter tries to address. To do this involves recognition of the interplay between emotions and politics and particularly the unconscious processes and strategies that are generated through this interplay.

> Many of the processes that contribute to organizational difficulties are unconscious in nature. By this I mean that the leadership, the management and the members are not aware of what the underlying factors are that motivate their behaviour, nor are they in touch with the fact that their behaviour has a destructive effect on the organization. In fact, they often believe the opposite.
>
> (Obholzer 1999: 87)

In practice, the focus of HRD has been on the monitoring and development of individual knowledge in order to inform action. This strategy can be successful in the development of individuals' rational and intellectual capabilities however it is unlikely to assist in the development of knowledge about the emotional and relational nature of learning and organizing. 'The human individual is a political animal and cannot find fulfilment outside a group and cannot satisfy any emotional drive without expression of its social component' (Bion 1962: 118). Bion's famous quotation is a reminder that emotional experience is located in a social as much as an individual context. This idea has important consequences for understanding HRD. It implies a shift from the development of cognitive processes and concepts towards a better understanding of the type of social engagements that provide a context for learning. For example, this will involve a shift away from the idea that change is a process that can be planned and implemented through the development and understanding of various models for the application of change or coherent 'steps in a change process'. Understanding the emotional as well as the social and relational context of change involves an awareness that any attempts to make change happen are sought at the same time as efforts to contain or control it. An approach to HRD that goes beyond the current focus on the development of individuals will serve an important purpose. It will help individuals and collectives to better understand the impact of unconscious processes on organizing and to explore how these can be harnessed in the service of creative institutional functioning.

Organizational obstacles to learning

Human behaviour and relations tend to contribute to the construction of organizational processes that become obstacles to learning. These include the fears and anxieties that the possibility of learning generates; habits of mind that privilege doing over reflecting; managerial strategies to avoid conflict and difference; the protection of personal empires; or perceptions of work pressure and expectations. As the (conscious and unconscious) emotions and relations behind these processes intermingle with decisions, strategies and political developments, the need to try and control and contain learning and change are reinforced.

There is a continuous tension between the need in organizations to have coherent and communicable values and structures that inform organizing as well as having the means to reflect on and revise the organization that is being created. In other words organizing involves a continuous tension between attempts to control and to change. Organizational learning, therefore, can inform changes in the establishment that has been constructed through the very processes of organizing. Organizational learning involves making an impact on the assumptions that both guide and are created from organizational behaviour, and that inform organizational structures and designs. The assumptions that underpin and inform organizing are shaped from and shape individual and collective behaviour in organizations. To learn, therefore, may involve letting go of habits that have formed about how to do things, attachments to knowledge that relates to the past, or ideas that have previously informed actions. Such habits and attachments can inhibit the development and utilization of new knowledge. Learning provokes anxiety, defensiveness, fear and retrenchment as much as it excites, stimulates, motivates and empowers organizational members. The tensions inherent in organizing reflect the continuous pull between the desire to learn and the need to avoid learning, and the ways in which such tensions are played out in organizational processes and designs.

Politics refers both to social forces that influence organization as well as all the many strategic processes that arise or are employed and deployed to maintain or change power relations. There are politics that are located in, and reflect broader social and societal contexts, which can be seen as *social politics*. These may include the politics emerging from social power relations, of gender, race, class, disability or other socially constructed differences or inequalities. It may include social and economic forces that are linked to national opportunities and identities or stereotypes. It may include world events that have an impact on the social context within which organization takes place. The second aspect to my understanding of politics concerns *strategic politics* that are associated with the history and actions of the organization itself. Strategic politics emerge from and express the nature of the relatedness between individuals, groups and other collectives. For example, strategic politics include conflicts that get repeated, habitual behaviour that reflects usual or characteristic approaches to leadership or authority, and patterns of communication or organization that have become taken-for-granted. Strategic politics therefore are concerned with the strategic consequences of behaviour in organizations and how this links to the emergence of organizational structures and designs that then have an impact on behaviour.

I want to illustrate the nature of strategic politics with an example. Hyder plc was Wales' largest private company (it was recently taken over and split up). An action-research project begun in 1998 highlighted various organizational obstacles to organizational learning in Hyder, and provided clues to the strategic politics that were created and reinforced within the company. These can be summarized as follows:

- The individual orientation of Hyder's learning strategy and the expectations on individuals to put learning into practice.
- Limited and self-limiting notions of reflection.
- Fears about engaging with the interplay between politics and emotion in the organization, particularly conflicts between sub-systems, and the effects of this on leadership and authority in practice.

One assumption that informed Hyder's HRD strategy was that an emphasis on individual learning would improve personal performance as well as contributing to the development of new ideas and forms of practice as well as their implementation. Hyder had a highly competent and developed range of learning processes available to individuals, collected under the general idea of a 'learning journey'. These included personal opportunities for formal and informal training and development linked to individual appraisal and supported through mentoring. New skills, knowledge and perceptions were developed through this process and individuals were enthusiastic as a result of their learning.

However, individuals' learning had little impact on processes of organizing, strategic decision-making, existing power relations or entrenched political positions. In fact, despite the enthusiasm surrounding personal learning there was a general feeling from staff that learning initiatives have little effect on the organization as a whole; that they tended to 'sink into the sand'. The individual orientation of Hyder's approach to learning remained uncritical of the ways in which strategic politics was experienced and enacted within the organization. This inevitably had an impact on the emotions experienced by staff. One department in Hyder organized a consultation process aimed at stimulating change within the department. Considerable energy and resources were given to the project and it succeeded in generating much enthusiasm from the front-line and middle-management staff involved because it seemed that they were being asked to shape the strategic direction of the department. Over time it became clear that the initiative was going to have little or no impact on the senior managers who had supported it, and gradually staff enthusiasm was replaced by staff cynicism about the ability of the senior managers and therefore the organization to change. This emotional journey from enthusiasm to cynicism in the face of established organizational politics is a common aspect of individual and collective experience in organizations.

Difficulties of reflection and development in Hyder were experienced individually as well as in relation to collective attempts at participation and involvement. As in many organizations, managers in Hyder experienced continuous pressure to deliver and develop performance. For example:

> You find yourself in a scenario where it is all happening around you and you have a problem that you have got to solve and you are so bloody happy to accept the first logical explanation that comes into your mind that of course you apply it, if it works then it is fine, then you get on and face the next thing you have to do. It is just not part of the culture that says, you take time out now and examine and understand how we did it and could it have been done better.
>
> (Hyder senior manager)

The way in which reflection was imagined, experienced and implemented created restrictions on the ability of organizational members to engage with the relationship between learning and organizing. Reflection was seen as *standing back* from what is happening, *thinking back* about what has been done, and *examining personal thinking or performance*. The emphasis here was on the individual evaluating something past, rather than on reflection as an active and organizationally focused process within the present. Reflection was understood as an individual responsibility, something that individuals do, when they have the time, in order to solve or think back about a problem or issue, and the way they dealt with it. A limited practice of reflection in Hyder meant that reflection served a limited purpose, contributing little to an understanding of the organizing processes that were being created and sustained.

Underlying both an individualized perspective on learning and a restrictive practice of reflection there were powerful emotions connected to organizational politics. Organizational members felt fear and anxiety about engaging with conflicts or differences either across hierarchical lines of accountability or across the political intricacies mobilized by competition, envy or ambivalence between various organizational subsystems. They would rather ignore or avoid such conflicts. The effects of this (largely unconscious) decision had considerable impact on the practice of leadership and expressions of authority in Hyder. Competition between different subsystems minimized partnership and understanding across organizational boundaries, as well as discouraging risk. In an environment that lacks risk there is a greater tendency toward control. Anxieties over either losing or retaining control contributed to reticent managers who feared change, failure and conflict. Through these organizing processes a culture of authority and leadership was created in Hyder that, despite being consensual or collegial in intention, was in practice cautious, controlling and reactive.

What I am attempting to illustrate with my example from Hyder plc is that, despite considerable investment of time and money in learning and development for individual managers, efforts towards learning made little impact on established ways of organizing. When the organizational processes or dynamics I have described are added together Hyder can be understood as a company with very little orientation towards organizational learning (despite the creative developmental processes present for individuals). This therefore raises the question of what can be done in organizations like Hyder to assist the development of a more comprehensive connection between learning and organizing?

Learning from organizing

The individual orientation in HRD practice has been perpetuated both through approaches to university-based management education and approaches to HRD that privilege individual learning and development. Since the mid-1990s there has been a growing recognition of the need for critical perspectives that inform both management education and HRD (French and Grey 1996; Reynolds 1999a, 1999b). My argument for an organizational orientation in HRD is developed through discussion of both management education and in-company HRD, since these connected areas of scholarship and action are both subject to the same individual orientation. Both management educators and company managers find it difficult to engage directly with the power relations that define their roles, either those aspects of power that are inherent in the student–teacher or manager–subordinate relationship, or those power relations that impact on educational or organizational designs. A focus on the (real and imagined) power relations mobilized and enacted from a role are a key starting point for the transformation of the organizing processes within which that role is embedded. This is not a new issue for educators or managers. The work of Paulo Freire (1972, 1974), critical thinking in adult education (Kemmis 1985) and critical approaches to action learning (Willmott 1994) have, for example, provided many clues about forms of education and approaches to management that work with and through power relations. In practice, however, it continues to be an issue that is more avoided than addressed.

In management education, the emphasis on 'learning from experience' (Revans 1983; Kolb 1984) is an acknowledgement that managers' own experience is central to their education and development. However, approaches to learning from experience have again placed the individual at the centre and obscured the politics that are constructed in any collective or group-based effort to learn (Vince 1998). There is therefore an increasing need for an organizational form of learning from experience, which I shall refer to as 'learning from organizing'. Learning from organizing places the emphasis on learning through collective experience, on the conscious and unconscious structures that are inevitably created through attempts to learn and on the reflexive relationship between collective experience and the politics that both construct and constrain learning. The practical focus of learning from organizing is the development of different ways of undertaking processes and approaches to reflection, a different interpretation of what leadership means and involves, and the need to engage with the interplay between politics and emotions.

Transforming the organizational processes within which management roles are embedded involves the development of approaches to reflection that encourage the questioning of the assumptions that organizing has created. Assumptions emerge, take shape and institutionalize for important reasons, giving security and coherence to the uncertainties of organizing, and defining the parameters of how to belong and develop. That assumptions promote constraint as well as coherence is an integral and inevitable part of organizing. The questioning of assumptions is a challenge to the rationality and stability that underpins organizing. However, many business failures are seen to be the result of an inability to reflect, especially breaking through assumptions (Hammer and Stanton 1997). Learning from organizing involves reframing the questioning of assumptions as an organizational imperative rather than a responsibility for individuals. This will mean that reflection is concerned with more than looking or thinking back. The idea is also to show managers that they need to be continually involved in an inquiry into what the organization may become.

A more developed, organizational approach to reflection can make a contribution to a revised understanding of leadership and the nature of managerial authority. In many organizations, managerial authority is constructed and enacted as an individual responsibility for making decisions (whether these decisions are made with others or not). Individual managers' reasoning involves assumptions such as 'I am the one who ultimately makes the decisions' and 'the buck stops with me'. However, to promote learning, managers' authority may need to be based on their ability to open leadership and decision-making to the critique and imagination of others. Authority is in the act of creating processes of inquiry involving other stakeholders. This does not mean that managers must 'facilitate' others' learning, rather that they can be responsible for creating containers for dialogue and action. The managers' role here is not about having responsibility for making decisions; it is about creating shared responsibility for decision-making. Management can then be understood less as an individual skill and more as an organizing process, one that involves making the thinking and politics behind decisions public, as well as involving others in processes of reflection on and about decisions. Such an approach inevitably leads to a shift in understanding of the role of manager (Vince 2000).

From such a shift of role, words like participation and involvement begin to acquire new meaning. They can more readily become an integral part of the way in which management is thought about and undertaken. Managers can contribute to a conceptualization of, say, leadership that involves the creation of critical processes of reflection, exploration and inquiry. From this position, the resentments that are created through prevailing politics and power relations in organizations become the starting point of attempts to learn and change not the consequence of them. Managers' approaches to learning and change can be based on how the organization is reflected and enacted within their own practice, and what this means in terms of transforming the particular organizational context that surrounds them. Managers will have learned that the current social and strategic politics that characterize an organization are an integral part of their own thinking and ways of working.

Learning from organizing is not a prescription for better or effective learning. In fact, the result of engaging with characteristic emotions, politics and assumptions are often uncomfortable and unpredictable. However, it is possible for managers to learn how they contribute to the creation of patterns of organizing that limit their and others ability to learn. An understanding of the complex nature of managerial authority, and its enactment as leadership, can emerge from creating such opportunities and processes for an organizational orientation towards learning. This then leads to the question of what these processes might look like in practice? I explore two examples to move towards answering this question.

Example 1 General method: group relations

What methods of education can offer opportunities for learning from organizing? Clearly, any method that seeks to question assumptions, engage with emotions and politics looks significantly different from many current approaches to both management education and HRD. It is unlikely, for example, to be a didactic method since this does little to challenge student or manager dependency on either expert or external knowledge, or to question established power relations. It is equally unlikely to be the common conceptualization of facilitation, which with its emphasis on empowerment has reinforced the primacy of individual learning in organizations.

One method that offers opportunities for individual learners to think about and experience how organizational designs are generated by collective learning is the Group Relations approach, pioneered at the Tavistock Institute of Human Relations in London, and since developed throughout many countries (French and Vince 1999). Group Relations is an experiential learning method that reveals the complexities of emotions, interactions and politics that are integral to processes of organizing. Participants in Group Relations conferences or workshops have the opportunity to engage with what is happening to them within the various conference events and how these relate to the 'organization' that the participants are collectively creating around themselves. The general themes of such events are authority, leadership and 'political relatedness' (Sievers 2001).

Group Relations conferences provide opportunities for reflection on organizational dynamics and their impact on individuals and groups. For individuals, they offer the possibility for review of how they express authority and enact different roles, as well as experiencing the consequences of both leadership and followership. They offer opportunities for reflection on relational experience, inevitably surfacing individual and collective defensive mechanisms, avoidance strategies and projective identification. They offer chances to explore organizing into subsystems, the experience of belonging or not belonging, what it means to represent a group, and the issues that occur across the boundaries of subsystems. More generally they provide opportunities for reflection and insight on the ways in which an institution becomes established through collective emotional experience, politics, patterns of leadership, authority and attempts at change.

Group Relations events, therefore, are designed to emphasize the exploration of learning within a collective context. 'It is the group that is the focus, not the personality characteristics of the people present' (Lawrence 2000: 16). Generally speaking, this would be an unusual starting point for HRD. The utilization of group relations as a method for development implies an interest not only in the ability of organizational members to engage in learning from experience, but also a commitment to understanding the emotional and political contexts within which the (individual and collective) experience of learning is contained and constructed. The emotions and politics that are created in collectives as they evolve over time are necessarily the starting point for developing actions orientated towards strategic learning.

When people meet in such events, emotions, fantasies, histories and politics immediately have an effect on both behaviour and structure. These effects contribute to the creation of the organization that conference members find themselves in, and to the subsequent difficulties that they have in changing the behaviours and structures that they have consciously and unconsciously created. A Group Relations event is a collective process of learning from organizing. The extent to which individuals can reflect, act and learn is important, but this is not undertaken in isolation from comprehension of the system and subsystems that are being collectively imagined and implemented. An individual involved in Group Relations might improve his or her ability as a 'reflective practitioner'; however, Group Relations events are concerned with *social* reflection-in-action and with understanding both the conscious and unconscious processes that impact on organizing. The educational value of the method is that it offers opportunities to experience and review how an institution is created and sustained. Within 'inter-system' and 'institutional events' participants can simultaneously explore both collective organizing and the consequences of individual or shared attempts to manage. The importance of the method is that it affords reflection on the relationship between learning and organizing at an individual, collective and organizational level. Group Relations conferences are designed to provide an environment within which to inquire into individual and collective emotional experience, to think about the power relations that are being collectively created, the politics that are constructed through organizing, and to explore ways in which such relations can be transformed.

Group Relations conferences provide safe (if somewhat confusing) environments for people to learn outside of the organization to which they belong. Such events have also been transferred into specific organizational contexts (Gutmann *et al.* 1999) but it is not always easy or politic to set up educational processes that engage so directly with emotions and politics within an organization. The methodology can be employed alongside other, more usual, approaches, for example an MBA (see Daunton *et al.* 2000) and assist in a more gradual transformation of the relationship between role and organization. In order to develop this idea further I want to provide a second example.

Example 2 Specific application: the guided doctorate in organizational leadership and change

The guided doctorate in organizational leadership and change (GD) at the University of Glamorgan is a group-based doctoral programme with a focus on organizational leadership and change. It started in 1996 and usually recruits twelve (senior) managers into each annual intake. The programme lasts four years and (as with all PhDs) students are required to produce a doctoral dissertation that constitutes 'a unique contribution to knowledge'. The GD attempts to provide a context for an in-depth process of knowledge creation, recognizing that knowledge changes as we live it. The aim, both in terms of understanding the temporary learning group and the organizational context within which individual research takes place, is to study 'the living enterprise in action' (Amado 1995: 351). Inquiry inevitably raises the question of power (for example, what is said, what can be said, social power relations), as well as conscious and unconscious relations to others and to a social context. In the GD, reflection on emotions and politics – both internal to the group and within the organizational context of the research – provides the impetus for learning from organizing.

As a temporary organization for learning, the GD programme itself reflects the possibility of organizational learning, challenging the politics of PhD study as supervision between a professor and her or his student. The GD programme does not intend to create and sustain an institution driven by dependency on staff experience and expertise. For example, it is not seen as the role of the professors to dispense knowledge, nor is it the role of students to project their anxieties in such a way to turn professors into experts (even if they are expert). Students and staff need to acknowledge their different roles in the GD, expressing different responsibilities and expectations. It is easy for staff and students to fall back on traditional positions in relation to each other. A strong emphasis on peer supervision and group engagement in learning sets is important, as is providing opportunities to focus on whole group dynamics through the integration of Group Relations methods into the course workshops.

A key aspect of the staff role is in sustaining and developing the relationship between learning and organizing. There are various aspects to this. First, the different emotions, politics and power relations that are inherent in the roles of staff and students are raised at the beginning of the programme. This involves exploring the different types of authorities that are an aspect of each role. For example, staff and students may be anxious at the start of the programme in different ways. Rather than ignoring the anxiety and tensions generated by beginning the programme, they are raised in the group. This is not to claim that such dynamics (apprehension, envy, rivalry and so on) are necessarily understood or managed by staff or students. The importance in raising such issues out loud at the start is that they become an aspect of organizational memory and afford opportunities for future reflection. Second, a particular perspective on leadership informs the programme. The notion of a leader as a flexible individual with the sole authority to creatively direct operations is seen as a fantasy that minimizes thought and ultimately gives rise to controlling and compliant organizational designs. In the GD the underlying assumption that informs learning about leadership (for both staff and students) is that leadership is expressed in the collective capacity to create learning. In terms of learning from organizing, therefore, it is seen as helpful to explore the distinctions that emerge between the expression of authority (in a role) and leadership. Third, work-based research at a doctoral level is a powerful intervention into the organizational systems and subsystems within which the management role is enacted. In our experience at Glamorgan, an action-research project leading to a PhD inevitably becomes more than the inquiry of one individual. In the GD, through the inquiry brought about by being in the role of researcher as well as manager, individuals are provided with an opportunity to question and to transform the patterns of organizing within which the role of manager is contained and constrained. Such research has a collective orientation; it is necessarily with others rather than on them (Reason 1988). To construct inquiry is to mobilize possibility with and through others, and this is a process that invariably connects learning and organizing, going beyond what individuals may learn from their experience. This approach to knowledge is significantly different because it acknowledges the idea that 'knowledge is not something people possess in their heads, it is something people do together' (Weick 2002: S12).

The GD provides an example of a shift of emphasis in the delivery of management education and human resource development away from the individual learner and towards educational processes that recognize and work with the complex relationship between individual and collective learning and organizing. In the final section of this chapter, I shall summarize the key points I have made about this approach as well as discussing the implications for management education and HRD.

'Learning from organizing', management education and HRD

At this point I shall briefly review what I have claimed should be the theoretical and practical focus of learning from organizing and its impact on HRD. I have indicated the need for theory that acknowledges the interplay between emotion, politics and learning. This involves recognition of how collective emotional responses become political and then impact on processes of learning and organizing. Human behaviour and relations can contribute to the construction of ways of organizing that become obstacles to learning. One consequence of ignoring the interplay between emotion and politics has been that the practice of HRD has become overly focussed on individuals' learning to the detriment of organizational learning. This then implies rethinking HRD in order to develop a more *organizational* focus, what I am calling learning from organizing. I have said that learning from organizing will involve different ways of thinking about and doing reflection, a different understanding and enactment of leadership, and the need to engage with the interplay between emotions and politics.

In my examples I have attempted to illustrate how the *general method* of Group Relations and a *specific application* of these ideas within the University of Glamorgan's guided doctorate programme constitute an organizational rather than an individual focus on management education and HRD. I have summarized these ideas in Table 9.1.

Table 9.1 provides a summary of 'learning from organizing' from one theoretical and practical position. The method of Group Relations has informed the development of an approach to a doctoral programme. I would not claim that the guided doctorate programme is radical or particularly new. Indeed, the importance of 'backyard research' is already well established (Jacobs 1997; Swanson 1997). There are several such programmes (the Centre for Action Research in Professional Practice at the University of Bath, for example) and similar ground is covered in various doctorates of business administration (DBA) and individual programmes of research study, as well as the 'New Route PhD', devised by a consortium of British universities. The GD may be one of very few action-based research initiatives that also utilize group relations methods to reveal unconscious processes and political relatedness. The thinking behind the programme and its design are an explicit attempt to emphasize the politics and emotions involved in organizational learning as well as integrating this with individual learning.

An understanding of the role of manager involves an awareness that a key aspect of managers' role is to transform the system within which the role is embedded (Neumann 1999). The emphasis here is not on what an individual knows, can learn or may change; rather it is on how the transformation of

Table 9.1 'Learning from organizing': key aspects of general method and specific application

General method: *group relations*	• A form of experiential learning that raises the complexities of 'political relatedness'. • Reflection on organizational dynamics – how the organization is created and recreated through the interaction of behaviour and structure; and the importance of *social* reflection-in-action. • The emotions and politics that are created in collectives as they evolve are a key starting point for an understanding of strategic learning.
Specific application: *the guided doctorate*	• The 'living enterprise in action'. Programme members study the relationships between organizing and learning that are being created within the GD at the same time as undertaking inquiry into such relationships within their own organizations. • The 'political relatedness' of different roles. Programme members and staff reflect on the nature and enactment of authority, leadership and change in the GD. The emphasis is on opportunities for collective and critical reflection, attempts to develop a collective enactment of leadership, understanding the potency of inquiry as intervention in the social and political context of an organization.

the system that creates and constrains management roles can occur through social reflection-in-action. Social reflection-in-action implies a relational, political and emotional understanding of organizing, since both unconscious processes and politics are mobilized within any social context. To have a meaningful impact, HRD (whether undertaken in the academy or in-company) has to engage with the contextual politics, power relations, and emotions that shape the possibilities and limitations of learning. This is not a complicated shift of understanding. At present the emphasis is on the relationship between a person and his or her role in an organization (learning to be a more effective manager, leader or follower, say). A revised emphasis can be on the relationship between role and organization (for instance, on what I have been calling learning from organizing).

For example, the chief executive of a company is not just a person, but is in a powerful role within the organization, one that attracts many relations, perceptions and fantasies. Whatever the behaviour of the person it is often the collective interpretations of his or her behaviour over time which come to define the person *within their role*. The chief executive might be seen as aloof from most staff, charismatic, a political animal, a fearsome ogre, ineffectual . . . the list is endless. However, as collective perceptions of the individual are reinforced, escaping them becomes more difficult, they can become seen as expected forms of behaviour that then impact on collective behaviour in the organization. Examining the relationship between role and organization involves inquiry into the ways in which organizational designs, assumptions, values and expected behaviour create and constrain the ways in which the authority of a role is enacted, and vice versa. Strategic learning therefore may involve an examination of the way senior managers are seen and experienced in order to understand the organizational structures that have been created from collective perceptions in action.

In general, approaches to management education and HRD that are seeking to explore the complex relationship between learning and organizing are likely to be informed by the following propositions.

- There is a difference between the sum of individuals' learning in an organization and organizational learning. Organizational learning supposes an interest in how social, political, emotional and relational processes are created, sustained and challenged through the interaction of learning and organizing. This signifies a shift from an analysis of what individuals or collectives may or may not learn, towards engagement with the politics that shape and are shaped by learning and organizing.
- The interaction between learning and organizing, emotion and politics constructs a temporary institution or state that helps to identify what the organization is in the minds of its members. This has the effect of both promoting and limiting learning and organizing (in Hyder plc for example, it particularly shaped processes of reflection, communication and authority).
- Learning from organizing provides a critical, conceptual framework for an organizational perspective, an addition to 'learning from experience'. It suggests engagement with characteristic emotions and politics that impact on both learning and organizing. For individuals this implies a shift from inquiring into the relationship between the person and his or her role (as manager, leader, follower) towards inquiring into the enactment of that role within the context of organizing. The focus is therefore on what is constructed through collective experience and on the conscious and unconscious behaviours and structures created through organizing.

There are implications of these propositions for both university-based management education and in-company human resource development. The starting point for exploring key managerial concepts like leadership, authority and change involves social reflection-in-action on the emotions and politics that construct and constrain the roles of both manager and educator. In university-based management education, for example, this means placing less emphasis on approaches to learning that are didactic or even experiential approaches that are designed for individual awareness. An understanding of the political relatedness that creates and constrains organizing comes from opportunities to explore the organizational dynamics that are being created as individuals and collectives participate in organizing. In practical terms this involves questioning and exploring the emotions and politics present in the roles of tutor and student, and the impact of these on the structure, content and outcomes of learning. It involves creating dialogical processes for learning, and identifying the dynamics of learning and organizing that are being created within a learning group. Group Relations methods provide one way of achieving an understanding of learning from organizing.

In terms of in-company HRD, less emphasis needs to be put on individual processes of appraisal and personal development. Individual training programmes orientated to skills and knowledge production play a significant part in learning, but do little to support an understanding of the relationship between learning and organizing. This occurs not through training interventions or individual appraisal and mentoring but through collective attempts to redefine how reflection, leadership, communication across subsystem boundaries, authority and decision-making are done. To engage with the development of these themes in an organization means engaging with the emotions and politics that characterize the relationship between learning and organizing. The focus here is on attempts to collectively transform the ways in which organizing is imagined and implemented in order to transform the constraints on learning in a managerial role.

Conclusion: reflections on HRD

To conclude this chapter I shall provide the following reflections about developments in HRD, related to the three main themes proposed by McGoldrick *et al.* (2002) mentioned in the introduction. Clearly, HRD has a central focus on and concern with learning, but the emphasis of this focus in practice has been on individual rather than organizational learning. HRD currently underemphasizes strategic learning, avoiding the development of approaches that might reveal and include the emotions and politics that are inevitably mobilized in any attempt to organize. Emotions and politics are often ignored, seen as irrelevant aspects of organizational life, certainly considered to be secondary considerations to organizational success and improved performance. However, a broader accountability than organizational performance, whether this relates, for example, to local and global responsibilities, sustainable development, or interorganizational partnerships and networks, cannot be created without making such organizational dynamics overt, an integral part of the creativity and imagination necessary to dismantle empires and to transform defensive organizational relations and designs.

The words 'business driven', therefore, necessarily include taking into account emotions and politics that organizational members would rather ignore or avoid. Of course, the fact is that there will always be actions, events, feelings and relations that members of an organization would rather ignore or avoid. This means that HRD will continue to be a pivotal political activity within organizations. Just like other members of the organization, HRD staff will respond to and enact the power relations and control processes that are collectively (and unconsciously) constructed by leaders and managers in their everyday behaviour and interactions. However, HRD staff members can undertake an important role for the organization. The HRD function is one part of the organization that can be responsible for revealing and reflecting on the emotions and politics that characterize 'the way we do things here'. It can be the focal point of a critical practice of HRD.

I can summarize what I think will be involved in a critical practice of HRD that addresses the complexities of the interplay between learning and organizing. This will include the following.

- The revelation of characteristic emotions and politics that have been created and are perpetuated through organizing, that are enacted in management roles, and that have a continuous impact on both organizational behaviour and organizational design.
- The development of reflective practices capable of contributing to the questioning of established assumptions. This implies the development of forms of reflection that are organizational rather than individual in orientation and that focus on the present rather than on the past.
- The implementation of a revised understanding and practice of leadership, one that promotes a shift of emphasis away from individual and towards the 'collective capacity to create something of value' (Senge *et al.* 2000).

What these components of a critical practice of HRD actually mean in day-to-day terms will emerge from future attempts at implementation, and from the critiques and dialogues inspired by this chapter and this book. My contribution to this emerging dialogue is the idea that in the future, one thing that both academics and practitioners have to better understand is the ways in which development initiatives are not simply about improving individual performance or organizational effectiveness. Future developments in HRD will have to support the advancement of knowledge about emotional, relational and political processes affecting management and organization, as well as the implementation of this knowledge in practice. At this time, further knowledge about individual development is not imperative. More important now is a better understanding of the complex relations between people in an organizational context, what people collectively create and can imagine. For this to happen there will have to be increased interest in the emotional responses that are integral to organizing, as well as how these create, reflect and represent the politics and power relations that underpin emerging organizational experience and designs.

Acknowledgement

I am very grateful to Dr Chris Kayes at George Washington University for his comments on two previous versions of this chapter.

References

Amado, G. (1995) 'Why psychoanalytic knowledge helps understand organizations: a discussion with Elliot Jaques', *Human Relations*, 48, 4: 351–357.

Bion, W. R. (1962) *Learning from Experience*, London: William Heinemann.

Clegg, S., Hardy, C. and Nord, W. (1996) *The Handbook of Organization Studies*, London: Sage.

Daunton, L., Hole, C., James, C. and Vince, R. (2000) *The Development and Evaluation of Experiential Learning Methods on the Masters in Business Administration (MBA)*, 'Pont Dysgu' Papers series, Glamorgan: University of Glamorgan.

Easterby-Smith, M., Araujo, L. and Burgoyne, J. (eds) (1999) *Organizational Learning: Third International Conference*, 2 vols, Lancaster: Lancaster University.

Fineman, S. (ed.) (1993) *Emotion in Organisations*, London: Sage.

Freire, P. (1972) *Pedagogy of the Oppressed*, Harmondsworth: Penguin.

Freire, P. (1974) *Education as the Practice of Freedom*, London: Readers and Writers Publishing Co-operative.

French, R. and Grey, C. (1996) *Rethinking Management Education*, London: Sage.

French, R. and Vince, R. (1999) *Group Relations, Management and Organization*, Oxford: Oxford University Press.

Gherardi, S., Nicolini, D. and Odella, F. (1998) 'Towards a social understanding of how people learn in organizations: the notion of a situated curriculum', *Management Learning*, 29, 3: 273–297.

Gutmann, D., Ternier-David, J. and Verrier, C. (1999) 'From envy to desire: witnessing the transformation', in R. French and R. Vince (eds) *Group Relations, Management and Organization*, Oxford: Oxford University Press.

Hammer, M. and Stanton, S. A. (1997) 'The power of reflection', *Fortune Magazine*, 24 November: 291–296.

Jacobs, R. L. (1997) 'HRD partnerships for integrating HRD research and practice', in R. Swanson and E. Holton III (eds) *Human Resource Development Handbook: Linking Research and Practice*, San Francisco, CA: Berrett-Koehler.

Kemmis, S. (1985) 'Action research and the politics of reflection', in D. Boud, R. Keogh and D. Walker (eds) *Reflection: Turning Experience into Learning*, London: Kogan Page.

Kolb, D. (1984) *Experiential Learning*, Englewood Cliffs, NJ: Prentice Hall.

Lawrence, W. G. (2000) *Tongued with Fire: Groups in Experience*, London: Karnac.

Lee, M. (2001) 'A refusal to define HRD', *Human Resource Development International*, 4, 3: 327–341.

Lipshitz, R. and Popper, M. (2000) 'Organizational learning in a hospital', *Journal of Applied Behavioural Science*, 36, 3: 345–361.

McGoldrick, J., Stewart, J. and Watson, S. (2002) *Understanding Human Resource Development*, London: Routledge.

Neumann, J. (1999) 'Systems psychodynamics in the service of political organizational change', in R. French and R. Vince (eds) *Group Relations, Management and Organization*, Oxford: Oxford University Press.

Obholzer, A. (1999) 'Managing the unconscious at work', in R. French and R. Vince (eds) *Group Relations, Management and Organisation*, Oxford: Oxford University Press.

Reason, P. (1988) *Human Inquiry in Action*, London: Sage.

Revans, R. (1983) *The ABC of Action Learning*, Bromley, Kent: Chartwell Bratt.

Reynolds, M. (1999a) 'Grasping the nettle: possibilities and pitfalls of a critical management pedagogy', *British Journal of Management*, 9, 3: 171–184.

Reynolds, M. (1999b) 'Critical reflection and management education: rehabilitating less hierarchical approaches', *Journal of Management Education*, 23, 5: 537–553.

Senge, P., Heifetz, R. A. and Torbert, B. (2000) 'A conversation on leadership', *Reflections*, 2, 1: 57–68.

Sievers, B. (2001) '"I will not let thee go, except thou bless me!" (Genesis 32:26): some considerations regarding the constitution of authority, inheritance and succession', *Human Resource Development International*, 4, 3: 357–381.

Swanson, R. (1997) 'HRD research: don't go to work without it', in R. Swanson and E. Holton III (eds) *Human Resource Development Handbook: Linking Research and Practice*, San Francisco, CA: Berrett-Koehler.

Vince, R. (1998) 'Behind and beyond Kolb's learning cycle', *Journal of Management Education*, 22, 3: 304-319.

Vince, R. (2000) 'Learning in public organizations in 2010', *Public Money and Management*, 20, 1: 39–44.

Vince, R. (2004) *Rethinking Strategic Learning*, London: Routledge.

Vince, R. and Broussine, M. (2000) 'Rethinking organizational learning in local government', *Local Government Studies*, 26, 1: 15–30.

Weick, K. (2002) 'Puzzles in organizational learning: an exercise in disciplined imagination', special issue: 'Organizational Learning: New Directions', *British Journal of Management*, 13, September: S7–S15.

Willmott, H. (1994) 'Management education: provocations to a debate', *Management Learning*, 25, 1: 105–136.

10 Getting to the heart of HRD

Some thoughts on the relationship between quality and performance in higher education in the United Kingdom

Heather Höpfl

A system under pressure

The expansion in UK higher education since the late 1980s has brought with it a number of unintended consequences, not least the problem of greater pressures on staff and students alike. This situation is true of both 'old' universities and the former polytechnics or 'new' universities' income from research and a greater emphasis on teaching. This chapter seeks to examine some of the ways in which such pressures are experienced and the implications for staff development practices. For those working in higher education significant work pressure is a matter of day-to-day experience. The dramatic increase in student numbers has brought attendant problems which have serious implications for staff. Although it is not perhaps politic to say it, students come with a more diverse range of abilities. Some students have very poor literacy skills. There has been a vast increase in the number of overseas students to provide an income stream and there is often a conflict between recruiters and their agents and academic staff. Anecdotes about the sometimes dubious entry qualifications and language skills of some students abound. There is a widespread feeling of powerlessness in relation to academic standards and a feeling that even with recent 'lighter touch' approaches to quality, there is a concern with cosmetic constructions rather than improvements in the standard of academic work. Clearly, this is a large subject to tackle and one which can be approached from a number of different angles. This chapter gives particular emphasis to the question of the sustainability of a system subjected to such pressures and so redolent with contradiction. In particular, it considers some of the ways in which the increase in pressure on university staff is evident in a range of organizational behaviours and a widening gulf between the pursuit of academic quality and the day-to-day experiences of staff expected to interpret aspirational vision statements.

A report of a survey conducted by the Association of University Teachers (AUT 1998) found evidence of increasing workloads damaging the health of staff and jeopardizing the quality of work. The survey identifies increased student numbers, funding cuts and the proliferation of external assessment mechanisms as being the main cause of stress for staff in higher education. Indeed, two-thirds of the respondents reported that they found their work 'stressful' and one-quarter had taken time off with work-related stress illnesses in the previous year. Three-quarters of staff reported that they had too much paperwork to deal with. Inevitably, under such circumstances the quality of work with students is compromised, as the respondents to the survey indicated in their answers. Exhortations to quality improvement and initiatives which rigorously monitor outputs lead to a situation where quality is jeopardized by the very mechanisms which regulate it. Many staff in the survey reported that the emphasis on performance indicators had damaged quality. For students, the picture is not so different. Pressures on students to fund their studies, to deal with accumulating debts, and frequently to work part-time to supplement their incomes have resulted in considerable pressure on students' abilities to keep up with their academic work. More students are looking to academic and counselling staff for emotional support. Suicides amongst students have increased significantly since the early 1990s (Utley 1998) and it has been suggested that universities are not doing enough to help students. Yet, staff say they cannot cope with the increased demands on them. Every aspect of staff behaviour becomes subject to scrutiny to the extent where it becomes simply impossible for university staff to respond to all the demands which are placed on them.

Unfortunately, these issues are not merely about discrepancies between abstract terms. The implications of increased pressure are real and physical. The system is groaning under the weight of proliferating regulation, increased student numbers, competing demands for time, exhortations to justify performance and to bring in money. In *The Times Higher*, Ruth Payne, former president of the AUT in Aberdeen, reported that she had started to experience panic attacks and says 'there are far more students who need some kind of support. There is pressure on everyone all the time to make money . . . it is not considered good if you haven't published' (quoted in Utley 1998). This is familiar territory to many staff in institutions of higher education. Staff feel that they are not valued and that their efforts to keep up with multiple and changing demands are not recognized.

Normative assumptions about the need for change

The sources of such pressures are in the process of change itself and in the almost mystical quality of the rhetoric of change management. The management of change is about moving organizations from one state to another. For illustrative purposes I have frequently referred to Cummings and Worley's (1993) book, *Organization Development and Change*, to make this point. This is rather unfair to Cummings and Worley since I could have chosen any one of many books within arm's reach from my desk. However, to make the point, I shall again refer to this text bearing in mind that it is one of many which identifies the ways in which changes *should be* introduced. It lays the foundations for a motivational approach to the management of change by identifying five activities essential to the process of organizational change. The text is primarily normative. It explains what should be done to achieve desired objectives. It talks of *motivating change*: moving organizational members towards these objectives. It says that change will bring resistance which has to be overcome and it talks of creating a vision to guide the direction of the change towards the desired future state. In this respect, it is no different from countless others which address these issues. The capacity to move, in various senses of the word, an organization from one state to another is clearly a significant part of the change process and of the rhetoric of change. However, such rhetoric needs to be subjected to careful deconstruction as many of the contradictions which emerge in the experience of organizational change lie in the assumptions which lie concealed within the change agenda (Billig 1987).

In relation to this, it is interesting to consider the etymology of the word *management* but, in this context, it is useful to trace the word management – as meaning 'to handle' (from the Latin *manus*, meaning hand) – and the maniple which refers to 'a handful' (L. *manus*, hand, plus *dim plenum*, full) of common soldiers and was the name given to a bundle of hay tied by Romulus to the standards of the various companies of soldiers as a symbol of their common identity and *purchase*. This may be related to the *fascis* which was a bundle of rods and an axe carried before the highest ranking magistrate as a symbol (and the implements of) the power to scourge and behead. The populus was expected to surrender (L. *dedere*) to the power of the symbol, to be placed 'under the burden' of the *fascis*. The maniple came to refer to an ecclesiastical vestment, a piece of cloth two to four feet long, worn suspended from the left (sinister) arm as a symbolic handkerchief for wiping away the tears shed by the celebrant for the sins of the world. Tears which might indeed be shed for those under the maniple.

A related term is manciple (L. *manus/capere*, hand/to take) which refers to an official who purchases provisions or slaves; indeed, originally *mancipium* referred to one obtained by legal purchase, a slave. Of course, manipulate, as a method of handling, comes from the same root and brings the notion of taking and handling back to this particular etymology of management. 'Management' then might be seen to refer to the notion of training, as in urging in a particular direction, and in disciplining – the correction of deviation, and to handling and controlling. This movement is not without consequences as this discussion of the implications for higher education seeks to demonstrate.

Objectives and movement

In broad terms, the argument presented here is concerned with the relationship between motivation and emotion both of which share a common etymological root (L. *movere*, to move). Movement, therefore, carries the notion of *something moved*, something which has to be *borne or carried*. Of course, in the change literature what is carried is the forward movement of the organization towards its objectives. What is rarely acknowledged in the literature is the inevitable emotional counterpart to such movement which has to be borne by organizational members. Where the costs of change are referred to it is as if the consequences of change were unfortunate obstacles to progress and should be overcome. For those affected by organizational change the issue is not so easily addressed. So, for example, the rhetoric of change in higher education might be set against the AUT survey in order to reveal its impact on employee experience. This is particularly important where the consequences of the changes are perceived by those who must implement them as detrimental to the very objectives which they seek to achieve.

Textbook accounts of change express a concern to overcome *resistance to change* and, in the case of Cummings and Worley (1993), advocate the creation of dissatisfaction in order to press home the need for change. Implicitly this involves an extension of the psychological contract of work. The contract of work now requires not only that people change with the demands of their work roles but also that they experience 'a felt need for change' (Cummings and Worley 1993: 138). Inevitably, this has consequences for the individual but 'people and organizations [*as if these were different from the people who make them up*] need to experience deep levels of hurt before they will seriously undertake meaningful change' (Cummings and Worley 1993: 138): all this without reflection or acknowledgement of the ideological imperative of strategic rationality. The individual is available to the reified organization, and without question, as an available and consumable collection of attributes: 'the individual learns . . . which parts of himself [*sic*] are unwanted and unworthy' (Gouldner 1969: 349).

Arguably, since the early 1970s there has been an increasingly specific attention to those attributes of the person which are desired and those which are not. Of course, to many this many seem an entirely inconsequential necessity to ensure the predictability of organizational behaviour. However, more is at stake than a simple and necessary classification of behaviours. Only a part of what might be held by the individual to be a coherent identity is required in the construction of the organizational role so, for example, the increasing use of performance measures is made to appear as a neutral arbiter of performance. However, as is apparent in the AUT survey, many staff in higher education institutions experience performance measures as intimidatory and are highly suspicious of the use of the categorizations which are frequently used to make apparently *logical* decisions about its staffing during a period of culture change. So, staff may feel their skills are undervalued, that teaching is privileged over research in some of the new universities, that generating income is more important than generating ideas. Older staff may feel that their values are increasingly compromised by changing expectations and younger staff may lose sight of the meaning of their roles as academics and the responsibilities that go with that. The tough minded strive, and ambition and the pursuit of personal goals have displaced a good deal of collegiality and collaboration.

Performance and performers

An emphasis on performance and presentation – of information, of outcomes, of rhetorical texts – has implications for self-perception (Goffman 1969; Hare 1985; Holt 1989). In a *theatrical* performance, the task of the actors is to present the action of the play, to comport themselves to a successful end and to use their skills to support the performance. The role is everything in performance and eclipses the personality of the actor who may, in support of the action, draw on personal experience and emotions to emphasize the role. In order for the performance to be achieved with authority and propriety, ambivalence needs to be concealed by a mask: literal or figurative. Given this emphasis on the role, the actor's skill has been described as the 'histrionic dissimulation of emotion used to create controlled illusions' (Roach 1985: 138). Actors have always been regarded with suspicion as professional dissimulators; indeed, at one time they were excommunicated from the Church. The issue here is with the way in which the acting performance is one which requires either a distortion of personal experience, or a simulation of behaviours in order to present a required performance, or a mechanical interpretation of a script. The emphasis on performance has led to extraordinary interpretations and evaluations of the 'performances' of academics on the basis of notions of 'customer satisfaction'. So, academics might be assessed on the quality of their slides, style of interaction or clarity of exposition. Now, while there is some merit in such assessments, they do little to recognize the quality of the ideas presented. In most student feedback, competence is assessed in a relatively superficial way in relation to a performance well executed. The presence of eccentricity is a rare occurrence on the modern campus having been regulated out by standardization and normalized expectations.

If this perception is accurate, then it is not surprising that academic life is replete with casualties. According to some, only medicine or liquor would remedy the pathological consequences of prolonged involvement in acting and 'habitual self-transformation' (Gayton, 1654). This notion of perpetual self-transformation is an acknowledged feature of change. A part-time student who works for an organization which has been through over ten years of relentless change was recently off work with a psychosomatic skin disease: 'the story of the change is written all over my body', he explained. Habitual self-transformation incurs costs. In a theatrical performance, the actors comport themselves to the task of presenting the action of the play; to the skills they employ in carrying off the performance (Hopfl and Linstead 1993). 'To carry it off' implies a successful outcome: a performance delivered with propriety. The ability to continually transform oneself led to the acting profession being regarded as a tawdry and degrading way of earning a living. The actor is thus a *tabula rasa* or blank surface, lacking personal affections, friendships, family ties, identities like the beggar, the seducer, the prostitute and the unbelieving priest – a professional illusionist who trades in the dispassionate embodiment of the passions (Sarbin 1986). The point here is to make a comparison between the perceived problems of staff in higher education and the changes which are being introduced. The discrepancy between the desired objective of the change and perceptions by academic staff of a deterioration in their actual performance leads to a similar sense of dissimulation as that experienced by the actor. The increasing emphasis on performance and presentation and the extent of bureaucratic regulation, leads to increasing pressures on academic staff to present themselves in a favourable light, and to give attention to appearances. For many, it seems, this gulf lays the individual open to a range of stress-related illnesses, to loss of sleep, to problems in personal relationships, to the need to manage their own ambivalence, to deteriorating performance. At the same time, the commitment to continuous improvement, to quality as *a mountain without a plateau*, means that there is a fundamental contradiction which has to be managed but which is rarely addressed.

Creating contempt

There is an important implication in all this for the playing out of staff–student, staff–management relationships to which those concerned with quality need to give serious attention. By imposing demands on academic staff which leave them feeling disoriented, abused and aware of the implications for this for their professional practice, bureaucratic initiatives in higher education stand the risk of increasing disregard and contempt. Although it is rarely acknowledged, contempt does seem to have a place in the actor–audience relationship. Apart from the obvious celebrity cults which attach to 'great' actors, the public seems to love theatre but dislike actors. After all, theatre is dirty work and contact with actors carries the danger of contamination. The standing of academic staff has changed dramatically since the early 1980s with a consequent erosion of self-esteem within the profession. The supermarket view of education has added to this. One of the most significant outcomes of the AUT survey is that staff want 'cuts in academic red tape, more formalised working hours and conditions, more open and skilled management, reduced departmental and institutional competition, higher pay, less emphasis on performance indicators and, above all, stability' (Swain 1998). The general secretary of the AUT, David Triesman, says that 'staff feel ever less valued, where job satisfaction is falling and where the worst features of management attitudes – bullying and intimidation – are perceived as increasing' (quoted in Swain 1998). This is particularly true of the new universities which, as 'managed institutions', have developed a cadre of those who manage academic work. Such staff may have little or no academic credibility but who, often for their bureaucratic skills, find themselves managing the work of others and frequently stifle the possibility of academic development. Of course, this is a broad generalization but it will be familiar to many people in new universities. Both from working in such institutions and through external examining at several new universities, I have seen this development at first hand and have been saddened for those who try to do good academic work in teaching and research but who find themselves working for people who have little understanding and even less sensitivity to what would be necessary to achieve a genuine improvement in quality.

What is being argued here is that the contradictory demands which academic staff experience in their day-to-day working lives are at the root of the problem and the primary cause of a feeling of disempowerment and alienation. Actors are frequently ambivalent in their attitudes to the audience. The intimacies of the actor – friendship, respect and admiration – are found in the companionship of the rehearsal room and, however else it is dressed up for public consumption, the relationship between actor and audience is curiously saprophytic. The actor knows the world behind the curtain to be fraudulent, to be both magical and tawdry. The actor knows the point at which he or she must 'enter' the role and the costs of surrender to it (Averill 1976). In short, the secret knowledge of stagecraft alienates the actor from the audience. The partial knowledge of the audience, albeit essential to the creation of the illusion, is experienced by the actor with disdain. Actors offer themselves in performance to people who do not and cannot understand the true worth of their transformations. As demands on academic staff to construct themselves for external consumption imposes more demands on their time students suffer from reduced availability of contact time and staff come to feel increasingly dissatisfied with the mechanisms of regulation and have no confidence in their worth. This cycle of behaviours nurtures a contemptuous relationship where staff who do not themselves feel wanted or worthy struggle to manage their ambivalence towards the demands placed on them by students as against the demands placed on them by bureaucratic systems.

People values

This travesty is rooted in the fundamental inauthenticity of the contemporary preoccupation with the debased notion of 'people values', customer service and quality. It seems that only the naive and those who might seek to gain from the pursuit of training for such values are able to discuss quality metrics and performance indicators without apprehension and, perhaps, more commonly cynicism. The theatricalities of organizational life have produced corporate actors who are humiliated, debased and undervalued. By turning contact staff at whatever level in the organization into performers, organizations have appropriated the interpersonal and replaced it with a package of skills, performance indicators and quality metrics. Only fellow performers understand the sense of misappropriation which they share. The customer cannot understand the personal costs to the performer and will rarely glimpse the off-stage cursing or despair. The donning of the mask becomes associated with a boundary: a step into and out of role. To a great extent, this is not the case in higher education. The personal value system and commitment that attracts staff into academic posts is not easily compromised. It is observably the case that the vast majority of academic staff struggle to manage the competing demands they face and, in consequence, come to embody their own ambivalences rather than jeopardize student needs. The health implications of this embodiment are obvious.

Likewise, the audience qua customer, being now separated from the performance, which has become self-serving and appropriative, finds its dignity in a scornful abhorrence of the actor's craft. The customer is led to expect delight, arousal and even magic from the encounter with the organization through its actors but now approaches the performance arena as a sceptic with some revulsion for the counterfeit experience at the heart of the performance: alienated actors playing to alienated audiences. The apparent coherence and consensus regarding the definition of the event depends on masking. The dramatic mask conceals ambivalence about the role, about performance and about the play itself but it is not infallible. When the mask fails the performance is thrown into question. For the actor, the extent of his or her degradation is revealed. The most important implication for organizational behaviour of the argument presented above rests on the commitment to the regulation of behaviour via manipulation of the role and attempts to replace professional identity with action check-lists. The individual comes to resent the feeling that they are simply a series of items to be checked off on a list. Such a view of the person, in blatant contradiction of the notion of people values, is bound to result in a cynical view of what the individual can contribute to the organization. Yet, despite this, organizations reproduce themselves without regard to the obvious.

The practical implications of this assertion need further consideration. Clearly, organizations in general and institutions of education in particular need to give attention to the implications of intensive *actor* training and the pursuit of *appearances* in performance. Unlike a theatre company (where the exhilaration of performance is accompanied by serious play, fun and a strong sense of an identity as an acting company however transient) the reluctant surrender of personal attributes and dramatistic experiences in the pursuit of organizational performance appears to produce cynicism and despair. After all, the intention of corporate actors is not to offer a travesty of service but genuine service. Academic staff have come under increasing pressure to perform in ways which are detrimental to students, to their own well-being and to the profession. Moreover, as the social aspects of work break down there is little comradeship in work for consolation. If there is a message for organizations in this analysis, it is that there is a need for an honest contract and understanding of the need to attack the contradictory demands imposed on staff. This is confirmed by the findings of the AUT survey. Organizations must give attention to the personal costs of performance, make more explicit the demands on employees, and acknowledge the implications of increasing demands.

Bureaucracy as a baroque construction

The emphasis on regulation in higher education has involved the construction of something akin to a baroque edifice with all its fuss and frippery. Bureaucracy proliferates in an overabundance of elaboration, intricacy, caprice, whimsy, stylization, indulgence, exaggeration. It is high baroque at its most supreme. According to Buci-Glucksmann (1994) the baroque paradigm employs a common range of tropes and stylistic devices: allegory, oxymoron, open totality and discordant detail; *relations of insistence*, permanent excess which eroticizes the real by staging phantasm *founds meaning on matter and not on concept . . . imperialism of seeing*, a delight in detail as the promise of happiness (Buci-Glucksmann 1994: 140–141, after Barthes 1977, original emphases). These characteristics of the seventeenth-century baroque are recognizably those of the regulatory mechanisms employed in higher education: the seduction of consumption in student choice which often results in a paralysing charade of heterogeneity, a compulsive pursuit of and delight in detail and bewildering and overwhelming massification – the pursuit of more and more emblems or indicators of success. Barthes 'saw in the baroque and the pansemic nature of the image, the site of excess meaning, *obtuse* meaning, a signifier without a signified, which governs aesthetic pleasure' so that 'meaning is destroyed beneath the symbol' (Buci-Glucksmann 1994: 140, original emphasis). It is the weight of such baroque constructions which produces the pressure which is reported in the AUT survey.

Regulation and monitoring is experienced as an overwhelming presence of great weight. The analogy between bureaucratic regulation and the baroque is precisely about the way in which such a weight of meanings might oppress. The experience of awe one might have in the face of a physical edifice of great elaboration, lavish detail, meticulous and impressive intricacy is very much akin to the experience of elaborate bureaucracy and regulation by an excess of words. The very nature of such baroque constructions seems to go hand in hand with decadent management and the pursuit of a greedy self-interest. The splendour of the baroque period is silencing and disempowering. There is no space left for any other response than awe. There is too much detail. There is overwhelming excess. The individual is crushed by proliferating meanings and demands and a contradiction between lavish indulgences of management and the impoverished reality of the classroom teacher. The consequence of this is paralysis. The individual is so bombarded that he or she can no longer act. The social world is reduced to a series of categories which shape and define experiences as if by their construction they constitute 'realities' to which experiences must conform.

In this way, the regulatory mechanisms of higher education have become a touchstone for quality without regard for their consequences. Consequently, too much meaning is invested in the construction of quality as a series of categories, as a sublime object, as the object of desire. Yet, quality is precisely what is sacrificed to the regulatory mechanism and with two consequences: frenetic activity which might, in the short run, protect against the inescapable melancholia occasioned by the recognition of loss. Put simply, of the loss of a sense of professional identity, of self-esteem, of value, of what is offered to the students and, furthermore, a crushing despondency which ironically translates into poor performance, ill-health, a deterioration of what is offered, a vicious circle of failing performance.

Erections and the mastery of the matrix

There is another aspect of regulation which requires some comment and about which I have written extensively elsewhere, the ubiquitous use of the matrix as an instrument of regulation. This is intriguing because it is about constructions which regulate, simplify and reduce organizational complexity in the service of strategic objectives. In part, it is the imposition of taxonomic structures which seek to render experience subject to science that cause much of the anguish which is evident in the academic stress survey. The *matrix* was formerly the term used to apply to a female breeding animal and not used to apply to women. In late Latin it came to be the term used for the human uterus; this is somewhat ironic. Yet, the capture of the matrix and its conversion into a space of regulation is easily demonstrated by recourse to any management *text*-book. The mastery of the matrix is achieved by the removal of the ovaries which renders the uterus impotent. Embodied reproduction is then replaced by the reproduction of text and the fertility of the site is surrounded to the fertility of words and regulation. So, the matrix is an instrument of management which locates and characterizes relationships on the basis of power. In the substitution of words for children, the natural products of the matrix, the space is regulated, and the reproduction of homologues guaranteed. This is, of course, why the matrix is such a favourite tool of bureaucracy. To bring this back to the subject of this chapter, the demands on staff in higher education, this means that the veneration of the word, the text, the taxonomy, and so on, has left an abyss of meaning between such constructions and the embodied experience of those regulated by such constructions. This chapter has argued that the site of the ambivalence thus becomes located in the person. The individual must bear the discrepancy. What is felt in the body and experienced in ill-health is the gap between the word and the body. For example, in a recent post, I was a member of the vice-chancellor's special group on Diversity and Fairness, which was chaired by a clever and competent woman, the only female Dean in the university, who was extremely popular and well regarded both for her academic work and her management skills. Following a restructuring of the university, this woman was displaced and chose to leave. The gulf between the rhetoric of Diversity and Fairness statements and policies and the day-to-day practices were immediately transparent. Six months later I also decided to resign.

Conclusion

This chapter is a tentative attempt to examine some of the reasons for the pressures on academic staff in higher education. The argument has presented a number of possible influences – the emphasis on performance, the personal costs of excessive and competing demands, a lack of academic management, the baroque scale of bureaucracy, the relationship between strategic trajectory and personal costs, of practices which lead to contempt and degradation, of management aggrandizement based on power and not academic standing, and the use of the matrix structure to simplify, standardize and regulate organizational practices. At the heart of the chapter is the assertion that these mechanisms are counter-productive and jeopardize the very outcomes which they seek to realize. Such strategies are not only unsustainable but actually damaging to organizations: staff and students. Short-sighted managerialism is successful only in its own terms and by its own measures. The risk is that the paradoxical disregard of the needs of students will result in universities having nothing no offer to their students, however elaborately gift-wrapped. Consequently, this chapter is an exhortation to address the very real needs of academic staff and to enshrine staff matters at the heart of change programmes and initiatives. Clearly, this involves doing more than merely paying lip-service to staff values. Human resource development must undertake a serious look at its contribution to this issue and come to some important conclusions about where its *heart* lies.

Acknowledgement

This chapter is a revised version of H. Höpfl (2000) 'Getting to the heart of HRD: some thoughts on the relationship between quality and performance in higher education in the UK', *Human Resource Development International*, 3, 2: 195–206 http://www.tandf.co.uk/journals/routledge/13678868.html

References

Association of University Teachers (AUT) (1998) 'Profession under pressure', *AUT Update*, issue 50, 30 April.

Averill, J. R. (1976) 'Emotion and anxiety: sociocultural, biological, and psychological determinants', in A. O. Rorty (ed.) (1980) *Explaining Emotions*, Berkeley, CA: University of California Press.

Barthes, R. (1977) *Sade, Fourier, Loyola*, London: Jonathan Cape.

Billig, M. (1987) *Arguing and Thinking: A Rhetorical Approach to Social Psychology*, Cambridge: Cambridge University Press.

Buci-Glucksmann, C. (1994) *Baroque Reason*, London: Sage.

Cummings, T. and Worley, C. (1993) *Organization Development and Change*, 5th edn, Minneapolis, MN: West.

Gayton, E. (1659) *The Art of Longevity; or, A Diaeteticall Institution*, London; (1654) *Pleasant Notes on Don Quixot*, London: Hunt, both in J. R. Roach (1985) *The Player's Passion, Studies in the Science of Acting*, Newark, DE: University of Delaware Press.

Goffman, E. (1969) *The Presentation of Self in Everyday Life*, Harmondsworth: Penguin.

Gouldner, A. (1969) 'The unemployed self', in R. Fraser (ed.) *Work*, vol. 2, Harmondsworth: Penguin.

Hare, A. P. (1985) *Social Interaction as Drama*, Beverly Hills, CA: Sage.

Holt, D. (1989) 'Complex ontology and our stake in the theatre', in J. Shotter and K. Gergen (eds) *Texts of Identity*, London: Sage.

Höpfl, H. and Linstead, S. L. (1993) 'Passion and performance, suffering and the carrying of organizational roles', in S. Fineman (ed.) *Emotion in Organizations*, London: Sage.

Roach, J. R. (1985) *The Player's Passion: Studies in the Science of Acting*, Newark, DE: University of Delaware Press.

Sarbin, T. R. (1986) 'Emotion and act: roles and rhetoric', in R. Harre (ed.) *The Social Construction of Emotion*, Oxford: Blackwell.

Swain, H. (1998) 'Too young, too far, too fast?', *The Times Higher*, 20 February.

Utley, A. (1998) 'Parents alarmed at suicide risk', *The Times Higher*, 1 May.

Part IV

HRD in the future

11 The knowledge revolution and the knowledge economy

The challenge for HRD

Joseph Kessels

Introduction

The economy is rapidly being transformed into a knowledge economy. Therefore, individuals, teams and companies need to develop the necessary competencies to be able to participate in a working life that is mainly based on knowledge productivity. Traditional approaches to management, training and development will not provide the learning environment that is required for knowledge work. Therefore, each company needs to design a corporate curriculum that turns the day to day work environment into a powerful learning environment.

The knowledge economy offers the possibility of prosperity to those who can join the new elite of knowledge workers. It also inherently creates new imbalances. The learning environment should help individuals to develop their talents and take part in various forms of knowledge work. The concepts of knowledge productivity and the corporate curriculum raise also the question of how far knowledge productivity can be managed. These concepts may even question the role of managers in a knowledge economy.

Perceptions of the role of human intervention in economic transactions have changed. The emphasis upon individual physical labour and ability to regulate and coordinate transactions has given way to an emphasis upon the potential human contribution to the production and application of knowledge. Of the products manufactured and services rendered by organizations, material items (such as commodities), capital and physical labour, are now less significant than the combination of knowledge embodied in the product or service. It is widely accepted that we are moving away from an industrial economy to a knowledge economy. Of course, traditional economic aspects such as labour and materials are still important, but it is now critical to be able to add value to products and services through knowledge (Drucker 1993). Economic success requires the ability to improve and innovate.

This slow but dramatic change in the economy will have a tremendous impact on organizing work and the meaning of learning. As a consequence, professionals in the domain of human resource development will have to reconsider their role and their potential contribution to a 'knowledge productive' work environment. This chapter aims to explore the changes brought about by the emerging knowledge economy, their implications for the HRD profession and the need for work-related collaborative research.

A knowledge revolution

One of the views underlying the knowledge economy is that the application of knowledge adds more value than the traditional economic factors like capital, raw materials and labour. Many writers have commented on such an economy, using a variety of synonymous terms including: the 'information society' (Giddens 1994), the 'learning society' (Commission of the European Communities 1996), the 'network society' (Castells 1998), the 'learning economy' (Field 2000; Lundvall and Borrás 1998) and 'economies of expertise' (Venkatraman and Subramaniam 2002). In all these concepts learning and collaboration are key aspects. Organizations must learn quickly, drawing on information from many external as well as internal sources, in order to be able to repeatedly improve and innovate. Sustained competitive advantage depends on the rapid generation and application of 'dynamic capabilities', defined as the firm's ability to integrate, build and reconfigure uniquely valuable competencies (Eisenhardt and Santos 2002). Venkatraman and Subramaniam (2002) argue that the key resources that drive value creation are knowledge and expertise. In economies of expertise strategic capability emerges from knowledge, which is embodied in people. Therefore the authors suggest that we may find a direct and significant link between the talent pool of the employees and the performance of the firm. Here the need for collaboration and networking of employees becomes crucial for the development of an organization.

The Organization for Economic Cooperation and Development (OECD) adopted the idea of an emerging knowledge economy and developed supporting policies in its reports *Lifelong Learning for All* (1996), *Literacy Skills for the Knowledge Society* (1997) and *Knowledge Management in the Learning Society* (2000). In 2001 two OECD publications, *The Well-being of Nations: The Role of Human and Social Capital* (2001a) and *The New Economy: Beyond the Hype – The OECD Growth Project* (2001b), contained a strong plea for major investment in education, training and lifelong learning to enhance economic growth.

An economic necessity for individual learning

In the current timeframe, it is challenging to investigate the characteristics and requirements of an emerging knowledge economy and its implications for individual development in the context of work-related learning. Such analysis might lead to the fresh hypothesis that externally imposed performance goals, power-based managerial positions and the concept of ownership of knowledge-intensive companies in the hands of anonymous shareholders could well inhibit knowledge productivity.

The defence of such propositions resides in the economic necessity for an individual-centred perspective on HRD, with a strong emphasis on the emancipated and autonomous professional. Such a perspective is not restricted to the highly educated service worker: even manual workers must be cooperative, responsible, creative and autonomous (Salling Olesen 2000). It could be argued that the cultural shift from social solidarity and collectivity to individual lifestyles and independent membership might hamper the socially embedded process of knowing. However, the social context of an organization should counterbalance the potential risk of individual self-centeredness, and should foster networks that find their cohesion through the mutual attractiveness, reciprocal appeal, shared interest and the passion of their members (Kessels 2001). Traditional virtues like obedience and loyalty do not propel improvement and innovation. Human capital as a resource for organizational performance will not be enough. It needs to be supported by social capital, based on shared responsibility, integrity, trust, respect for human dignity and environmental awareness (OECD 2001a). All these elements require high levels of critical individual learning.

HRD in Europe

Human resource development is not an exclusive corporate interest. More than ever before, individuals want to master their own lives and expect to contribute to the economy and society. The International Labour Organization (2002) places the individual at the centre of the knowledge and skills-based society and reports impressive growth results in Danish enterprises that combined learning activities and innovation. In Sweden, the Adult Education Initiative (AEI) is the largest adult education investment initiative ever undertaken in the country and explicitly puts the focus on the individual. In Europe, the development of individuals as active citizens of society is given a central place in statements of learning and education objectives (Commission of the European Communities 1996). Learning opportunities and decent work underpin individuals' independence, self-respect and well-being, and, therefore, are the key to overall quality of life. The European Council held a special meeting on 23–24 March 2000 in Lisbon to agree a new strategic goal for the European Union in order to strengthen employment, economic reform and social cohesion as part of the knowledge-based economy. Investing in people is the focal point in the European Union's policies, not only to play an important role in the knowledge economy, but also to resolve existing social problems of unemployment, social exclusion and poverty. Economic growth, innovation, social cohesion and lifelong learning are considered as inseparable (Lisbon European Council 2000). More recently, the 2002 European Council in

Barcelona stressed the importance of education and training in the achievement of the Lisbon ambitions, by setting a new overall goal 'to make Europe's education and training systems a world quality reference by 2010' (Commission of the European Communities 2002). These policies put HRD at the core of a learning society and a knowledge economy.

Knowledge management: an anachronism

The managerial tendency since the 1920s has been based upon routine work and mass production, an approach characterized by standardization with a focus upon efficient procedures and regulations controlled by the 'brains' at the top of the organization, who set the strategy. The problem with this is that in the knowledge economy, where the complexity of work increases and the role of knowledge creation is gaining importance, (top) management is no longer equipped to direct and control the organization in a traditional way. Management now has to be done at every level, and it also requires a contribution of knowledge from all employees at all levels. As a consequence an entirely new approach to employing and managing workers is called for. The old work contract was based upon obedience and loyalty, in return for a decent salary and the company taking care of you and managing your performance. As soon as employees offer an entirely different input to the company, in terms of contributing ideas and proposals to improve and radically innovate, they become part of the collective ambitions of the organization. This is already happening in consultancy businesses and small, knowledge intensive networks.

When capital is displaced by the capability to create knowledge, the legitimate base for a company shifts from ownership by anonymous shareholders to knowledge workers. This leaves managers in an insecure position: the traditional role of the middle person between capital and labour becomes obsolete, and controlling brainwork is hardly possible any more. Many recognize the importance of organizational knowledge and the capability to develop new knowledge, but they often apply the traditional management principles to exploit this potential resource. From a classical business perspective it was inevitable that 'knowledge management' entered the organizational area. Yet, the move to the knowledge economy has been accompanied by an *engineering* approach to knowledge management, based upon building knowledge systems, extracting knowledge and making it explicit – which is far from *knowledge sharing*. When in the new economy knowledge comes to be regarded as an individual capability that cannot be directed, handled, controlled and assessed in a manner familiar to managing financial capital, commodities and physical labour, then knowledge management will appear to be an anachronism, using an outdated term to facilitate a new phenomenon.

However, the concepts of knowledge productivity and the corporate curriculum do raise the question of how far knowledge productivity can be managed. These concepts may even question the role of managers in a knowledge economy. Managerial ability to develop strategies, procedures and control work processes turned top management into the ruling business class of the twentieth century, a position that they inherited from the company owners. In exchange for security and material support employees carried out their jobs in a disciplined and obedient fashion. As knowledge productivity becomes the driving force in the twenty-first century and, as this knowledge production will be found at every level of economic activity, knowledge workers and autonomous professionals will take charge. The corporate curriculum, as a collective learning space, might become the binding force of knowledge networks, and smart communities that heavily depend on shared intrinsic motivation and personal affinity with the content of the job.

Knowledge productivity and HRD

Although the capability of knowledge creation already plays an important role in the new economy, the breakthrough of the knowledge revolution will occur as soon as we are able to apply knowledge systematically to the production of knowledge (Drucker 1993). Understanding the processes of knowledge productivity (Kessels 1995; Kessels and Keursten 2002), organizing a knowledge productive work environment and supporting employees in their ongoing work-related learning will probably become one of the main challenges for HRD.

Where knowledge is dominant – not just among upper management but at all levels of organizations – daily operations should be designed to support *knowledge productivity* (Kessels 2001). This process entails signalling, identifying, gathering, absorbing and interpreting relevant information, using this information to develop new capabilities and applying these capabilities to incremental improvement and radical innovation of operating procedures, products and services. Most of the elements in the description of the concept of knowledge productivity are supported by learning processes. In fact the process of knowledge productivity is a way of facilitated individual, team and organizational learning. These notions on the development of knowledge and making it productive are closely related to human resource development if not at the core of it. In the years ahead, knowledge productivity will become an increasingly critical economic factor. Understanding how knowledge productivity arises and the competence to promote knowledge productivity are becoming critical capacities for participation and survival in a knowledge economy.

The knowledge productivity concept is based on the view that knowledge is a personal competence. More specifically when 'knowledge' is defined in terms of a personal, individual capability, capacity, craftsmanship or expertise, it involves a subjective skill that is inextricably linked with the individual(s) concerned (Malhotra 2000). The objective is not merely to apply rules and procedures in dealing with standard problems but also to improve on such rules, analyse new situations, devise new concepts and improve understanding of the mental and learning processes underlying the capabilities stated. Thus, knowledge development is seen as a combination of individual knowledge application within teams and the company's coordination capabilities in providing the direction and resources for these teams. As Tomassini (2002: 96) concludes: 'the firm is a mechanism for the governance of economic activities, coordinating processes that integrate the knowledge of different individuals for the production of goods and services'.

An environment for knowledge work

For organizations, knowledge becomes productive when the creation and application of knowledge results in gradual improvements and radical innovations of operating procedures, products and services. These processes take place in collaborative work relationships. Knowledge work and learning cannot be enforced on the basis of power, control or contract. It requires a shared ambition that is attractive, comprehensible and meaningful for both employees and the organization. New ways of organizing work for knowledge production need to be developed. The idea that management does not set the goals nor determines the direction of employee development, is central to the concept of knowledge production and the supporting learning. Knowledge workers and autonomous professionals take charge of their own development. The main principles for this concept are self-control and self-organization, integration of working and learning, coaching, leadership and collaboration. Such learning processes take place among staff members and clients in the course of their work. In addition, people are becoming increasingly aware that learning for knowledge work may be stimulated and supported through a variety of means other than formal training programs. Options include issuing special assignments, changing positions or seconding staff members, and actively participating in quality teams and discussion groups. Alternative possibilities entail organizing the work through project management and equipping the workplace with electronic performance support systems (Winslow and Bramer 1994).

Given the vital importance of the learning processes involved, leaving the necessary learning to random opportunity would be imprudent. A systematic approach with a clear purpose therefore appears necessary. Yet the feasibility of managing such learning processes is open to question and is hardly possible in the manner in which we are accustomed to running other industrial processes. Ascertaining knowledge creation appears far from simple, as the necessary learning processes will not appear on command. Alternatives have been presented by Tjepkema (2003) when she studied the learning infrastructure of self-managing work teams. In fact her research introduced a different language to describe the nature and quality of a work-related learning environment. Adopting a socio-constructivist approach, she uses terms such as a 'rich landscape for learning' where learners become motivated, not on the basis of hierarchy and power, but through relevant, authentic and meaningful work, in collaboration with colleagues. Instead of 'managing' the required learning processes, nurturing and supporting the learning ecological system is advised.

Knowledge work probably requires a transformation of work processes. Tapscott (1999) describes this transformation as follows:

> When knowledge is the basis of value creation, work and learning are the same. Knowledge workers, whose 'products' often don't exist in the physical world, have a different relationship to their work and their employers, and different expectations about their professional growth.
>
> (Tapscott 1999: ix)

Similarly one of the main conclusions of Stewart and Tansley's (2002) research on training in the knowledge economy is that this transformation has major implications for HRD:

> Informal and work-based learning is of increasing importance in the knowledge economy. Highly developed learning skills are necessary to maximise the potential offered by conscious and deliberate learning through work.
>
> (Stewart and Tansley 2002: ix)

With her pioneering book on building and sustaining the sources of innovation, Leonard (1998) was among the first to probe the relationship between successful innovators and the way they create, nurture, and grow the experience and accumulated knowledge of their organization. Her research at Harvard on behavioural interaction with technology led her ultimately to a powerful conclusion on enthusiasm for the knowledge content of every activity, that could easily form the core of modern HRD theory:

> This love of learning is woven throughout the organisation, whether the activity be problem solving across internal boundaries, creating knowledge through experimentation, importing from outside, or transferring it to other sites and nations. People who are knowingly engaged in building core technological capabilities are *curious:* they are information seekers. There is a sense of enjoyment in the work – the lightness of step that suggests that building knowledge not only makes good business sense but is *fun.*
>
> (Leonard 1998: 261, original emphases)

These statements, findings and conclusions reinforce the main point that in a knowledge economy the characteristics of work processes can best be described in terms of learning processes, and that these do not appear on command, and require a mutual interest of employee, team and organization.

Principles for work-related learning in a knowledge economy

The traditional approaches to management, training and development will not provide the learning environment that is required for knowledge work. Therefore, each company should consciously develop an integrated plan for learning, 'a corporate curriculum' (Kessels 2001) that turns the day-to-day work environment into a powerful learning environment. On the basis of the argument made in the previous sections, participants in a knowledge economy who wish to integrate the necessary learning in their actual work, need to adopt a number of learning strategies, that involve reflecting on the meaning of their actual work in relationship to their talents and capabilities. These learning strategies also include regular discussions on how to turn the work environment into a rich and interesting setting. As teamwork is so important, members need to confer on how to improve their collaboration and make it more appealing. Individual professionals will search for the hidden factors that inhibit and support their motivation, involvement and commitment. In fact, these strategies aim at enhancing the learning infrastructure of knowledge work.

These considerations and strategies lead to three development principles for knowledge work that refer to the social context, the personal affinity with domain specific content, and deliberate interventions to support the learning culture.

Enhancing reciprocal appeal (the social context)

Knowledge-productive workplaces are rich learning environments in which the social context fosters collaborative efforts. No single manager, instructor or trainer is exclusively responsible. Participants work hard to maintain their reciprocal appeal, which means that they do their best to provide each other with a fruitful learning environment. Important characteristics of this social context for learning seem to be: reciprocal respect, appreciation and integrity, ample security and openness for constructive feedback and confrontations. The communicative and interactive skills of the participants are required to meet high standards. The need for reciprocal appeal is a keenly understood self-interest. Knowledge workers who are dissatisfied with the current learning environment cannot hold others responsible for improving it. If they are unable to improve the interactive setting, they have no choice but to seek out more appropriate surroundings. Teams may lose valuable colleagues this way, while overly eager 'jobhoppers' fail to cultivate their own appeal for others.

Searching for a passion (the content component)

People are clever only if they want to be. Nobody can talk somebody else into curiosity, motivation, interest and ambition. People cannot be 'smart against their will' (Kessels 2002). Discipline, loyalty and obedience may be welcome and valuable support systems for overcoming a temporary hurdle or an impasse. Without any substantive drive, however, they are likely to lead to mediocrity at best. Knowledge-productive environments encourage cultivation of a personal, substantive theme. Such an individual theme and passion for work inspires curiosity and enables information to be traced more quickly. It facilitates establishing connections with attractive, professional networks and stimulates exceptional achievements where others might give up. Knowledge workers need to become competent to navigate through the diffuse arena of affinity, motivation, passion and ambition to be able to develop and apply their capabilities in a productive way.

Enticement towards knowledge productivity (supporting the learning culture)

Cultivating reciprocal appeal serves primarily to create a favourable social context and a rich learning infrastructure, while searching for a passion establishes the foundation for substance and subject matter expertise. However, promoting knowledge productivity also requires the competence to work deliberately and systematically on the quality of the social context and the substantive component. The desire to manage, control and monitor in these matters is becoming increasingly difficult to fulfil. The growing interest in self-guidance is apparent in both work and learning contexts. If we touch here on issues that cannot be managed in the traditional way this raises the question of how we can tempt or entice each other towards knowledge productivity? The main objective is to develop the capability to design a work environment that fosters the development of capacities like learning to learn, organizing reflection, increasing reflexivity and basically applying knowledge to knowledge development.

These three principles for knowledge development directly support the learning infrastructures needed for the successful establishment of communities of practice as described by Wenger (1998) and Wenger and Snyder (2000), the ethical, social and psychological attributes of the social relationships in networks as identified by Lundvall and Borrás (1997) and the development of social capital marked by trust, cooperation and mutual sharing as explained by Putnam (1993) and Nahapiet and Goshal (1998).

In a knowledge economy, where improvement and innovation are required for long-term survival, standardization is not the goal, but rather the extraordinary, the surprising, the artistic. This assumption not only affects managerial thinking, but also influences our perception of the characteristics of almost every employee and knowledge worker. As a result, one of the arguments in the upcoming debate is that the required knowledge for improvement and innovation is basically an individual, subjective competence. Team learning and organizational learning provide the context for individual knowing. The knowledge economy will probably require the autonomous, independent individual to undertake learning for personal growth (Merriam and Caffarella 1999). However, this will happen in a context of communicative rationality: a process of reaching understanding through the cooperative negotiation of common definitions of a situation (Habermas 1984). Here the paradox of emancipation comes into play. Howell (2001) observed that when workers become active participants in process improvement, they also take on more and more responsibility. Doing so, they inevitably start questioning whether their interests match the interests of the organization.

Knowledge development, improvement and innovation require a high level of personal involvement from employees. This capability cannot exist without critical reflection and emancipation. Emancipated employees will critically examine the corporate goals, the ethics of governance and shareholder property of their knowledge work. In a knowledge economy, corporate success and individual emancipation will be difficult to separate. Are top managers and shareholders able and prepared to pay this price for sustainable economic growth?

Individual knowing at the basis of knowledge productivity

From such a perspective it is evident that the focus in HRD should shift to the individual, to individual learning, objectives, motivation and conditions. This means that work-related learning will inevitably comprise reflection, learning from mistakes, critical opinion sharing, challenging groupthink, asking for feedback, experimenting, knowledge sharing and career awareness. These characteristics of critical reflective work behaviour are identified in the research of Van Woerkom (2003) and point towards an emancipated, autonomous professional as the main protagonist in a knowledge intensive work environment.

Such work environments should encourage employees to become self-directed learners:

> to pursue their interests, to find personal meaning, and to adapt to and change their life circumstances . . . adult learners are assumed to be capable of framing their own choices, reflecting on their options, and making responsible, informed decisions that serve their interest.
>
> (Percival 1996: 138)

When the knowledge economy thrives on the basis of individual learning and critical knowing, this has major implications for organizing work, establishing knowledge networks and promoting professional development.

The deliberate choice of incorporating personal meaning, the social context and ethical values within the concept of knowledge productivity supports the prevalence of tacit knowledge. However, its inherent social embedding and implicit character rather than the formal scientific knowledge expressed in peer reviewed research and protected patents, will be central to organization-based knowledge development.

Implications for HRD

Research on knowledge development in the context of organizations is making it increasingly clear that far more attention needs to be focused on how to bring workplace communities of practice together in a shared organizational purpose, without, however, destroying the unique self-regulating properties that make them so attractive to individuals and so powerful in driving the knowledge process. This realization lends further weight to earlier conclusions that the emphasis in knowledge-creating organizations should be less on devising management systems to 'control' learning or to 'manage' knowledge, and more on encouraging people to think creatively and provide the skills and support systems to share and apply their findings to benefit the organization.

The concept of the corporate curriculum requires the HRD function to produce and promote processes and initiatives to support the acquisition of subject matter expertise, learning to identify and deal with new problems, cultivating reflective skills, acquiring communication and social skills, supporting self-regulation of motivation, affinities and emotions, promoting peace and stability, and stimulating creative turmoil (Kessels 2001).

It is quite widely agreed that HRD professionals need to become learning facilitators, and learning architects who can promote strategically valuable knowledge (Stewart and Tansley 2002; Tjepkema *et al.* 2002). The move away from training and the view that HRD is an organization-based process is widely recognized. McGoldrick *et al.* (2002: 396) conclude: 'HRD will be increasingly concerned with facilitating the learning of individuals, teams and organisations through the design, structuring and organisation of work itself.'

The concept of the knowledge productive work environment focuses not only on the social aspects of a favourable learning climate, but also on the need for individuals to explore and invest in their personal domains of interest, and to create meaningful work (Kessels and Keursten 2002).

To do so HRD is not an objective science of 'social engineering' but has a strong philosophical dimension which needs to be made explicit. When exploring knowledge as a social process of 'knowing' the key issue will become rather the *emancipation* of the knowledge worker – engendering a new freedom for knowledge workers, as it is they who are at the centre of knowledge development. Qualities of social capital, trust, respect, integrity, ethics, meaningful work, affective involvement and practical wisdom assume key significance, in order to generate knowledge that will bring benefits to all parties, whether in the board room or in the workplace.

This way of reasoning brings us back to the roots of adult education focusing on individual learning experiences (Lindeman 1926), critical consciousness and liberation (Freire 1970), interventions for promoting well-being (Ten Have 1975), emancipatory learning and critical theory (Habermas 1984), critical, reflective thinking and analysis (Brookfield 1987), the direct facilitation of the development of individuals through improving the educative quality of their environment (Knowles 1990) and lifelong learning and the new educational order (Field 2000).

This case for a critical and individual development perspective, leading to the emancipation of knowledge workers, may engender a strong reminiscence of the radical and politically engaged adult educators of the 1970s. However, the argument developed here is not a naive U-turn to a socialist, communist or anarchistic past, in a period of economic crises, following the collapse of an over-enthusiastic free market play.

Promoting the development in organizations of an appropriate learning culture does not only require critical thinking and emancipatory learning. When the focus shifts from the external and internal transfer of explicit knowledge to the social construction of tacit knowledge among members of informal networks (Brown and Duguid 1991), more emphasis has to be placed on creating favourable conditions for learning in the workplace than on organizing the provision of formal training. The new literature on technological change, improvement and innovation emphasizes an evolutionary process, which takes the form of the steady accumulation of a tacit capability through work-related learning processes. Thus, public knowledge can be effectively exploited only by firms that develop learning processes embodied in a form of social organization. Even economists start to acknowledge that successful linkage between science, research and technology requires face-to-face contacts in communicating the results of complex learning processes which embody a tacit element (Cantwell 1999). Improvement and innovation require individual learning in a favourable social context.

Conclusion: the agenda for HRD

The argument of this chapter is that HRD should build expertise in a number of domains. First, it should contribute to an understanding of the process of knowledge productivity, improvement and innovation, and the support of learning. Second, it should develop interventions to facilitate the learning functions of the corporate curriculum for knowledge work, and with an emphasis upon the learning infrastructure (Tjepkema 2003) and critical reflective work behaviour (Van Woerkom 2003). Third, it should start a dialogue on the need for emancipation as a prerequisite for sustainable growth. Finally, it should promote the development of social capital in which knowledge networks are embedded.

References

Brookfield, S. D. (1987) *Developing Critical Thinkers: Challenging Adults to Explore Alternative Ways of Thinking and Acting*, San Francisco, CA: Jossey-Bass.

Brown, J. S. and Duguid, P. (1991) 'Organizational learning and communities-of-practice: towards a unified view of working, learning and innovation', *Organization Science*, 2, 1: 40–57.

Cantwell, J. (1999) 'Innovation as the principal source of growth in the global economy', in D. Archibungi, J. Howells and J. Michie (eds) *Innovation Policy in a Global Economy*, Cambridge: Cambridge University Press.

Castells, M. (1998) *End of Millennium: The Information Age – Economy, Society and Culture*, vol. 3, Oxford: Blackwell.

Commission of the European Communities (1996) 'Teaching and learning: towards the learning society', *Le Magazine*, 5: 3–5.

Commission of the European Communities (2002) *Communication from the Commission. European Benchmarks in Education and Training: Follow-up to the Lisbon European Council*, Brussels: EU Com.

Drucker, P. F. (1993) *Post-capitalist Society*, Oxford: Butterworth Heinemann.

Eisenhardt, K. M. and Santos, F. M. (2002) 'Knowledge-based view: a new theory of strategy?', in A. Pettigrew, H. Thomas and R. Whittington (eds) *Handbook of Strategy and Management*, London: Sage.

Field, J. (2000) *Lifelong Learning and the New Educational Order*, Stoke-on-Trent: Trentham Books.

Freire, P. (1970) *Pedagogy of the Oppressed*, New York: Herter and Herter.

Giddens, A. (1994) 'Living in a post-traditional society', in U. Beck, A. Giddens and S. Lash (eds) *Reflexive Modernization: Politics, Tradition and Aesthetics in the Modern Social Order*, Cambridge: Polity Press and Blackwell.

Habermas, J. (1984) *The Theory of Communicative Action, vol. 1: Reason and Rationalization of Society*, Boston, MA: Beacon Press.

Howell, S. (2001) *The Production of Knowledge in Work Teams: The View from Below*, http://www.edst.educ.ubc.ca/aerc/2001/2001howell.htm

International Labour Organization (2002) *Learning and Training for Work in the Knowledge Society*, http://www.ilo.org/public/english/employment/skills/recomm/report/ch_int.htm

Kessels, J. W. M. (1995) 'Opleidingen in arbeidsorganisaties. Het ambivalente perspectief van de kennisproduktiviteit' [Training and development in organizations. The ambivalent perspective of knowledge productivity] *Comenius*, 15, 2: 179–193.

Kessels, J. W. M. (2001) 'Learning in organizations: a corporate curriculum for the knowledge economy', *Futures*, 33: 479–506.

Kessels, J. W. M. (2002) 'You cannot be smart against your will', in B. Garvey and B. Williamson (eds) *Beyond Knowledge Management: Dialogue, Creativity and the Corporate Curriculum*, Harlow: FT Prentice Hall.

Kessels, J. and Keursten, P. (2002) 'Creating a knowledge productive work environment', *LLinE, Lifelong Learning in Europe*, 7, 2: 104–112.

Knowles, M. (1990) *The Adult Learner: A Neglected Species*, 4th edn, Houston, TX: Gulf.

Leonard, D. (1998) *Wellsprings of Knowledge: Building and Sustaining the Source of Innovation*, Boston, MA: Harvard Business School Press.

Lindeman, E. C. (1926) *The Meaning of Adult Education*, New York: New Republic.

Lisbon European Council (2000) *Presidency conclusions*, http://www.ue.eu.int/Newsroom/LoadDoc.asp?BID=76&DID=60917&from+&LANG=1

Lundvall, B.-A. and Borrás, S. (1997) *The Globalizing Learning Economy: Implications for Innovation Policy*, Luxembourg: Office for Official Publications of the European Communities.

McGoldrick, J., Stewart, J. and Watson, S. (2002) 'Postscript: the future of HRD research', in J. McGoldrick, J. Stewart and S. Watson (eds) *Understanding Human Resource Development: A Research-based Approach*, London: Routledge.

Malhotra, Y. (2000) 'Role of organizational controls in knowledge management: is knowledge management really an "oxymoron"?', in Y. Malhotra (ed.) *Knowledge Management and Virtual Organizations*, Hershey, PA: Idea Group.

Merriam, S. B. and Caffarella, R. S. (1999) *Learning in Adulthood.* San Francisco, CA: Jossey-Bass.

Nahapiet, J. and Goshal, S. (1998) 'Social capital, intellectual capital and the organizational advantage', *Academy of Management Review*, 23, 2: 242–266.

Organization for Economic Co-operation and Development (OECD) (2001a) *The Well-being of Nations: The role of Human and Social Capital*, Paris: OECD.

OECD (2001b) *The New Economy: Beyond the Hype – The OECD Growth Project*, Paris: OECD.

Percival, A. (1996) 'Invited reaction: an adult educator responds', *Human Resource Development Quarterly*, 7, 2: 131–139.

Putnam, R. (1993) *Making Democracy Work*, Princeton, NJ: Princeton University Press.

Salling Olesen, H. (2000) *Life Long Learning and Collective Experience*, http://www.edst.educ.ubc.ca/aerc/2000/sallingolesenh1–final.PDF

Stewart, J. and Tansley, C. (2002) *Training in the Knowledge Economy*, London: Chartered Institute of Personnel and Development.

Tapscott, D. (ed.) (1999) *Creating Value in the Network Economy*, Boston, MA: Harvard Business School Publishing.

Ten Have, T. T. (1975) *Andragologie in blauwdruk* [Blue-print of andragology], Groningen: H. D. Tjeenk Willink.

Tjepkema, S. (2003) 'The learning infrastructure of self-managing work teams', doctoral dissertation, University of Twente, Enschede: Twente University Press.

Tjepkema S., Stewart, J., Sambrook, S., Mulder, M., Ter Horst, H. and Scheerens, J. (eds) (2002) *HRD and Learning Organisations in Europe*, London: Routledge.

Tomassini, M. (2002) 'Theories of knowledge development within organisations – a preliminary overview', in B. Nyhan (ed.) *Taking Steps Towards the Knowledge Society: Reflections on the Process of Knowledge Development*, Cedefop reference series 35, Luxembourg: Office for Official Publications of the European Communities.

Van Woerkom, M. (2003) 'Critical reflection at work: bridging individual and organisational learning', doctoral dissertation, University of Twente, Netherlands.

Venkatraman, N. and Subramaniam, M. (2002) 'Theorizing the future of strategy: questions for shaping strategy research in the knowledge economy', in A. Pettigrew, H. Thomas and R. Whittington (eds) *Handbook of Strategy and Management*, London: Sage.

Wenger, E. (1998) *Communities of Practice: Learning, Meaning, and Identity*, Cambridge: Cambridge University Press.

Wenger, E. C. and Snyder, W. M. (2000) 'Communities of practice: the organizational frontier', *Harvard Business Review*, January–February: 139–145.

Winslow, C. and Bramer, W. L. (1994) *Future Work: Putting Knowledge to Work in the Knowledge Economy*, New York: Free Press.

12 The evolution of HR?

Monica Lee

Introduction

As the various branches of social science have developed the way in which they build accounts of the world and our existence within it, they have moved away from each other and from the natural sciences. Barklow *et al.* (1992) note that the natural sciences have retained a common root in their development, such that any move forward needs not only to fit with its 'home' discipline, but also to be concurrent with all others in order to be accepted. This has not happened in a consistent way within the social sciences. In adopting a post-scientific perspective, postmodernism has challenged many of the contradictory yet self-sustaining frameworks that have developed. Yet in creating a world that is devoid of structure other than our own unique and individual structuring of it, postmodernism is actively engaged in preventing constructive (or 'with structure') dialogue between the various disciplines of the social sciences (though see Cilliers 1998). In this chapter I shall argue that there are processes that underlie the human condition, but before I do so it is worth noting (as I shall expand upon later) that I am using language loosely. By this I mean that each of the discipline areas that I bridge in this chapter has their own (often conflicting) terminology and reference points. In taking a bridging approach I stand the risk of offending the mores (and the adherents) of each discipline. My choice of words is therefore governed by the need to paint a coherent picture, rather than to meet the specific requirements of any one area of thought.

Underlying processes

In this section I shall explore what these processes might be through illustration. I do this to emphasize their metaphorical or representational nature. The words employed are used to represent concepts which are themselves socially constructed representations; in other words, while there might be some commonality of language between the various constructions discussed here it must be remembered that the meanings behind the words are dynamic, situated and ephemeral. One word may mean different things in different contexts and different things to different people (Jankowicz 1996).

I am therefore trying to explore the parameters of the concepts or meanings behind the words, while acknowledging that these concepts are also socially constructed and essentially indefinable.

Four main views of 'management' can be identified within research and writing on the subject: the classical, scientific, processual and phenomenological (Lee 1997a). Within the classical view, managers must be able to create appropriate rules and procedures for others to follow, they must be good judges of people and able to take independent action as and when required. Good managers are assumed to be 'born' rather than 'made' and so management development is a matter of selecting the 'right' people with leadership potential. The *scientific* view assumes that human behaviour is rational, and that people are motivated by economic criteria (Taylor 1947). Within this view 'correct' decisions can be identified and implemented appropriately through scientific analysis, and thus good management techniques can be acquired by anyone with the right training, and 'training departments' systematically identify and fill the *training gap*. Both of these approaches assume a structured and known world based upon rational principles and in which rationality leads to success. The other two approaches to management assume a world in which agency (rather then structure) is the predominant force. The *processual* view of management assumes that economic advantage will come to those who are best able to spot opportunities, to learn rapidly, and to create appropriate commitment among colleagues. Human resource development is seen to help managers develop leadership and interpersonal skills, creativity, self-reliance and the ability to work in different cultures. Although the individual is the main stakeholder in his or her own development, the direction of the organization (and thus of an individual's development) remains at the behest of senior management who, through initiatives such as Business Process Re-engineering (BPR), aspire to mould the organization and the people within it. *Phenomenological* management differs from processual management by the way in which the activities drive the functions, strategies and even leadership of the organization. For many, management is about 'purpose' and 'doing' while phenomenology is about the 'study' of 'being'. All individuals are seen to collude with their situation and, through that collusion, are together responsible for the running and development of the organization (despite some being senior management and others from the shop floor). 'Management' is about being part of a system whose activities change as a function of the system and of its relationship to its environment.

These four approaches link quite closely to the four ways in which the word 'development' is used in the literature, as delineated through an entirely different line of research (Lee 1997b). Development was used to indicate a form of *maturation* – the (inevitable or natural) progression through series of stages of life cycle. When used to indicate *shaping* it similarly implied a known end-point to which the individual or organization was steered by the application of various tools, within a known, quantifiable and manageable environment. In contrast, the other two uses of the word 'development' that were identified did not have a known end-point. Development as a *voyage* was evident in literature about personal development – in which the self was the agent and the object, and development as *emergent* was evident in social science literature particularly, in which the lines between the individual and the organization became blurred and the focus was upon co-development and co-regulation.

Figure 12.1 shows a representation of these four forms of development, presented as a typology (in which the lines of the figure indicate the strength of spheres of influence, and not delineations or divisive categories) and maps on to these the four views of management discussed earlier. This latter point is important and worth emphasizing. I am *not* here discussing 'real' differences and saying that there exist four ways of 'doing' management or development, or that management or development are 'things' that can be done, or can be done to. In contrast, I am saying that there appear to be differences in the way that people talk about, or enact, whatever it is that constitutes 'development' or 'management' in their eyes, and, that there appears to be some consistency within the realization of those differences. These points of similarity could, of course, merely be a product of my imagination – my own research being the common factor between the two; however, others have reached the same conclusion.

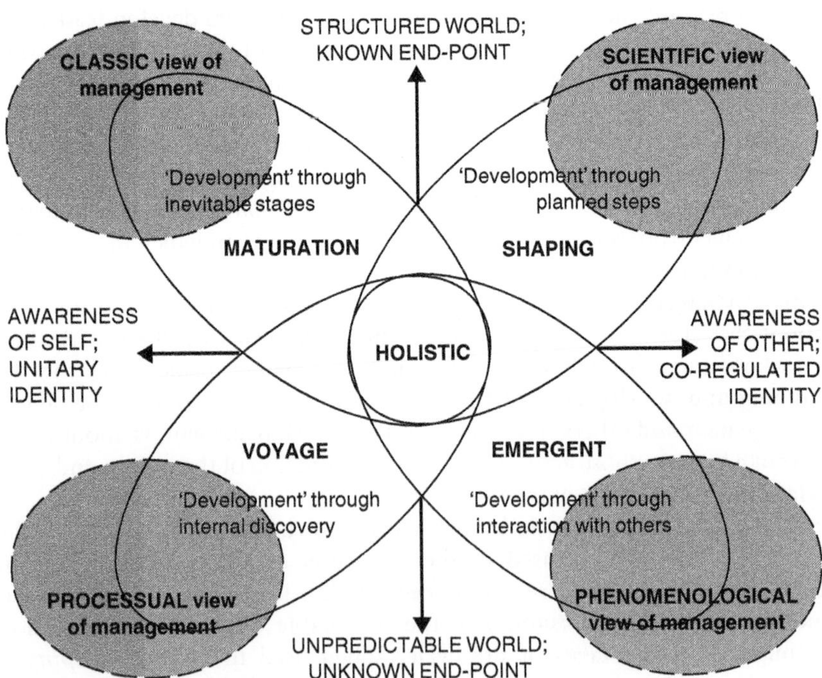

Figure 12.1 Four types of 'development' (after Lee 1977b).

Parallels to these notions can be seen in the work of Carl Jung (1964, 1971). Jung suggested that while everyone seeks to make sense of the world around them, they do not focus on the same things. He suggested that there exist two processes (perception and judgement) which are independent of each other, and both are bi-polar. Perception is the process by which individuals make sense (consciously or subconsciously) of their surroundings, and is thus mediated by previous understandings, expectation and anticipations, memory and unconscious influences (from the 'promissory notes' of metaphor, myth and rhetoric (Soyland 1994) to primal drives). When gathering information people *prefer* to focus *either* on the 'here-and-now' information from their senses, *or* on the 'what-if' information they 'intuit' from the possibilities and patterns they see developing. Judgement is the process of deciding which of the many alternative perceptival interpretations available at any one instant to adopt as 'reality'. Judgement is influenced by previous understandings and is more likely to be based upon *post-hoc* rationalization than the traditionally accepted view of 'scientifically' weighing up the alternatives and rationally choosing the best option in advance of the final decision. When deciding about the information they have gathered, people *prefer* to make decisions based on objective thinking, by analysing and weighing the alternatives from a wide perspective, *or* to make decisions based on their feelings for each particular situation in an individualized manner.

There is strong evidence of individual variation in preferred perceptual and judgemental styles (see, for example, Mitroff and Kilmann 1978; Reason 1981). Such variation forms the basic premise of the Myers Briggs Type Indicator (MBTI), a management assessment and development tool for individuals and organizations that is being increasingly used worldwide. It is beyond the remit of this chapter to go into the MBTI based literature in any depth, though see Briggs Myers and McCaulley (1985), Krebs Hirsh and Kummerow (1987) for more detail. I raise the issue here to record general acceptance of the MBTI tool, and thus (by implication) the assumptions on which the tool is based. Other researchers have used Jungian dimensions as a basis upon which to build an analysis of their area, for example, Tufts-Richardson (1996) links Jungian typology to individual spirituality by mapping four types of spiritual path, while McWhinney (1992) maps four paths of change, or choice, for organizations and society. Similarly, as can be seen in Figure 12.2, the work of other researchers who make no claim to root their work in Jungian typology, such as that of Hofstede (1991), can also be mapped onto these dimensions.

I have included different approaches to learning in this figure as I shall refer to them in the next section. However, before moving on I wish to emphasize that we cannot label the dimensions in a fixed and unique manner, but we do need to understand their qualia better if they are fundamental to our way of describing and enacting self and society. In the following section I shall explore the underlying dimensions of these quaternities further

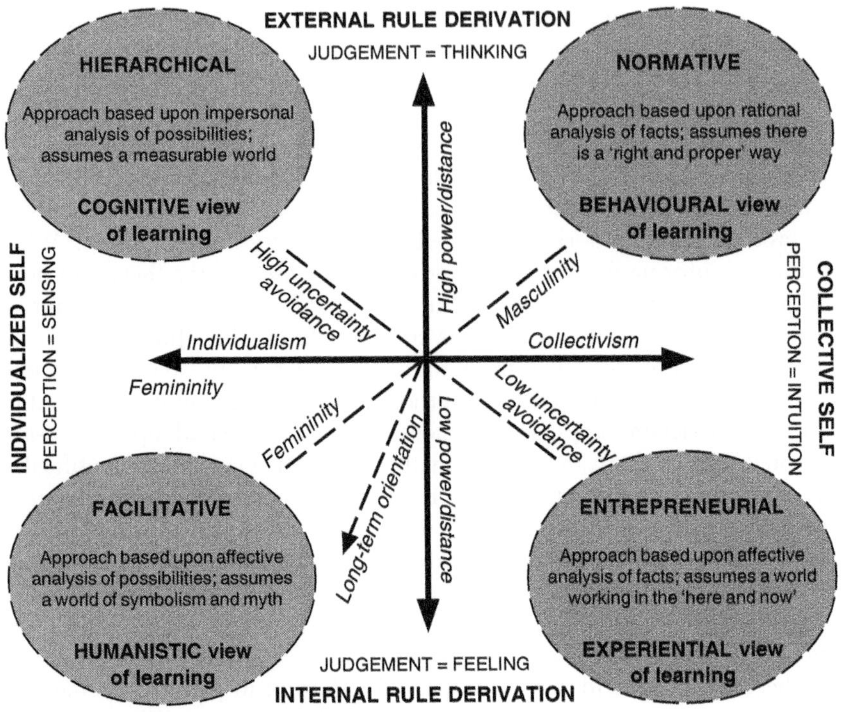

Figure 12.2 Mapping of typologies.

by positing their evolutionary basis, and the way in which they might be promulgated.

An evolutionary basis?

Research into evolutionary psychology and psychiatry (Barklow *et al.* 1992; Bradshaw 1997) suggests that human (and primate) affectional development progresses through the maturation of specific affectional systems, and that 'All major psychiatric syndromes may thus be conceived as inappropriate expressions of evolved propensities concerned with adaptive behaviour in the domains of group membership . . ., group exclusion . . ., and mating' (Stevens and Price 1996: 29). They argue that there exist two 'great archetypal systems'. The first formative experience faced by our proto-human ancestors would be that associated with parenting and family. As our ancestors developed the pattern of bearing live young that needed parental care for survival, they also developed the pattern of behaviours and emotions that bonded parent and child in a dependent relationship. Thus their first great archetypal system has to do with attachment, affiliation, care-giving, care-receiving and altruism. As the child grew, was replaced by other children, and eventually became a parent themselves, so 'self' – and as a necessary and integral part of that process, 'not-self', or the 'other' – emerged. Therefore, the first fundamental dynamic played out in each person's life is that of self and other. This pervades the whole of our existence and is the core of self-development literature.

The second formative experience was that of collectivity. For 99 per cent of its existence, humanity has lived in 'extended organic kinship groups' of about forty to fifty individuals, comprising six to ten adult males, twelve to twenty child-bearing females, and about twenty juveniles and infants (Fox 1989). As predators, they were sufficiently effective not to need to develop large aggregations, flocking behaviour and high sensitivity to others in the group in order to survive, but they were sufficiently weak that they could only exceptionally survive as solitary individuals. We are therefore left with an awareness of society and its necessary structures and hierarchy, and also of individual agency. This equates to Stevens and Price's (1996) second great archetypal system, that concerned with rank, status, discipline, law and order, territory and possessions. Stevens and Price posit that the search for achievement of archetypal goals occurs throughout the whole of the life cycle, though the presenting face of the goals we seek changes as our circumstances change with age. These dual aspects of our collective psyche (self and other, and the structured law and the anarchic body: Höpfl 1995) can be seen mirrored in the tensions between sociology and psychology, or between structure and agency, as elucidated by Giddens (1976).

In other words, we can identify two fundamental processes derived from our evolutionary history that continue to affect our humanity and our enactment of our existence. I want to make a clear distinction between the discussion here about the existence of fundamental or underlying processes and our day-to-day appreciation of them. Our daily lives and ways of seeing them are framed by our sense making of our past and by our anticipation of the future; we each live in our own self-constructed worlds. The surface diversity of our own worlds does not, however, detract from the existence of underlying processes. Our existence is interpreted differently across the spread of our civilizations, but that is a matter of the ways in which we choose to make sense of our existence.

Autopoietic mechanism for promulgation of the subsets

Socialization can be seen as a mechanism by which the tensions and their resolution between self and other, and between structure and agency, are promulgated and emphasized through succeeding generations. I base my argument on the view that social development is a process of creative interaction in which 'individuals dynamically alter their actions with respect to the ongoing and anticipated actions of their partners' (Fogel 1993: 34; Smith 1992; McWhinney 1992; Lee 1994). Relationships exist within mutually constructed conventions or frames of reference (Kelly 1955;

Duncan 1991: 345; Moreland and Levine 1989) and a dynamic view of culture is facilitated (Hatch 1993). 'Society' exists in so far as people agree to its existence – and could be a family unit or a nation. In some way (whether by being born into and thus socialized within it, as in a family or nation; through meeting like-minded people and thus forming friendship groups; or formally through induction into an organization) individuals come to identify (and be identified by others) as part of a community. In doing so they help create and collude with underlying values and norms. This process starts at birth and is a basal acculturation mechanism in which the underlying processes are the same whether the focus is upon family and friendship groupings, temporary micro-cultures, small or large organizations, or national culture (Burns 1977).

There is empirical evidence of correlation between form of parenting and the child's life stance (Baumrind 1973; Bee 1985) and between career and family history (Cromie *et al.* 1992). Similarly, there is evidence that choice of curricula, methodological approach and course design are partially governed by the value base of the providers, and thus perpetuate that value base (Ashton 1988; Boyacigiller and Adler 1991). Thus the approach to learning adopted by each society has a fundamental effect upon the continuation of the parameters of that particular society (Lee 1996). In Figure 12.1 different forms of learning were mapped against the archetypal parameters of self and other, and of structure and agency. In practical terms, the 'cognitive' environment carries with it group norms about received wisdom and the value of qualifications. Power is vested in those who have achieved qualifications and those who can give them. Cogent argument carries more importance than does applicability or individual difference. The 'problem' student (or heretic: Harshbarger 1973) would be someone who lacked sufficient intelligence to master the required concepts. The 'behavioural' environment focuses upon activity, functionalism and the importance of the end result. Norms are about identifying competence, and filling the 'training gap' to achieve appropriate levels of competence. The heretic is someone unable to demonstrate the required competence. The 'humanistic' environment focuses upon difference and equality. Received wisdom (in so far as it epitomizes a particular view of reality) is inappropriate, as are identifiable and assessable 'competencies' (in so far as they epitomize a 'right' way of doing things). The problem participant is unwilling to explore and share their affective and attitudinal aspects. In the 'experiential' environment the focus is on actionable outcome; the end justifies the means. The heretic is someone who questions the route, or prefers inactivity. 'The confidence to act is a prerequisite for learning' (Blackler 1993).

It is rare, in real life, that 'learning' occurs only within one approach. Instead, it is much more likely that in any situation one learns more 'holistically' (Lee 1996). Honey and Mumford (1989) suggest that 'experience' plays a part in any learning, regardless of whether or not it is acknowledged or focused upon within the educational process. One of the best known models of experiential learning is that of Kolb (1974, 1984) who suggests that the process of learning is cyclical, revolving through experience, reflection, theorizing and planning. In Figure 12.3 this is represented by the large (arrowed) circle. From this perspective, we really learn only by engaging in all aspects of the activity.

Transformative experiences, therefore, appear to be those that force us to (re)examine our worldview (Emery and Trist 1965; Pascale 1990). Any 'experience' is an opportunity for learning; however, as Dewey (1938) pointed out, 'It is not enough to insist upon the necessity of experience, nor even of activity in experience. Everything depends upon the quality of experience which is had . . . every experience lives in further experiences.' Vasilyuk (1984) takes it further, building the case that all learning that has a transformative effect upon us is derived from a clash between our understanding of the world and our experience, such that learning and change are painful processes of redefinition. Romanelli and Tushman (1994) offer empirical support for rapid, discontinuous change in organizations being driven by major environmental changes.

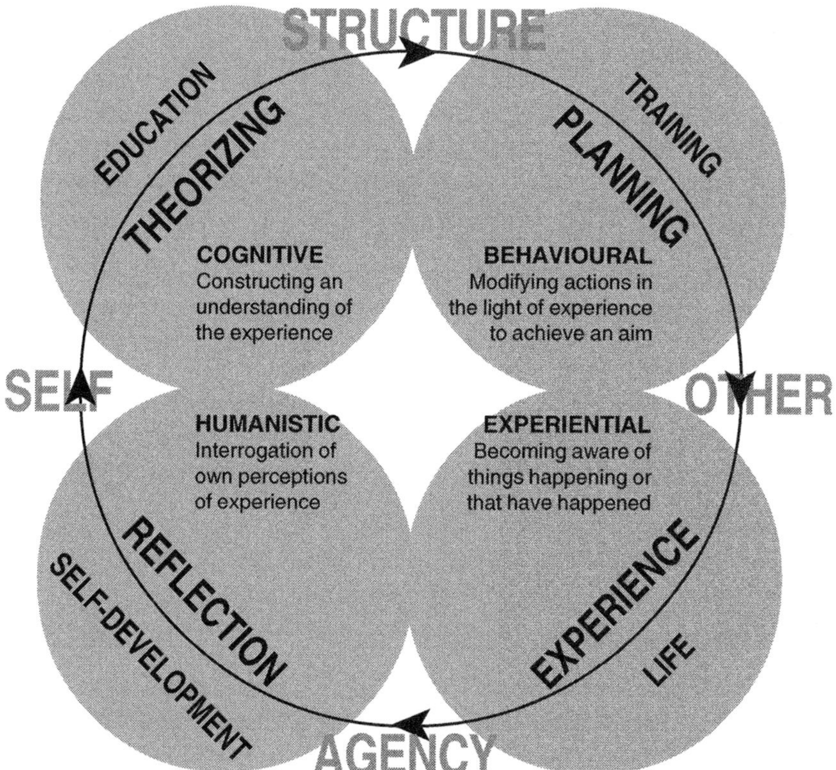

Figure 12.3 Movement through typologies (after Lee 1996).

Similarly, Stevens and Price argue that our changing lives necessitate renegotiating our position with respect to the great archetypal systems, and that 'Psychopathology results when the environment fails, either partially or totally, to meet one (or more) archetypal need(s) in the developing individual' (Stephens and Price 1996: 34). In the terms of complexity theory, transformative experiences occur at bifurcation points, when the system and the environment impact in such a way that the system can either continue in its current, well travelled pattern, or shift to some way of being that is new and unpredicted (though not necessarily unpredictable). Indeed, the current analysis would suggest that the system is likely to shift to incorporate qualia of a different worldview.

I have argued that there exist two main bi-polar underlying processes by which the human condition is structured, and that these give rise to four main archetypes. The processes of socialization, or learning, emphasize particular aspects of our worldview, such that the various systems or subsystems, be they individuals, organizations or nations, have a tendency to enact the qualia of a single archetype. However, although I have talked of the qualia of the archetypes, I have deliberately failed to define them other than by example. Archetypes, by their nature, are indefinable in the scientistic sense, and also, as discussed earlier, the qualia are unmeasurable other than dialectically (Pascale 1990) by reference to their 'opposite'. Furthermore, that 'opposite' might be different under different occasions or interpretations. For example, in one situation it was found that the word 'conflict' was interpreted by some people to be 'contested negotiation' while others saw it as 'a fight to the death', and acted accordingly with misunderstanding on both sides (Lee 1998). We could extrapolate that for these people the opposite to their views of conflict would be the similar but subtly different qualities of 'easy negotiation' and 'peaceful life'. We live within our own worldview yet in order to understand or even describe it we need to compare it with that of others in a dialectic manner. In other words – to know what we are, we also have to know what we are not. We can not categorize the human condition in a positivistic mutually exclusive sense, but we can use the arguments above to develop a dialectically based typology.

A metatypology has been developed, but a few pages of text are too limiting to explore it. The benefit of a metatypology is that it helps model the variability of social form. Different parts of the system might well adopt different configurations, and configurations might change as 'needed'. The activities of the system are emergent and feed back into it (Weick 1977), they can influence all other aspects of the system, and the system itself can be 'far-from-equilibrium' (Stacey 1993). This approach, therefore, denies the ability to 'plan' or 'control' organizational development; it argues for a resource-based view of the organization in which the role of 'managing' is fragmentary (Mintzberg 1979) and offers a valuable critique of the established discipline of strategy. In addition, because this view eschews ideas of (real) control by a hierarchy, as well as questioning the ability of the organization to (really) predict or plan, it is more in tune with work that questions the serial and causal nature of our existence (Lee and Flatau 1996).

From Heraclitus onwards (ca 500 BC) it has been suggested that humanity is in a state of always 'becoming' despite the appearance of structured categorization and 'being' fostered by western scientism (Lee 2001; Stacey *et al.* 2000). In other words, our lives are dynamic, and in a state of constant change. Fixed goals, known end-points and clear delineations are tools that we use to provide a sense of stability, but that sense is merely a mechanism and is false with respect to the wider reality of existence. The meta-typology, presented here with lines and detail, is merely an attempt to indicate underlying structures; those structures exist, however, not as things in themselves but are presented as a possible pattern of relationships: a representation of the relationships between other representations. As noted earlier, even the terminology used is just a representation. For example, Campbell and Muncer (1987) show that both occupational role and gender are indicative of whether a person views 'aggression' as a functional act aimed at imposing control over other people, or in expressive terms as a breakdown of self-control over anger. Thus understanding of the word 'aggression' co-varies with the axes and will be interpreted by different readers in different ways.

HRD as the relationship between representations

As illustrated in Figures 12.1 and 12.2, one's view of the nature and role of HRD is dependent upon one's worldview. This chapter, however, suggests that, regardless of one's 'understanding', or the terminology used, that which might be called the development of human resources is actually located at the dynamic and co-creative interface between the elements of the system, and between subsystems, such that interacting, they become more than the sum of the parts. Thus the business of HRD, in so far as it exists as a concept and a practice, is concerned with the relationship between the representations. Research into HRD is, in effect, research into the processes that underlie the human condition, and the practice of HRD is about influencing the relationships that comprise the glue of the human condition.

As we research into HRD it means that we need to be aware that we are researching the intangible and unmeasurable. We can catch glimpses of what we are looking for and we can try to represent or model it, but we need to avoid the temptation to overly objectify or embody that which we research. The 'individual' and the 'organization' are not unitary bounded concepts; they are part of a whole and are identifiable by their relationship to the whole. It is the interactions that are of importance, rather than descriptions of 'purpose'. Similarly, a change in approach requires a change in the language and meaning that is used. For example, it would be inappropriate to talk of 'organizations' as if they had a body and could be anthropomorphized, or of 'people' as if they were machine cogs within 'the organization' whose function was to 'operate' if we were to adopt a loosely bounded or relativistic view of these elements of the system.

As practitioners of HRD we intervene in the human condition with some aim in mind, yet both the *outcomes* and the *value* of them are subject to interpretation. There is no longer necessarily a clear and obvious route between cause and effect – and one person's preferred 'outcome' might be someone else's feared possibility or cause. In both theorizing about HRD and in the practice of HRD we can no longer assume that a particular intervention at a particular time will produce a known effect. We lose the gloss of certainty that many HRD professionals feel is necessary for their work as academics, consultants, trainers etc. HRD and learning are becoming more central to the needs of the nation (as in Watson 1994) and this shift in provision further increases the complexity and uncertainty of inquiry into the nature (and practice) of HRD.

These points suggest that we need to develop a new language to reflect a different way of looking at our theory and practice, and, indeed, our existence. Neither the certainty of scientism nor the dissolute nature of post-modernism captures these ideas. In contrast to this, the notions of complexity provide the ideal vehicle by which a metaview of human existence can be established within which apparently contradictory worldviews can be accommodated. In brief, the idea that a complex system is more than 'just' a complicated system is central to the notion of complexity. A complicated system or a problem might be very complicated indeed, but with time and effort all its parts and its whole can be measured and understood. In contrast, a complex system might be quite simple, yet its parameters cannot be measured or quantified (in the normal sense) and the whole is more than the sum of the parts. However much we atomize the different parts, we can never get to the essence of the whole. In this there is similarity between post-modernism and complexity theory; however, unlike postmodernism, complexity theory suggests that while aspects of complex systems cannot be measured in the normal sense, we can infer relationships between the constituent parts and subsystems, and we can deduce global underlying principles. Put another way, however we choose to view the world, there exist processes that underlie all of humanity, and the principles of complexity theory might provide a language by which we can get closer to an appreciation of them (Tsoukas and Hatch 2001). In addition, there is no requirement that a complex system be uniform in nature. It may have subsystems that appear in structure and function to be significantly different from each other and to the whole yet each is in relationship to the others and to the 'environment' of the whole, and the whole is in relation to the wider environment. This relationship might be one that is in a state 'far from equilibrium' (Stacey 1993) yet the system maintains dynamic coherence through autopoietic processes, and adheres to its global underlying principles. The diversity apparent between individuals and nations is indicative of self generating and autopoietic subsystems that might be complex in their own right, but which are still parts of the whole, as each derives its identity or being from its opposite (as perceived from the whole), and 'development' in any of these subsystems is synonymous with interaction with the whole.

Conclusion

I have suggested that there exist 'great archetypal structures' that underlie the human condition, and that these can be identified by their effect upon it, such that human society and thought clusters into four main archetypal worldviews, termed here, for the sake of convenience and bearing in mind the fragility of language, hierarchical, normative, entrepreneurial and facilitative. The axes by which these are located are bi-polar and termed, again, for convenience, self and other, and structure and agency. I suggest that these great systems and their products are most fruitfully discussed using the language (and thus concepts) of complexity. This recognizes that while the whole system cannot be pulled apart and understood, it can be accessed by examining the relationships between the multiplicities of representations that are located within it. Thus the study of the system is the study of the relationships within it, and that study is that which we might commonly call HRD. It follows from this that the practice of HRD is about *agency* in a pluralistic, relativistic and interpretative world. This involves the search for the patterning of the whole, for dynamic structures, an understanding of the possibilities and their links; in short, a *holistic* approach. Holistic agency (Lee 1996) is therefore about individual action (or non-action) within a relativistic yet structured world, and thus is about the 'doing' and 'becoming' of HRD.

Acknowledgement

Parts of this chapter have appeared in M. Lee (2003) 'The complex roots of HRD', in M. Lee (ed.) *HRD in a Complex World*, London: Routledge, pp. 7–24.

References

Ashton, D. J. L. (1988) 'Are business schools good learning organisations? Institutional values and their effects in management education', *Personnel Review*, 17, 4: 6–14.

Barklow, J. H., Cosmides, L. and Tooby, J. (eds) (1992) *The Adapted Mind: Evolutionary Psychology and the Generation of Culture*, New York: Oxford University Press.

Baumrind, D. (1973) 'The development of instrumental competence through socialization', in A. D. Pick (ed.) *Minnesota Symposium on Child Psychology*, vol. 7, Minneapolis, MN: University of Minnesota Press.

Bee, H. (1985) *The Developing Child*, New York: Harper and Row.

Blackler, F. (1993) 'Knowledge and the theory of organisations: organisations as activity systems and the reframing of management', *Journal of Management Studies*, 30, 6: 863–884.

Boyacigiller, N. and Adler, N. J. (1991) 'The parochial dinosaur: organisational science in a global context', *Academy of Management Review*, 16, 2: 262–290.

Bradshaw, J. L. (1997) *Human Evolution: A Neuropsychological Perspective*, Hove: Psychology Press.

Briggs Myers, I. and McCaulley, M. H. (1985) *A Guide to the Development and Use of the Myers-Briggs Type Indicator*, Palo Alto, CA: Consulting Psychologists Press.

Burns, T. (1977) *The BBC: Pubic Institution and Private World*, New York: Holmes and Meier.

Campbell, A. and Muncer, S. (1987) 'Models of anger and aggression in the social talk of women and men', *Journal of Theory for Social Behaviour*, 17: 489–511.

Cilliers, P. (1998) *Complexity and Postmodernism: Understanding Complex Systems*, London: Routledge.

Cromie, S., Callaghan, I. and Jansen, M. (1992) 'The entrepreneurial tendencies of managers: a research note', *British Journal of Management*, 3: 1–5.

Dewey, J. (1938) *Experience and Education*, New York: Kappa Delta (then Collier).

Duncan, S. (1991) 'Convention and conflict in the child's interaction with others', *Developmental Review*, 11: 337–367.

Emery, F. E. and Trist, E. L. (1965) 'The causal texture of organisational environments', *Human Relations*, 18: 21–32.

Fogel, A. (1993) *Developing through Relationships: Origins of Communication, Self and Culture*, Hemel Hempstead: Harvester Wheatsheaf.

Fox, R. (1989) *The Search for Society: Quest for a Biosocial Science and Morality*, London: Rutgers University Press.

Giddens, A. (1976) *New Rules of Sociological Method: A Positive Critique of Interpretive Sociologies*, London: Hutchinson.

Harshbarger, D. (1973) 'The individual and the social order: notes on the management of heresy and deviance in complex organisations', *Human Relations*, 26, 2: 251–269.

Hatch, M. J. (1993) 'The dynamics of organisational culture', *Academy of Management Review*, 18: 657–693.

Hofstede, G. (1991) *Cultures and Organisations, Software of the Mind: Intercultural Cooperation and its Importance for Survival*, London: McGraw-Hill.

Honey, P. and Mumford, A. (1989) *The Manual of Learning Opportunities*, Maidenhead: Peter Honey.

Höpfl, H. (1995) 'Organisational rhetoric and the threat of ambivalence', *Studies in Cultures, Organisations and Societies*, 1, 2: 175–188.

Jankowicz, D. (1996) 'On "resistance to change" in the post-command economies and elsewhere', in M. M. Lee, H. Letiche, R. Crawshaw and M. Thomas (eds) *Management Education in the New Europe*, London: International Thompson.

Jung, C. G. (1964) *Man and his Symbols*, London: W.H. Allen.

Jung, C. G. (1971) *Collected Works*, revised trans. R. F. C. Hull, vol. 6, *Psychological Types*, Princeton, NJ: Princeton University Press.

Kelly, G. (1955) *A Theory of Personality: The Psychology of Personal Constructs*, New York: Norton.

Kolb, D. (1974) 'On management and the learning process,' in D. A. Kolb, I. M.

Rubin and J. M. McIntyre (eds) *Organizational Psychology*, 2nd edn, Englewood Cliffs, NJ: Prentice Hall.

Kolb, D. (1984) *Experiential Learning*, Englewood Cliffs, NJ: Prentice Hall.

Krebs Hirsh, S. and Kummerow, J. (1987) *Introduction to Types in Organizational Settings*, Palo Alto, CA: Consulting Psychologists Press.

Lee, M. M. (1994) 'The isolated manager: walking the boundaries of the micro-culture', *Proceedings of the British Academy of Management Conference*, Lancaster, UK.

Lee, M. M. (1996) 'Holistic learning in the New Europe', in M. M. Lee, B. H. Letiche, R. Crawshaw and M. Thomas (eds) *Management Education in the New Europe*, London: International Thompson.

Lee, M. M. (1997a) 'Strategic human resource development: a conceptual exploration', in R. Torraco (ed.) *Academy of Human Resource Development Conference Proceedings*, Baton Rouge, LA: AHRD.

Lee, M. M. (1997b) 'The developmental approach: a critical reconsideration', in J. Burgoyne and M. Reynolds (eds) *Management Learning*, London: Sage.

Lee, M. M. (1998) 'Understandings of conflict: a cross-cultural investigation', *Personnel Review*, 27, 3: 227–242.

Lee, M. M. (2001) 'A refusal to define HRD', *Human Resource Development International*, 4, 3: 327–343.

Lee, M. M. and Flatau, M. (1996) 'Serial logic in a parallel world', in M. Mitzla (ed.) *Facilitating ISO900 Training: Report for the European Commission*, Brussels: European Commission.

McWhinney, W. (1992) *Paths of Change: Strategic Choices for Organizations and Society*, Newbury Park, CA: Sage.

Mintzberg, H. (1979) *The Structuring of Organisations*, Englewood Cliffs, NJ: Prentice Hall.

Mitroff, I. I. and Killman, R. H. (1978) *Methodological Approaches to Social Science: Integrating Divergent Concepts and Theories*, San Francisco, CA: Jossey-Bass.

Moreland, R. L. and Levine, J. M. (1989) 'Newcomers and oldtimers in small groups', in P. Paulus (ed.) *Psychology of Group Influence*, 2nd edn, Hillsdale, NJ: Lawrence Erlbaum.

Pascale, R. T. (1990) *Managing on the Edge: How Successful Companies Use Conflict to Stay Ahead*, London: Viking Penguin.

Reason, P. (1981) '"Methodological approaches to social science", by Ian Mitroff and Ralph Kilmann: an appreciation', in P. Reason and J. Rowan (eds) *Human Inquiry: A Source Book of New Paradigm Research*, Chichester: John Wiley.

Romanelli, E. and Tushman, M. L. (1994) 'Organisational transformation as punctuated equilibrium: an empirical test', *Academy of Management Journal*, 37: 1141–1166.

Smith, P. B. (1992) 'Organisational behaviour and national cultures', *British Journal of Management*, 3: 39–51.

Soyland, A. J. (1994) *Psychology as Metaphor*, London: Sage.

Stacey, R. D. (1993) *Strategic Management and Organisational Dynamics*, London: Pitman.

Stacey R., Griffin, D. and Shaw, P. (2000) *Complexity and Management: Fad or Radical Challenge to Systems Thinking?* London: Routledge.

Stevens, A. and Price J. (1996) *Evolutionary Psychiatry: A New Beginning*, London: Routledge.

Taylor, F. W. (1947) *Scientific Management*, London: Harper and Row.

Tsoukas, H. and Hatch, M.-J. (2001) 'Complex thinking, complex practice: the case for a narrative approach to organisational complexity', *Human Relations*, 54, 8: 979–1014.

Tufts-Richardson, P. (1996) *Four Spiritualities: Expressions of Self, Expressions of Spirit*, Palo-Alto, CA: Davies-Black.

Vasilyuk, F. (1984) *The Psychology of Experiencing: The Resolution of Life's Critical Situations*, English trans. 1991, Hemel Hempstead: Harvester Wheatsheaf.

Watson, J. (1994) *Management Development to the Millennium: The New Challenges*, London: Institute of Management.

Weick, K. (1977) 'Organizational design: organizations as self-organizing systems', *Organizational Dynamics*, 6, 2: 31–46.

Index

Abbreviations: Fig = Figure; HRD = human resources development; Tab = Table.

For Product Safety Concerns and Information please contact our EU representative GPSR@taylorandfrancis.com Taylor & Francis Verlag GmbH, Kaufingerstraße 24, 80331 München, Germany

Printed and bound by CPI Group (UK) Ltd, Croydon, CR0 4YY
11/04/2025
01843977-0009